MARX AND KEYNES

The Limits of the Mixed Economy

MARX AND KEYNES

The Limits of the Mixed Economy

By

PAUL MATTICK

EXTENDING HORIZONS BOOKS
Porter Sargent Publisher
11 Beacon St., Boston, Mass. 02108

EXTENDING HORIZONS BOOKS

W. H. TRUITT, Co-Editor

*This book is set in 10 point Baskerville, a fine transitional
type face named for the eighteenth century English printer.
Cover design by John Coyne.*

CONTENTS

INTRODUCTION

This book was written during a time hailed by the President of the United States as "the greatest upsurge of economic well-being in history." Others, in other nations, spoke of an "economic miracle," or else claimed that "we never had it so good." Professional economists were overjoyed that their "dismal science" had finally turned out to be the hope of the world. They impressed governments and businessmen alike with their theoretical erudition and its practical applicability. With the unfortunate exception of an inarticulate minority, from the "High" down to the "Low" there was general agreement that business was excellent and that it would stay that way. There was some concern with a residue of poverty and with the few bottle-necks of unemployment which still marred the otherwise beautiful face of Western prosperity; and there was something more than just concern with the unsolved problem of "underdevelopment" which prevented the large part of the world from partaking in the general prosperity. But some day the poor nations too would "take off" and emulate Western success, and the blessings of capitalism would spread over all the globe.

Although I have witnessed this period of "unprecedented prosperity," I also experienced the Great Depression between the two world wars. At that time, confidence in the resilience of capitalism was at a low ebb and theories abounded regarding its decline and predicting its certain demise. Marxism was once again in the ascendancy, if only as an expression of a growing discrepancy between capitalist ideology and reality. The climate of despair was ended by government interventions in the economy and by World War II. Meanwhile, John Maynard Keynes had evolved his theory, which suggested monetary and fiscal policies capable of assuring full employment in a stagnating capitalist economy. Governments applied the Keynesian suggestions to secure some measure of social and economic stability in their nations. Because these endeavors proved successful, an old slogan was modified to proclaim that "we are all Keynesians now."

It is my contention that the Keynesian solution to the economic problems that beset the capitalist world can be of only temporary avail, and that the conditions under which it can be effective are in the process of dissolution. For this reason the Marxian critique of political economy, far from having lost its pertinency, gains new relevance through its ability to comprehend and transcend both the "old" and the "new" economics. I shall subject Keynesian theory and practice to a Marxian critique, and beyond that, I shall try to elucidate political and economic events and trends with the aid of Marxian analysis.

This book is not presented as a consecutive narrative, however; various of its parts have been written on different occasions and at different times. These are necessary parts and all of them relate to the single theme of the mixed economy and to the differences between Keynes and Marx. There is some unavoidable overlapping and even repetition which, I hope, will enhance rather than encumber the book's readability.

CHAPTER I

THE KEYNESIAN "REVOLUTION"

The theories of bourgeois economists down to David Ricardo were developed before there was a real awareness of the class issues that dominate capitalist society. Ricardo, as Marx wrote, "made the antagonism of class interests, of wages and profits, of profits and rent, the starting point of his investigations, naively taking this antagonism for a social law of nature. But by this start the science of bourgeois economy had reached the limits beyond which it could not pass,"[1] for a further critical development could lead only to the recognition of the contradictions and limitations of the capitalist system of production. By doing what could not be done by bourgeois economists, Marx felt himself to be the true heir, and the destroyer as well, of bourgeois economy.

Though bourgeois economy was indeed unable to advance as Marx had said, it was able to change its appearance. Classical economists had emphasized production and the system as a whole. Their followers emphasized exchange and individual enterprise. Economic theory became increasingly apologetic until the whole problem of the social relations that underly economic processes was done away with through the rejection of the classical value theory in favor of the subjective value concept of the marginal-utility school. Increasing economic difficulties, however, created an interest in the business cycle, in the factors that make for prosperity, crisis, and depression. The neo-classical school, whose best-known proponent was Alfred Marshall, attempted to transform economy into a practical science; it sought ways and means to influence

1 K. Marx, *Capital,* Kerr ed., Vol. I, p. 17.

1

market movements and to increase both the profitability of capital and the general social welfare.

In the midst of the Great Depression there appeared John Maynard Keynes' work, *The General Theory of Employment, Interest and Money,* which was soon hailed as a "revolution" in economic thought and which led to the formation of a school of "Keynesian economics." While persistent "orthodox" economists opposed this school as either "socialistic" or "illusory," inconsistent socialists attempted to blend Marx with Keynes, accepting Keynes' theories as the "Marxism" of our time. Marx's scepticism about the future of bourgeois society was now said to indicate only his inability or unwillingness to criticize the classicists *constructively.* And of Keynes it was said that he made real Alfred Marshall's aspirations for a reformed and improved capitalism.

John Maynard Keynes' popularity is of long standing and was created by his book *The Economic Consequences of the Peace.* Keynes opposed the harshness of the Versailles Treaty because around "Germany as a central support the rest of the European economic system grouped itself, and on the prosperity and enterprise of Germany the prosperity of the rest of the Continent mainly depended."[2] It was suggested that Keynes' conciliatory reasoning was motivated by his fear of an anti-capitalist revolution in the wake of the war. Others suspected that his constructive proposals with regard to the peace were merely subtle ways of furthering British post-war foreign policies. Though these two concerns undoubtedly played a part in the formulation of his opinion, Keynes' opposition to the treaty was based mainly on economic considerations and was determined by his conviction that the capitalist world could operate rationally.

The war itself was to Keynes only an accidental and unhappy interlude in the liberalistic process of capital formation. In 1919, he feared an impairment of capital accumulation because "the laboring classes may no longer be willing to forego so largely, and the capitalist classes, no longer confident of the future, may seek to enjoy more fully their liberties of consumption so long as they last,

2 J. M. Keynes, *The Economic Consequences of the Peace,* New York, 1929, p. 146.

and thus precipitate the hour of their confiscation."[3] The disturbed "accumulative habits" had to be restored; for at this time Keynes still unreservedly favored the "inequality of the distribution of wealth" as the best means for a vast amassing of capital. With the war's end he expected a return to international free trade and unlimited investment opportunities. The simplest way to restore "normalcy" was, of course, to reinstitute pre-war conditions. This implied treating Germany as if there had been no war at all.

But after experiencing the period of "war-socialism" in England and on the Continent and witnessing the Bolshevik "experiment" in Russia, Keynes ceased to think that capitalism was restricted to *laissez-faire* economics; in fact, he now considered *"laissez-faire* a legend, a bit of metaphysical thinking." He was convinced that the capitalist economy could be regulated so as to function better without losing its capitalist character. And if the national economy could be steered into definite, desirable channels, it might also be co-ordinated with the economic needs of the world. Because schemes of control were conceivable, Keynes was confident that their practical realization merely depended upon the presence of wise men of good will. "He believed in the supreme value of intellectual leadership, in the wisdom of the chosen few,"[4] and in their ability to influence the economic processes in a socially satisfactory way.

In bourgeois economic theory men behave rationally in a market where self-interest meets self-interest, each vying for advantage and each limiting the other. Through all the unhampered individual attempts to maximize want-satisfaction, the market establishes price relations which tend toward the most economical allocation of resources. Keynes did not challenge the assertion that the optimum of economic self-interest leads to the maximum of social well-being; but he did find that people seldom know their real interests. The individualistic principle was not enough to recognize *true* self-interest. Savings and consumption restrictions, for instance, at times suit both the individual and society; but at other times they may impoverish both. To find out just when one or another policy is appropriate requires a social point of view.

3 *Ibid.,* p. 22.
4 R. F. Harrod, *The Life of John Maynard Keynes,* London, 1951, p. 332.

The notion that the satisfaction of individualistic self-interest demands a consideration of the social system's needs forced Keynes to turn from "micro-economics" to the "macro-economics" of the classicists. This involved a partial return to the labor theory of value; for the terms that describe the single firm and individual price determination are not suited to a theory discussing social aggregates such as total income, consumption, investment, employment and their economic interdependence. This change on Keynes' part has been considered an "implicit fundamental criticism of the existing social order."[5] In reality it attests only to Keynes' great concern for governmental controls "both as the only practical means of avoiding the destruction of the existing economic forms in their entirety and as a condition of the successful functioning of individual initiative."[6]

In an attempt to cope with growing economic difficulties, economists turned to monetary theory in order to influence the business cycle. Keynes was well suited to serve this trend. A speculator in international currency, Keynes was occupied with money questions and monetary reforms from his first publication *Indian Currency and Finance* (1913), down to his last contribution on the *International Monetary Fund*. The control of the monetary system had become essentially a control of credit by means of the rate of interest. In Keynes' view, excessive inflation as well as excessive deflation — both capable of disturbing the stability of the economy — could be attributed to a disparity between savings and investments. If investments exceeded savings, inflation would occur; and if the reverse were true, deflation would set in. He traced the discrepancy between savings and investments to a lack of regulation of both. As individuals and groups made their separate decisions on savings and investments, there was no guarantee that these decisions would complement each other. Economic well-being depended, then, on a rate of interest that would keep savings in conformity with investments and thus stabilize the general price level.

Keynes held that production is limited by the rate of interest

5 D. Dillard, *The Economics of John Maynard Keynes*, New York, 1948, p. 195.
6 J. M. Keynes, *The General Theory of Employment, Interest and Money*, New York, 1936, p. 380.

because this rate defines the standard for the profitability of invest-ments. The rate of investment depends on entrepreneurs, who make investments according to their expected profitability. These entrepreneurs are supposed to compare their profit expectations with the current interest paid on borrowed money. Thus, lowering the interest rate would increase the inclination to invest. Keynes did not deny that a prolonged depression would reestablish a "proper" relationship between profit, interest and wages. But he felt sure that an inflationary course would accomplish the same results with fewer hardships. He looked upon his inflationary pro-posals not as a contrast to the classical doctrine, but as an answer to the violation of that doctrine which was already accomplished through artificially-maintained interest rates. He was convinced that control of the money and credit supply could establish an equilibrium rate of interest which would equate savings and in-vestments and create the psychological conditions for "normal" capital expansion.

There is no need, for the moment, to follow Keynes' numerous proposals on how to alleviate the economic ills by monetary means. His "originality" did not lie in this field: here he shared honors with Hawtrey, Harrod, Cassel, Wicksell, Fisher and a host of long-forgotten "money-cranks," particularly Proudhon and Silvio Gesell.[7] Proudhon envisioned an economic system of "mutualism" without exploitation, to be achieved by rendering capital incapable of earning interest. He proposed the establishment of a national bank, which would gratuitously grant credits to all callers in a society of independent producers and workers' syndicates. While Proudhon imagined that the abolition of interest was the surest way toward "socialism," Silvio Gesell found nothing wrong with the "Man-chester system." He was opposed to interest and rent as detriments to the continuous expansion of production. Money, according to Gesell, since it was not only a medium of exchange but also a store of wealth, had the tendency to leave the circulation process, thereby causing stagnation and decline. If the hoarding of money could be prevented, production could go on uninterruptedly. He suggested imposing a carrying-charge for money. Taxing all liquid

7 S. Gesell, *Die Natürliche Wirtschaftsordnung durch Freiland und Freigeld*, Berlin, 1916.

funds would make the holding of money an expensive affair. He assumed that people would invest their money in "real capital" rather than pay a price for hoarding; and that the increase in investments would lead to an economy of abundance and general well-being.

While Keynes did not share Proudhon's utopian longings, he was in full agreement with the attack upon the payment of interest, and he favored the gradual "euthanasia of the rentier." And though he found Gesell's theories rather impractical, he regarded them as sound in principle. He, too, thought the *laissez-faire* doctrine wrong in its assumption that a self-adjusting mechanism balanced the rate of interest and the volume of investment. Although he appreciated Gesell's "pioneer work," Keynes thought it unnecessary to apply it: a manipulated rate of interest could control investment well enough to maintain the necessary rate of capital expansion.

In distinction from those economists who believed that all economic problems could be solved by monetary means alone, Keynes presented his ideas as a "complete theory of a monetary economy" integrating monetary and value theory. He called his work a "General Theory of Employment, Interest and Money," because in his opinion "the postulates of the classical theory are applicable to a special case only and not to the general case, the situation which it assumes being a limiting point of the possible positions of equilibrium. Moreover, the characteristics of the special case assumed by the classical theory happen not to be those of the economic society in which we actually live, with the result that its teaching is misleading and disastrous if we attempt to apply it to the facts of experience."[8]

Traditional or standard theory did not account for unemployment; until the *General Theory*, Keynes' own arguments overlooked the problem. To be sure, his *Treatise on Money* (1930) anticipated the later attempt to approach the question of output and employment as a whole. But only in the *General Theory* does he seriously begin to deal with both the distribution and the quantity of employment, and with the forces that determine its changes.

Traditional theory was bound to the imaginary conditions of

8 *The General Theory*, p. 3.

full employment because its proponents felt sure that wage levels would react to the forces of supply and demand and would never be so high for so long a time as to create or maintain unemployment. They were convinced that lower wages would increase employment, and they were confident that unemployment would reduce wages. Keynes shared their conviction but not their confidence. He found that a given "propensity to consume" and a given rate of investment determine between them a definite level of employment consistent with economic equilibrium. Although this level cannot be greater than full employment, it can be smaller. An equilibrium including full employment may exist; but it would be a special case. Generally, an increase in the level of employment necessitates a change either in the propensity to consume or in the rate of investment.

Keynes did not question the assertion that under certain conditions unemployment indicated the existence of real wages that are incompatible with economic equilibrium, and that lowering them would increase employment by raising the profitability of capital and thus the rate of investment. But he found that wages were less flexible than had been generally assumed. Workers had learned to resist wage reductions. And as long as the "socialist method" of wage-cutting by government decree was not, he said, a reality, the available methods of wage-cutting were not efficient enough to secure uniform wage-reductions for every class of labor. He also noticed that workers' resistance is greater to a cut in money wages than to a lowering of real wages. This is true, of course; if only because it is easier to go on strike than resist rising prices. Keynes saw that this allowed for more subtle ways of wage-cutting than those traditionally employed. The subtle way was also the more general and effective way, he felt. A flexible wage policy could be created by a flexible money policy: an increase in the quantity of money would raise prices and reduce real wages if money-wages remained stationary or rose more slowly than the general price level. "Having regard to human nature and our institutions," he wrote, "it can only be a foolish person who would prefer a flexible wage policy to a flexible money policy, unless he can point to advantages from the former which are not available from the latter."[9]

9 *Ibid.*, p. 268.

Beyond these observations, however, Keynes held that employment in a developed capitalism is determined not by wage-bargains between workers and employers but by the existing "effective demand," which depends on the propensity to consume and on the rate of capital expansion. Even with perfectly flexible wage-rates, unemployment would exist if there were a declining demand. The ruling assumption of "Say's law" that "supply creates its own demand" is simply not true; capitalism is not the self-adjusting system it was supposed to be. While it is true that a reduction in money-wages which leaves the existing aggregate demand intact will increase employment, this will not be the case if the aggregate demand declines. From a "social" point of view, wage-reductions make sense only if they lead to an expansion of production which increases effective demand. And the market will not provide wage policies to secure and enlarge effective demand until full employment is reached. To this end, interferences of a monetary and, perhaps, an extra-monetary character are needed. The purpose of these interferences, however, is to make the market's economic equilibrium operate under conditions of full employment. Say's unworkable law of the market is to be made to work by extra-market means.

According to Say, all people produce either to consume or to sell and all sell in order to buy some other commodity to use or to consume; consequently, supply and demand are bound to balance. If there is too much of a particular commodity, its price will fall; if there is not enough, its price will rise; these price changes, tending to economic equilibrium, exclude the possibility of general overproduction. The market mechanism is here seen as a self-adjusting equilibrium mechanism which need only be left alone to produce the most economical and rational allocation of productive resources and distribution of commodities. As a corollary of the same doctrine, Keynes said, "it has been supposed that any individual act of abstaining from consumption necessarily leads to, and amounts to the same thing as, causing the labor and commodities thus released from supplying consumption to be invested in the production of capital wealth."[10]

10 *Ibid.*, p. 19.

Notwithstanding some theoretical inconsistencies, modern economic thought, according to Keynes, "is still deeply steeped in the notion that if people do not spend their money in one way they will spend it in another."[11] Keynes admitted the plausibility of the idea "that the *costs* of output are always covered in the aggregate by the sale-proceeds resulting from demand." This idea makes it natural to suppose "that the act of an individual, by which he enriches himself without apparently taking anything from anyone else, must also enrich the community as a whole; so that an act of individual saving inevitably leads to a parallel act of investment. For, it is indubitable that the sum of the net increment of the wealth of individuals must be exactly equal to the aggregate net increment of the wealth of the community." But Keynes concluded that "those who think in this way were deceived, nevertheless, by an optical illusion, which makes two essentially different activities appear to be the same."[12]

From the assumption that the demand price of output as a whole equals its supply price follow all the other assumptions of neoclassical equilibrium theory, including its theory of employment. This theory allows only for "voluntary" or "frictional" unemployment, not for involuntary unemployment. Keynes, however, acknowledged the existence of involuntary unemployment: he described its absence as a state of "full employment." It is not very plausible, he wrote, "to assert that unemployment in the United States in 1932 was due either to labor obstinately refusing to accept a reduction of money-wages or to its obstinately demanding a real wage beyond what the productivity of the economic machine was capable of furnishing. Wide variations are experienced in the volume of employment without any apparent change either in the minimum real demands of labor or in its productivity."[13]

For Keynes the very fact of large-scale and prolonged unemployment indicated that "Say's law" is not a general economic law but holds true only under the special conditions of equilibrium with full employment. In Keynes' view, the economic system may be in equilibrium under conditions of less than full employment.

11 *Ibid.,* p. 20.
12 *Ibid.,* p. 21.
13 *Ibid.,* p. 9.

That is to say, a given level of employment short of full employment may be the most profitable for the entrepreneurs. No force
then exists within the equilibrium to raise the level of employment
to full employment. This can be brought about only externally,
by selecting out of the mutually interdependent economic variables
"those variables which can be deliberately controlled or managed
by central authority in the kind of system in which we actually
live."[14] For Keynes, these determinable variables were the propensity to consume and the incentive to invest. Manipulation of these
variables was to lead to a state of economic equilibrium with full
employment. Once this was established, the static equilibrium analysis would hold good again. Keynes did not question the possibility of such an equilibrium; he doubted only that the system
would adjust itself to create it. The theory which failed to fit the
practice was countered by a practice to fit the theory.

Keynes found it convenient to sympathize with the doctrine
"that everything is produced by labor," because "much unnecessary
perplexity can be avoided if we limit ourselves strictly to the two
units, money and labor, when we are dealing with the behavior of
the economic system as a whole."[15] The basic unit of employment
in his system is a working-hour of average productivity, as in Marx's
system skilled labor is reduced to unskilled labor. A wage-unit is
the quantity of money received for an hour of work. The aggregates of production, income, and employment represent certain
values in terms of wage-units and the latter are assumed to be of
constant magnitude. Quantities of employment measured in wage-
units serve as an index for measuring the changes in the economic
system.

Expressed in simplest terms, Keynes' model represents a closed
system divided into two departments of production — that of consumption goods and that of capital goods. The total money expenditures on consumption goods plus the total expenditures on capital goods constitute total income. When the aggregate demand —
the demand for consumption and capital goods — equals total
income, which implies that total savings equals total investments,
the system is supposed to be in equilibrium. A decline of aggre-

14 *Ibid.*, p. 247.
15 *Ibid.*, p. 43.

gate demand, implying a discrepancy between savings and investments, reduces total income and produces unemployment. In order to alter this situation, the aggregate demand must be increased to a point where total income implies full employment.

Because Ricardo "neglected the aggregate demand function," Keynes felt himself anti-Ricardian and pro-Malthusian in raising the issue of "effective demand" as the fundamental principle of an economy of full employment. But while "Malthus was unable to explain clearly how and why effective demand could be deficient,"[16] Keynes thought that he had discovered the reason in the psychological "propensity to consume." Malthus saw that in capitalism the demand of the workers could not be large enough to enable the capitalists to realize their profits. And since prices included profits, they could not be realized in intra-capitalist exchange. Capital-labor relations contained and created a lack of demand which destroyed the incentive to accumulate capital. Malthus concluded that this demand must come forth from social layers other than labor and capital. In this way he justified the continued existence of the non-productive feudal class: he deemed their consumption necessary for the proper functioning of the economy. However, "the great puzzle of effective demand with which Malthus wrestled vanished from economic literature,"[17] until resurrected by Keynes. His theory may thus be regarded as a modern version, elaboration, and possibly refinement of Malthus' theory of accumulation.

Consumption, for Keynes, is the obvious end and object of all economic activity. Capital, he wrote, "is not a self-subsistent entity existing apart from consumption"; therefore "every weakening in the propensity to consume regarded as a permanent habit must weaken the demand for capital as well as the demand for consumption."[18] He believed that it is a "psychological law" that individuals tend to consume progressively smaller portions of their income as this income increases. When aggregate real income is increased consumption increases too, of course, but not so much as income. It is only in an economically backward society, Keynes wrote, that the propensity to consume is large enough to assure the

16 *Ibid.*, p. 32.
17 *Ibid.*, p. 32.
18 *Ibid.*, p. 106.

employment of all hands. This propensity declines in a "mature" society. Since the propensity to consume declines with the enrichment of society, and since capital formation is the enrichment of society, it follows that to foster the enrichment of society is to support the decline of the propensity to consume. The accumulation of capital must, therefore, come to an end in the declining propensity to consume, which is the *key* to the decreasing effective demand. Keynes had set out to defeat Say's law of the market on its own ground, that is, on the assumption that production is carried on for the benefit of consumption. And how could he have been more successful than by showing that just because of the "fact" that production serves consumption, supply does not create its own demand?

Keynes views the consumption of the mass of the population, miserable as it may be compared with potential and even actual production, as the community's chosen consumption, which expresses its actual propensity to consume. Yet he thinks that even in the "mature" society effective demand might be increased by a change in the propensity to consume. He thus admits to a difference between what he considers the community's chosen propensity to consume and the actually existing social consumption needs. This admission implies, of course, that consumption is not the end of economic activity in capitalism. If it were there would be no problem of effective demand.

When employment increases, Keynes wrote, "aggregate real income is increased. The psychology of the community is such that when aggregate real income is increased aggregate consumption is increased, but not by so much as income. Hence employers would make a loss if the whole of the increased employment were to be devoted to satisfying the increased demand for immediate consumption. Thus, to justify any given amount of employment there must be an amount of current investment sufficient to absorb the excess of total output over what the community chooses to consume when employment is at the given level. For unless there is this amount of investment, the receipts of the entrepreneurs will be less than is required to induce them to offer the given amount of employment."[19] This refutes, of course, Keynes' own statement that cap-

19 *Ibid.*, p. 27.

ital is "not a self-subsistent entity," and that "consumption is the sole end of production."

It is true that, generally, bourgeois economy paid no attention to the question of effective demand. Marxism dealt with it, although, according to Keynes, only "furtively, below the surface, in the underworld" of economic theory. For Marx, capitalist production is oriented not towards consumption needs but towards the production of capital. Capitalism must produce in order to consume, it is true; but in order to produce it must first see the green light of profitability. Effective demand is composed of a demand for consumption goods and a demand for production goods. The relationship between the two sides of effective demand indicates whether the profitability of capital is rising or falling. Capital accumulation, implies a decline of consumption relative to the faster-growing capital. In *this* sense, capital formation does diminish the propensity to consume; yet this is only another way of saying that in capitalism, capital accumulates.

"A lack of effective demand" is just another expression for a lack of capital accumulation and is not an explanation of it. Even in Keynes' view, "employment can only increase *pari passu* with the increase in investments; unless, indeed, there is a change in the propensity to consume."[20] However, Keynes maintained that for the present the only rational and effective remedy for unemployment lay in the further expansion of capital. The problem could also be solved by a reduction of the working-time at the expense of investment and consumption; but, like most non-workers, Keynes was sure that "the great majority of individuals would prefer increased income to increased leisure."[21] Still, while Keynes was very much "impressed by the great social advantages of increasing the stock of capital until it ceases to be scarce," he was willing to "concede that the wisest course is to advance on both fronts at once . . . to promote investments and, at the same time, to promote consumption, not merely to the level which, with the existing propensity to consume, would correspond to the increased investment, but to a higher level still."[22] Under capitalist conditions,

20 *Ibid.,* p. 98.
21 *Ibid.,* p. 326.
22 *Ibid.,* p. 325.

however, this "higher level still" would reduce the profitability of
capital, decrease the level of employment, and initiate new demands for the increase of investments as a precondition for an
increase of consumption.

Traditionally, profit has been regarded as a reward received by
capitalists for their activity and, where there was no such activity,
as a reward for their willingness to invest rather than consume
their "savings." Profit also rewarded them for taking "risks," or for
their social importance in developing "round-about methods" of
production which, while leading to greater productivity, imply
waiting-periods for long-term investments. In either case, capitalists, by abstaining from consumption at one time, earned the right
to consume more at a later time; unless, of course, they wished to
abstain still further. But there have been times when capitalists
have refused to take "risks"; when instead of investing their and
other peoples' money they have held on to it, an attitude which
Keynes calls "liquidity-preference." Because recent history has recorded years of so-called "investment strikes," Keynes found it advisable to alter the abstinence theory of profit and interest. He
suggested that profit and interest should no longer be regarded as
rewards for saving and investing money but as rewards for overcoming the desire not to invest, for opposing "liquidity-preference"
— in other words, for the willingness on the part of the capitalist
to remain a capitalist.

Actually, of course, it makes no difference at all whether one
says that profits are rewards for investing capital or rewards for
opposing liquidity. Quarrels among economists in this regard
revolve around the question of whether liquidity-preference causes
stagnation or the other way around. "When things look black,"
wrote J. A. Schumpeter, "and people expect nothing but losses
from any commitment they might contemplate, then, of course,
they will refuse to invest their current savings . . . or they will
defer investment in order to profit by further reductions in prices.
At the same time, savings will not only be reduced but increased
by all those who expect impending losses of income, in their business or through unemployment. [But] no defense of any 'over-
saving' theory can be based upon it because it occurs only as a
consequence of a depression and hence cannot itself be explained

by it."[23] In Keynes' view, in contrast, "liquidity-preference" precedes stagnation because of the psychologically-determined tendency towards hoarding which is associated with the declining propensity to consume.

According to Keynes, to state his position once more, an increase of income increases consumption, but by less than income. On the assumption that all investment ultimately serves consumption needs, savings will increase faster than investments. As this occurs, aggregate demand declines and the actual level of employment falls short of the available labor supply. This happens in a "mature" society because the great size of the already-existing stock of capital depresses the marginal efficiency (profitability) of capital and thus depresses expectations about future capital yields. Wealth-owners would rather hold their savings in liquid form than invest in enterprises promising little or no reward. The short-run expectations of owners of wealth are, in Keynes' view, based on long-term expectations, which are necessarily gloomy due to the decreasing scarcity of capital. How this long-term trend — decreasing marginal efficiency of capital — affects immediate investment decisions, Keynes does not make clear. He merely asserts that capitalists see in any actual decrease of profitability a still greater future decline; and that this dark outlook causes present-day business to decline even faster. In other words, the short-term outlook determines the long-term outlook and the latter determines behavior in the short-run. Relying on this "insight," "foresight," or "instinct," capitalists show that they prefer a bird in the hand to one in the bush by not risking new investments.

Short of closing the gap between income and consumption, it follows from Keynes' theory that "each time we assure today's equilibrium by increasing investments we are aggravating the difficulty of securing equilibrium tomorrow."[24] But for the near future he thought these difficulties still surmountable and suggested a series of reforms designed to combat "liquidity-preference" and increase "effective demand," despite the decreasing propensity to consume. He was confident that a rate of investment which

23 J. A. Schumpeter, *Capitalism, Socialism and Democracy*, New York, 1947, p. 395.
24 *The General Theory*, p. 105.

would secure full employment was still a possibility. Even "pyramid-building, earthquakes, [or]. . . wars may serve to increase wealth, if the education of our statesmen on the principles of classical economics stands in the way of anything better."[25] Already the first world war had shown that "war-socialism unquestionably achieved a production of wealth far greater than we knew in peace, for though the goods and services delivered were destined for immediate and fruitless extinction, none the less they were wealth."[26] Aside from the "accident" of war, however, if employment as "a function of the expected consumption and the expected investment," was not full employment because expectations were pessimistic, these insufficient expectations could be augmented by an optimistic planning which need not destroy the basic fabric of capitalism. In Keynes' view, full employment did not have to involve warfare, capital destruction, or superfluous production, but could be realized by way of public works of either great or doubtful utility which would increase income without enlarging savings, and thus keep the laborers busy.

The actual crises or business-cycle fitted only imperfectly into Keynes' theory of "effective demand" based on the declining "propensity to consume," because the business-cycle accompanied the most important period of capitalist development, not just its "mature" stage. It had to be considered largely a thing of the past, and in this capacity it served as a rather hazy illustration of society's "maturing" process — a process in which, at intervals, the declining propensity to consume could still be immunized by profit expectations of considerable though diminishing force and by the "wealth-creating" power of numerous wars. Keynes often expressed the belief that capitalism had long since lost its ability to overcome depressions and that stagnation was the "normal" state of its existence unless government interventions in the investment market interrupted it. Some of Keynes' disciples did not think it an "exaggeration to say that inflation and full employment are the normal conditions of a war-time economy and that deflation and unemployment are the normal conditions of a peace-time economy in the present stage of capitalist development."[27]

25 *Ibid.,* p. 129.
26 J. M. Keynes, *Laissez-Faire and Communism,* New York, 1926, p. 48.
27 D. Dillard, *The Economics of John Maynard Keynes,* p. 241.

Whatever the objective reasons for depressions, as long as economists consider them unascertainable they have nothing to work on but the psychology of the class they represent. This psychology is explicable out of the real movements of capital production; it cannot in turn explain these movements. Even Keynes felt at times that such a procedure was insufficient and tried to give his psychological interpretations a material base. Quite in contrast to his general tone of argumentation, he pointed out that the "duration of the slump should have a definite relationship to the length of life of durable assets and to the normal rate of growth in a given epoch." At the outset of the slump, he continued, "there is probably much capital of which the marginal efficiency has become negligible or even negative. But the interval of time, which will have elapsed before the shortage of capital through use, decay and obsolescence causes a sufficiently obvious scarcity to increase the marginal efficiency, may be a somewhat stable function of the average durability of capital in a given epoch."[28]

The reason for the low marginal efficiency of capital at the outset of (and during) the slump appears to be that an abundance of capital causes a lack of profitability. It follows from this that hastening the use, decay, and obsolescence of capital should increase its scarcity-value and, with this, its profitability. One method of achieving capital-scarcity is liquidity-preference. It implies a lack of new investments; and in the slump situation, new investments would only increase the quantity of capital, which is already too large to have satisfactory yields. So liquidity-preference would be one way, among others — such as pyramid-building and warfare — to maintain the scarcity of capital and thus its profitability. But, unlike pyramid-building and warfare, liquidity-preference means unemployment. Keynes opposes it for precisely this reason.

In Keynes' view, capital stagnation expresses the capitalist inability or unwillingness to accept a decreasing profitability. The crisis results from an "over-investment" prompted by "expectations which are destined to disappointment." The crisis occurs not because "the community as a whole has no reasonable use for any more investments," but because "doubts suddenly arise concerning the reliability of their respective yields," and "once doubt begins, it spreads rapidly." During the boom "disillusion falls upon an over-optimistic and much over-bought market," and "leads to a sharp increase in liquidity-preference." This creates the crisis.

The "over-investment" exists because investments have been associated with profit-expectations that prove to be highly unrealistic. "Instead of getting a hoped-for 6%, for instance, investments may yield only 2% and this disappointment changes an 'error of optimism' into an 'error of pessimism' with the result that the investments, which would in fact yield 2%, in conditions of full employment, are expected to yield nothing; and the resulting collapse of new investments then leads to a state of unemployment in which investments, which would have yielded 2%, in condition of full employment, in fact yield less than nothing." The ensuing sudden collapse of the marginal efficiency of capital, "determined by the uncontrollable and disobedient psychology of the business world, lowers the existing propensity to consume by involving a severe decline in the market-value of stock equities."[29] And thus the decline feeds on itself, until it is arrested by an increase of the marginal efficiency of capital within the crisis situation or by an expansion of capital despite its lower marginal efficiency.

To hope for a rise of the marginal efficiency of capital within the crisis situation means to await the return of a sufficient scarcity of capital. In "mature" capitalism this may well be disastrous: large-scale unemployment of long duration has severe social consequences. To overcome the depression it is necessary both to improve the profitability of capital and to expand production beyond the limits of private capital formation. Although Keynes came to see interest-rate manipulations as a possibly minor, or even totally ineffective, instrument for raising the incentive to invest, he held on to it nevertheless as part of an extensive onslaught on "liquidity-preference." As we know, he favored a reduction in the rate of interest not only because "it plays a peculiar part in setting a limit to the level of employment, since it sets a standard to which the marginal efficiency of a capital-asset must attain if it is to be newly produced,"[30] but also because he favored the elimination of the "function-less investor" in principle, because "interest today

---

29 *Ibid.,* pp. 317, 319, 321, 322.
30 *Ibid.,* p. 222.

rewards no genuine sacrifice."[31] As "mature" capitalism signifies a lower marginal efficiency of capital, the greater risk implied in new investments could be at least partly reduced by eliminating the "lender's risk" altogether.

In view of the precarious state of investment markets, Keynes came finally to the conclusion that "the duty of ordering the current volume of investment cannot safely be left in private hands."[32] The goal of all governmental policies was to be full employment, for "only in condition of full employment is a low propensity to consume conducive to the growth of capital."[33] And as it is only during a boom that capitalism comes nearest to full employment, the "right remedy for the trade-cycle," in Keynes' view, is to be found in "abolishing slumps and thus keeping us permanently in a quasi-boom."[34] With full employment the criterion, the effectiveness of various government interventions in the market economy could be tested by experiment. Whatever did not lead to full employment was not enough.

31 *Ibid.*, p. 376.
32 *Ibid.*, p. 320.
33 *Ibid.*, p. 373.
34 *Ibid.*, p. 322.

CHAPTER II

MARX AND KEYNES

It is rather difficult to regard the theories of Keynes as a "revolution" in economic thought. However, the term may be used at will, and the Keynesian theory is called a revolutionary doctrine "in the sense that it produces theoretical results entirely different from the body of economic thought existing at the time of its development."[1] Yet since that "body of thought," was neo-classical equilibrium theory, Keynes' "revolt" may better be regarded as a partial return to classical theory. And this notwithstanding Keynes' own opposition to classical theory, which in his strange definition, included the whole body of economic thought from Ricardo down to his own contemporaries.

Although Keynes regarded himself as an anti-Ricardian, his critics saw, of course, that he tried "to arrive at economic truth in the manner of Ricardo and his followers"[2] through his analysis in terms of economic aggregates. His friends concluded that, because of Keynes, "the study of economic aggregates has taken its place in the centre of economic science, and can never again be pushed to the periphery where pre-Keynesian economists left it — one does not undiscover America."[3] But Keynes was no Columbus, for the concept of economic aggregates dates back two hundred years to Quesnay's *Tableau Oeconomique*, to Ricardo and to Marx.

It was Keynes' rejection of Say's "law of the market" which lent his theory the connotation, "revolutionary." Almost seventy-five years earlier, Marx had pointed out that only an accelerated capital

---

1   L. R. Klein, *The Keynesian Revolution*, New York, 1947, p. VII.
2   A. F. Burns, *Economic Research and the Keynesian Thinking of our Time*, New York, 1946, p. 4.
3   *The Economist*, London, January 27, 1951.

expansion allows for an increase of employment. The "dull and comical 'prince de la science,' J. B. Say," Marx did not find worth overthrowing, even though "his continental admirers have trumpeted him as the man who unearthed the treasure of the metaphysical balance of purchases and sales."[4] For Marx, Say's law of the market was sheer nonsense in view of the growing discrepancy between the profit needs of capital expansion and the rationally-considered productive requirements of society, between the social demand in capitalism and the actual social needs; and he pointed out that capital accumulation implies an industrial reserve army of unemployed.

There is a necessary connection between Marx and Keynes. Marx anticipated Keynes' criticism of the neo-classical theory through his own criticism of classical theory; and both men recognized the capitalist dilemma in a declining rate of capital formation. But while Keynes diagnosed its cause as a lack of incentive to invest, Marx traced the dilemma to its final base, to the character of production as *production of capital*. It is rather astonishing, then, to find Keynes relegating Marx to the "underworld of economic thought together with Silvio Gesell and Major Douglas."[5] Though he was ready to learn from the "underworld," as is demonstrated by his affinity with the ideas of Gesell, Keynes held "that the future will learn more from the spirit of Gesell than that of Marx." He thought so, he said, because, unlike Gesell, Marx based his theories "on an acceptance of the classical hypothesis, and on an unfettering of competition instead of its abolition."[6]

Even a superficial study of *Capital* would have shown Keynes that Marx's theories, which he considered "illogical, obsolete, scientifically erroneous, and without interest or application to the modern world,"[7] led to conclusions often quite similar to those that constitute the "revolutionary" content of his own reasoning. He did not study Marx seriously because he identified Marx's theories with those of the classicists. In a letter to G. B. Shaw,

4   K. Marx, *A Contribution to the Critique of Political Economy*, Chicago, 1904, p. 123.
5   *The General Theory*, p. 32.
6   *Ibid.*, p. 355.
7   J. M. Keynes, *Laissez-Faire and Communism*, p. 48.

Keynes related that he "made another shot at old Karl Marx. . .
reading the Marx-Engels Correspondence," but he still failed to
discover anything "but out-of-date controversializing." He also told
Shaw that he himself is "writing a book on economic theory which,
will largely revolutionize — not at once but in the course of the
next ten years — the way the world thinks about economic problems. There will be a great change, and, in particular, the Ricardian foundations of Marxism will be knocked away."[8] By opposing
the "classical theory," Keynes thought he was opposing Marxism as
well.[9] In reality, however, he dealt with neither of these theories,
but struck at the neo-classical market theory which no longer had
any significant connection with the ideas of Ricardo.

Keynes preferred Gesell to Marx because he favored economic
policies, particularly in the monetary and fiscal fields, which he
thought capable of alleviating the economic ills of capitalism
without altering its basic social structure. Marx, though dealing
with monetary questions exhaustively, emphasized the extra-monetary aspects of the economy. In his view, money questions could
be understood only in the light of the capitalist relations of production, which are relations "based on the class distinction between
buyers and sellers of labor power. It is not money which by its
nature creates this relation; it is rather the existence of this relation
which permits of the transformation of a mere money-function into
a capital function."[10] And only in this latter sense is it of contemporary interest.

According to Marx, money is important not as a measure of
value and a medium of exchange, but because it is the "independent form of the existence of exchange-value." In the capitalist
circulation process, value assumes at one time the form of money
and at another that of other commodities. In the form of money
it preserves and expands itself. The market economy and capital
accumulation are beset with difficulties which appear as monetary

8   R. F. Harrod, *The Life of John Maynard Keynes*, p. 462.
9   Class loyalty itself opposed Keynes to Marx: "When it comes to the class
    struggle as such," he wrote, "my local and personal patriotism . . . are
    attached to my own surroundings. I can be influenced by what seems to
    me to be Justice and good sense; but the class war will find me on the
    side of the educated bourgeoisie." — *Essays in Persuasion*, London, 1931,
    p. 324.
10 *Capital*, Vol. II, p. 39.

troubles. The buying and selling process itself, by providing money with two different functions, contains a crisis element, as the seller is not forced to buy but may retain his wealth in money form. An existing quantity of money, if not large enough to serve as additional capital, may necessitate a period of hoarding, which may also constitute an element of crisis. A relative lack as well as a relative abundance of capital may lead to economic difficulties which will appear as a crisis of the money system.

The need to amass money by hoarding in order to accumulate it as productive capital was largely eliminated by the development of the banking and credit system. The pooling of money resources helped extend industrial and commercial operations. The increasingly more speculative character of capital production enhanced the irrational aspects of capital competition by producing fail-investments and over-investments. Of course, these activities were not considered "speculative" in a derogatory sense,[11] as it was the presumed function of financial capital to "anticipate" further development and to "create" the conditions for an accelerated capital formation. There can exist, however, a strictly monetary crisis due to the relatively independent movement of money in the form of finance capital. Accordingly, Keynes distinguished between "finance" and "industry," favoring the latter and defining the former as the business of the money-market, speculation, stock-exchange activities, and the financing of production. Although he held that "speculators may do no harm as bubbles on a steady stream of enterprise," he found the situation "serious when enterprise becomes the bubble on a whirlpool of speculation."[12]

This distinction between "industry" and "finance," between "productive" and "parasitical" capital is as old as capitalism itself and gave rise to a pseudo-struggle against "interest-slavery" and irresponsible speculators. This strictly intra-capitalist affair is now

---

11 Even when his activities are considered in a derogatory sense, the successful capitalist, speculator, and financier becomes a benefactor of the nation. S. H. Holbrook, for example, writes that almost every one of the great American moguls would under present-day rules face a good hundred years in prison. Yet, he believes "that no matter how these men accumulated their fortunes, their total activities were of the greatest influence in bringing the United States to its present incomparable position in the world of business and industry." — *The Age of the Moguls*, New York, 1953, p. X.

12 *The General Theory*, p. 159.

largely a thing of the past, for the fusion of industry and finance
is so complete as to exclude a "moral" distinction between them.
But even previously, not only the financiers but all capitalists saw
production "merely as a necessary evil of money-making." And,
though profits arise out of the process of production, attempts were
always made "to make money without the mediation of the process
of production."[13] Particularly during times of "idle" capital
and a slackening rate of investments, capitalists increase their
efforts to make money at the expense of other money- and title-
holders by financial manipulations and stock-market activities.

Speculation may enhance crisis situations by permitting the
fictitious over-evaluation of capital, which then cannot satisfy the
profit claims bound up with it.[14] But speculative "money-gains"
represent so many "money-losses"; unless speculation serves as an
instrument of capital concentration it represents only a redistribution of the available exchange-value. The concentration of wealth
is economically meaningless unless it is accompanied by a reorganization of the capital structure which leads to its further expansion.

The division of surplus-value (profits) between "active" and
"inactive" capitalists, of which Keynes made so much, is for Marx
only a part of the general competition for the largest possible share
of the social surplus-value by all capitalists and all those living
on the surplus-product. He did not doubt that under definite
conditions a lowering of interest rates would affect investments
positively. For if too much of the realized profits goes into the
hands of the money-lenders, entrepreneurs will be less apt to
expand production. But no generalization regarding the behavior
and the importance of the rate of interest can be based on this
possibility. High interest rates are not incompatible with high
rates of profit. When all is well in the sphere of profit production,
a relatively high rate of interest will not hamper capital formation.
It may even quicken its pace, if productivity develops fast enough
to satisfy both loan capital and productive capital . In fact, the

13 *Capital*, Vol. II, p. 159.
14 "Once it becomes easier for people to make money faster by buying du
     Pont stock than the du Pont Corporation can make money by producing
     nylon, dacron, and chemicals, then it is time to watch out." The Senate
     Banking Committee's Report on its Stock Market Survey. *The New York
     Times*, May 27, 1955.

rate of interest may rise or fall with a decline of profits as well
as with a rise of profitability, for in either case the demand for
money may exceed the supply or *vice versa*.

Interest is for Marx only a portion of the average profit. It
results from the fact that capital appears in two roles — as loanable
capital in the hands of the lender and as industrial capital in the
hands of the entrepreneurs. As *capital*, however, it functions only
once, and only once can it produce profits. Aside from rent, this
profit is then divided into profit and interest. The division is
often arbitrary and does not affect the basic problems of capital
production. Being generally limited by the rate of profit, the rate
of interest cannot have the significance assigned to it by monetary
theory.

With regard to interest rate problems, it was not Keynes' but
Marx's point of view which found its verification in the crisis
situation. A decade of falling interest rates after 1929 did not
affect investment decisions seriously. Interest-rate manipulation
ceased to be regarded as a main instrument for the control of
business activities, and "in the academic view it seems that the
importance of the rate of interest was very much exaggerated in
traditional theory, and that Marx was after all not much at fault
in neglecting it altogether."[15] Soon it was quite widely acknowledged that investment decisions are seldom based on considerations of
the market-rate of interest[16] and that the "flow of savings appears
to be influenced in modern conditions only to a relatively modest
extent by the level of interest rates."[17]

Keynes himself was finally forced to concede the economic limitations of interest-rate manipulations; and he decided that "the
collapse in the marginal efficiency of capital may be so complete
that no practical reduction in the rate of interest will be enough"[18]
to stimulate investments. "With markets organized and influenced

---

15 J. Robinson, *An Essay on Marxian Economics*, London, 1942, p. 84.
16 The British Committee on the Working of the Monetary System (Rad-
    cliffe Report) came to the conclusion that the monetary means affecting
    the rate of interest are by themselves quite incapable of stimulating the
    economy and have meaning only in connection with a general economic
    policy which includes fiscal measures and direct physical controls. — Cumd.
    827, London, 1959.
17 *The Statist*, London, September 24, 1955.
18 *The General Theory*, p. 316.

as they are," he wrote, "the market estimation of the marginal efficiency of capital may suffer such enormous fluctuations that it cannot be sufficiently offset by corresponding fluctuations in the rate of interest."[19] From this he concluded that it may be necessary for the government to control and guide investments directly.

Prior to Keynes there were only two schools of economics; or, rather, there was only bourgeois economy and its Marxist critique. To be sure, bourgeois economy comprised a variety of viewpoints about the difficulties arising within the system and the means of overcoming them. There were theoretical deviations from the generally-held position of *laissez-faire*. Some of them related to the specific and changing needs of particular capitalist groups within the capitalist system; some discussed the problems created by the differences between the capitalist nations within the world economy. All of them, however, took the given capitalist system of production for granted; they did not attack profit production, private property or the competitive accumulation of capital. Against such critics *laissez-faire* theory could hold its own, as long as the market relations seemed to produce some kind of actual economic order.

But the great economic and social upheavals of twentieth century capitalism destroyed confidence in *laissez-faire's* validity. Marx's critique of bourgeois society and its economy could no longer be ignored. The overproduction of capital with its declining profitability, lack of investments, overproduction of commodities and growing unemployment, all predicted by Marx, was the undeniable reality and the obvious cause of the political upheavals of the time. To see these events as temporary dislocations that soon would dissolve themselves in an upward turn of capital production did not eliminate the urgent need for state interventions to reduce the depth of the depression and to secure some measure of social stability. Keynes' theory fitted this situation. It acknowledged Marx's economic predictions without acknowledging Marx himself, and represented, in its essentials and in bourgeois terms, a kind of weaker repetition of the Marxian critique; and its purpose was to arrest capitalism's decline and prevent its possible collapse.

19 *Ibid.*, p. 320.

CHAPTER III

MARX'S LABOR THEORY OF VALUE

Whereas Keynes' preoccupation with monetary questions was based on his desire to make the capitalist system work more efficiently, Marx's relative neglect of these issues stemmed from his goal of formulating a theory of capital development. This labor theory of value evolved out of his criticism of classical value theory.

In order to yield regulatory results, the market automatism presupposes a principle on which exchange is based, a principle that explains prices and their changes. If a price is given, it may vary in the interplay of supply and demand, but the question of what determines prices remains. For the classicists, price derived from value and value was determined by the labor incorporated in commodities. This conception does not rule out specific cases in which price has no relation to labor time. Marx found the labor theory of value indispensable for understanding the developmental tendencies of capital production and in fact, the only "rational basis of political economy."

The labor theory of value underlies both early bourgeois economic theory and its Marxian critique, and in both cases deals with social production and its distribution between different social classes. Classical economy, according to Marx, culminated in Ricardian economics and was an expression of the rising industrial capitalism within the decaying feudal regime. It represented itself as the theory of the *productive classes,* as opposed to the non-productive classes, which appropriated their privileges in the form of interest and rent. It did not as yet concern itself with the industrial proletariat and was thus able to see in labor the sole creator and measure of economic value.

The labor theory of value became an embarrassment for the capitalist class as soon as the newly-arising frictions between bourgeoisie and proletariat replaced and overshadowed those between the feudal and the capitalist regime. If the value of commodities is determined by the quantity of labor time required for their production, and the product of the whole of social labor is divided into rent, profit, and wages, it would seem to follow that the elimination of profit and rent would allow for an equal exchange of commodities in accordance with their labor-time. Ricardian economics gave rise to a school of "Ricardian Socialists," which demanded an exchange system that would assure producers the full value of their labors.

Marx did not draw similar conclusions from the labor theory of value. Nonetheless, as Friedrich Engels pointed out, "in so far as modern socialism, no matter of what tendency, starts from bourgeois political economy it almost exclusively links itself to the Ricardian theory of value."[1] It is for this reason that Marx has often been called "the last, as well as the greatest of the classical economists."[2] This fulfills the double purpose of granting Marx his undeniable greatness and yet dismissing his theory as outdated, along with all classical theory. Even though Marx accepted and developed Ricardo's value theory, he was not the "greatest" of the classical economists, but their adversary. He knew that the social labor process itself has nothing to do with either value or price but only with the time-consuming physical and mental exertions of the laboring population, and that "value" and "price" are fetishistic categories for existing social production relations. His criticism of political economy was conceived as part of a social struggle to abolish capitalism together with the economic theories which rationalized its existence.

Bourgeois economic theory sees the relations of bourgeois production as natural relations, that is to say, it holds "that these are the relations in which wealth is created and productive force developed in conformity with the laws of nature. These relations therefore are themselves natural laws independent of the influence of time. They are eternal laws which must always govern society. Thus there has

---

1 Preface to Marx's *The Poverty of Philosophy*, Moscow, p. 8.
2 G. Lichtheim, *Marxism*, London, 1961, p. 175.

been history, but there is no longer any."[3] For Marx, however, capitalism was only an historical form of social production. He recognized that underlying this specific form of social development is the general process of social development — comprehended in the materialist conception of history — which expresses itself in a variety of socio-economic formations bound up with different levels of labor productivity. This process has its source in man's struggle for existence in a natural setting that enables and forces him to increase his capacity for work and social organization. Its starting point is lost in prehistory, but in known history the different stages of human and social existence reveal themselves in the changing tools and modes of production.

When Marx speaks of the "law of value" as *relating* to a deeper reality which underlies the capitalist economy, he refers to the "life process of society based on the material process of production."[4] He was convinced that in all societies, including the hoped-for socialist society, a proportioning of social labor in accordance with social needs and reproduction requirements is an inescapable necessity. "Every child knows," he wrote to Kugelmann, "that a nation which ceased to work, I will not say for a year, but even for a few weeks, would perish. Every child knows, too, that the masses of products corresponding to the different needs require different and quantitatively determined masses of the total labor of society. That this *necessity* of the distribution of social labor in definite proportions cannot possibly be done away with by a *particular* form of social production but can only change the *mode* of its *appearance,* is self-evident. No *natural* law can be done away with. What can change in historically different circumstances is only the *form* in which these proportional distributions of labor assert themselves. And the *form* in which this proportional distribution of labor asserts itself in a state of society where the interconnections of social labor are manifested in the *private exchange* of the individual products of labor, is precisely the *exchange-value* of these products."[5]

It has been said that this and similar statements by Marx "dis-

---

3   K. Marx, *The Poverty of Philosophy,* p. 121.
4   K. Marx, *Capital,* Vol. I, p. 92 (Kerr ed.)
5   Marx-Engels, *Selected Correspondence,* Moscow, 1953, p. 251.

prove the generally accepted view that Marx regarded *all* economic laws as being of an historico-relative character."[6] According to Oscar Lange, for example, Marx's position seems to have been "that the economic laws of universal validity are so self-evident that there is scarcely need for a specific scientific technique for their study, and economic science ought to concentrate, therefore, upon investigating the particular form these laws assume in a definite institutional framework."[7] But all that Marx has said on this point is that there are natural laws and social necessities which no *economic law* can violate for very long without destroying society. Natural laws and social necessities are not "universal economic laws," even though, when unattended as in capitalism, they may assert themselves as manifestations of that system's economic law of value. In the preface to the second edition of the first volume of *Capital,* Marx quotes with approval the statement of a Russian reviewer of his work, to the effect that he, Marx, "directly denies that the *general laws of economic life* are one and the same, no matter whether they are applied to the present or the past . . . Such abstract laws do not exist. On the contrary . . . every historical period has laws of its own. As soon as society has outlived a given period of development, and is passing over from one given stage to another, it begins to be subject also to other laws."[8]

Like any other form of social production, value production, too, in Marx's view, implies an allocation of social labor in accordance with social and natural necessities. For Marx, the law of value represented the only *indirect* form that social organization of production could take in a commodity-producing society; but it was also, at the same time, a form restricted to such a society. He illustrated his view with actual and imaginary descriptions of similar processes under non-capitalist conditions. The pre-capitalist conditions Marx dealt with need not concern us here; with regard to the imaginary conditions, Marx referred first to Robinson Crusoe, who knew that his labor, whatever its form, was nothing but his own activity to secure his existence. This knowledge compelled him to apportion his time accurately between different kinds of work. Let us picture, Marx wrote, "a community of free individ-

6 O. Lange, *On the Economic Theory of Socialism,* Minneapolis, 1938, p. 132.
7 *Ibid.,* p. 132.
8 *Capital,* Vol. I, p. 23.

uals, carrying on their work with the means of production in common, in which the labor-power of all the different individuals is consciously applied as the combined labor-power of the community. All the characteristics of Robinson's labor are here repeated, but with the difference, that they are social, instead of individual . . . The total product of our community is a social product. One portion serves as fresh means of production and remains social. But another portion is consumed by the members as means of subsistence. A distribution of this portion amongst them is consequently necessary. The mode of this distribution will vary with the productive organization of the community, and the degree of historical development attained by the producers. We will assume, but merely for the sake of a parallel with the production of commodities, that the share of each individual producer in the means of subsistence is determined by his labor-time. Labor-time would, in that case, play a double role. Its apportionment in accordance with a definite social plan maintains the proper proportions between the different kinds of work to be done and the various wants of the community. On the other hand, it also serves as a measure of the portion of the common labor borne by each individual and of his share in the part of the total product destined for individual consumption. The social relations of the individual producers, with regard to both their labor and its products, are in this case perfectly simple and intelligible, and that with regard not only to production but also to distribution."[9]

No "law of value" enters this hypothetical arrangement; it is *directly* determined by the conscious considerations of the producers. It is also true that Marx wrote that even after the abolition of the capitalist mode of production, "the determination of value continues to prevail in such a way that the regulation of the labor time and the distribution of the social labor among the various groups of production, also the keeping of accounts in connection with this, becomes more essential than ever."[10] But the term *value* in this connection is a mere manner of speech; for, obviously, what Marx meant was that the abolition of capitalism does not end the need to allocate labor in accordance with social require-

9 *Ibid.,* p. 90.
10 *Capital,* Vol. III, p. 992.

ments. In a socialist society, Engels wrote with greater precision, "the people will arrange everything very simply without the intervention of the much-famed 'value'."[11]

As regards the allocation of social labor, it has also been said that socialism merely makes apparent, and therefore more effective, what in capitalism appears as the "regulatory force of the law of value." From this point of view, it is only the *mystification* of the social organization of labor as a "law of value" which comes to an end with the end of capitalism. Its *demystified* results reappear in a consciously-regulated economy. According to Rudolf Hilferding, for instance, the theory of value "is restricted to the epoch wherein labor and the power which controls labor have not been consciously elevated to the rank of a regulative principle of social metabolism and social predominance, but wherein this principle unconsciously and automatically establishes itself as a material quality of things . . . It is . . . because labor is the social bond uniting an atomized society, and not because labor is the matter most technically relevant, that labor is the principle of value and that the law of value is endowed with reality."[12] By defining labor as the principle of value, Hilferding continues, Marx recognized "the factor by whose quality and quantity, by whose organization and productive energy, social life is causally controlled."[13] For this reason the value principle is "identical with the fundamental idea of the materialist conception of history."[14]

Apparently, in Hilferding's view, the law of value fulfills the functions of Adam Smith's "invisible hand." But whereas in bourgeois theory it is the exchange process which assures the proper distribution of social labor and the products of this labor, for Hilferding it is labor itself and the necessary distribution of this labor which regulate social life behind the back of the producers. In either case, social necessities assert themselves independently of human activities and force a definite behavior pattern upon them.

Social necessity is here seen as a force which, recognized or not, overrules on its own accord all human activities by which it may

11   F. Engels, *Anti-Dühring*, Chicago, 1935, p. 325.
12   R. Hilferding, "Böhm-Bawerk's Criticism of Marx," in *Karl Marx and the Close of his System*, New York, 1949, pp. 133, 134.
13   *Ibid.*
14   *Ibid.*

be contradicted. For Hilferding, social necessity turns into a law of value in capitalism because social relations between persons are attached to things and appear as things, as commodity relations, and not as what they really are, namely, social production relations between persons. By doing away with the fetishism of commodity production, he believes, the law of value would be revealed for what it really is — the necessity to regulate the social labor process in accordance with social needs directly recognized in the needs of persons. And it is only in this sense, according to Hilferding, that the law of value is historical. In socialism, it will be replaced by a social organization of production and distribution based on the principle of labor and its appropriate distribution. This change, however, only makes apparent and direct what hitherto asserted itself indirectly and unconsciously in the form of value relations.

According to P. M. Sweezy, another Marxist, it is "one of the primary functions of the law of value to make clear that in a commodity-producing society, in spite of the absence of centralized and co-ordinated decision-making, there is order and not simply chaos. No one decides how productive effort is to be allocated or how much of the various kinds of commodities are to be produced, yet the problem does get solved and not in a purely arbitrary and unintelligible fashion. It is the function of the law of value to explain how this happens and what the outcome is." It follows from this, Sweezy says, "that in so far as the allocation of productive activity is brought under conscious control, the law of value loses its relevance and importance; its place is taken by the principle of planning. In the economics of a socialist society the theory of planning should hold the same basic position as the theory of value in the economics of a capitalist society."[15]

In Sweezy's view, then, the opposition of value production to planned production is one between unconscious and conscious control of production. The functions of the law of value, i.e. the regulation of "exchange ratios among commodities, the quantity of each produced, and the allocation of the labor force to the various branches of production,"[16] are also the functions of the planning

15 P. M. Sweezy, *The Theory of Capitalist Development,* New York, 1942, p. 53.
16 *Ibid.*

principle, with this difference, however, that the latter is accompanied by knowledge and foresight and the former is not.

According to Marx, "all economy is finally reducible to the economy of time."[17] But even though the "economics of time" determine the allocation of labor in both socialism and capitalism, the allocation itself will be different for the two systems. In capitalism it is determined by the production of capital as exchange-value; in socialism, production is supposedly a *value-free* production for use. The allocation of labor in capitalism is therefore not identical with the distribution of labor that prevails in other forms of social production. It is a capitalistically-modified form of this necessity to distribute labor in definite proportions. And it is precisely this modification which makes the allocation of labor in capitalism appear as an "economic law" operating blindly like a natural law. For the nature of the production process determines the allocation of labor within the necessities set up by the "economy of time." Although value production, too, rests on social labor and the economics of time, it is not derived from the laboring process itself. Rather, value production derives from the laboring process as the social relations of capitalism modify and change it. What Marx defines as the "rational and naturally necessary," and as the "life process of society based on the material process of production," is neither an economic category nor an "economic law of universal validity," but simply the rock-bottom condition of all social existence and development.

Despite Hilferding's assertion, the materialist conception of history is not identical with the labor theory of value. It discusses social development in general, of which capitalism is only a special case. The labor theory of value refers to the specific social relations which operate under capital production. Capital production transforms the laboring process into a value-producing process and the social relations into economic categories. The labor theory of value does refer to the inescapable need — common to all societies — to work and to distribute the social labor in definite proportions. But this general necessity is manifested in a law of value only in capitalism, and only because the market economy cannot divorce the

---

17 K. Marx, *Grundrisse der Kritik der Politischen Okonomie*, Berlin, 1953, p. 89 (from here on referred to as *Grundrisse*) .

value-producing process from the production process itself. The law of value does not operate apart from market relations and is not a necessary requirement for the social organization of labor. But the social organization of labor is necessary for social production, and capitalism finds its answer to this need in the law of value.

The type of regulation of production brought about by the law of value is also specific to capitalism. The proportional allocation of social labor is necessary in all systems of social production; but it will vary nonetheless with the differences between these systems. Even the most general requirements of social production, which may be valid at all stages of social development, take on a specific historical character when applied in different social systems of production. This is not merely a question of conscious as against unconscious regulation, as Sweezy seems to imply by referring to the displacement of the law of value by the planning principle; for the regulation of production under the planning principle will be quite different from that determined by the law of value.

For Marx, "even the most general categories, which possess universal validity just because of their abstract nature, are nonetheless historically conditioned and have full validity only for, and within, the historical relations in which they arise."[18] For instance, he pointed out, both the fact and the concept of abstract labor, of "labor in general," are rather ancient. Yet abstract labor as an *economic category* is a modern accomplishment. The *Physiocrats* still considered agricultural labor the only kind of labor that created value. With Adam Smith, however, it is already labor as such, whether applied to manufacture, commerce, or agriculture, which yields the wealth of nations. Wealth is brought forth by all kinds of labor, by labor in general. From this it may appear, Marx wrote, "that finally there has been found the abstract expression for the simplest and oldest of social production relations of general validity. In one sense this is true, of course, but in another sense not, for *the modern lack of interest regarding specific types of labor presupposes the great and actual variety of the labor activities of modern capitalism,* of which none in particular can be adjudged the ruling type of labor. . . . Labor as such, labor in general, this

18 *Ibid.,* p. 25.

simple abstraction, which is the starting point and the high point
of bourgeois economy, appears as a *practical truth* only as a category of modern society, even though it also expresses an ancient
and for all social formations valid relationship."[19]

It is because capitalism is the hitherto most developed organization of social production that its economic categories throw light
upon past social production relations. Just as the "anatomy of
man is a key to the anatomy of the ape," Marx said, so bourgeois
society is a key to the production relations of previous social formations. But not in the sense of bourgeois economic theory which, by
disregarding historical differentiations, discovers in all past societies
only its own economic categories. The economic categories of
bourgeois society may lead to the apprehension of the conditions of
existence common to all social formations; but they will not lead
to the discovery of "economic laws of universal validity." The labor
theory of value, i.e. the *equation of social wealth in general with
social labor in general,* which has also yielded insight into the
"rational and naturally necessary" common to all social formations,
will continue in the future as it has in the past to have general
validity in so far as it is *itself* an expression of the "rational and
naturally necessary," but not in so far as it is an expression of the
specific capitalist production relations.

As a measure of value and an allocator of social labor, the theory
of value evolved for, and within, the bourgeois relations of production. It is surplus-labor which leads to capital, and thus it is
labor time by which social wealth is measured. But the formation
of wealth as the accumulation of surplus-value is just a particular,
historically-conditioned form of wealth production, bound up with
the specific class and property relations of capitalism. Although
wealth as capital can only be increased through the increase of surplus-labor as surplus-value, this is due not to the process of material
wealth production as such, but to the form this process takes within the social relations of capitalism. Capital arises from labor time,
and grows the faster the more labor time becomes surplus-labor
time; but real social wealth depends only on the actual productivity
of labor and on the real conditions of production, and is not
necessarily tied to appropriated quantities of labor time.

19 *Ibid.*

For Marx and Engels economic value is "a category that belongs to commodity production and disappears with this mode of production, as it did not exist prior to this mode of production."[20] The ruling economic categories "are only abstractions of the social production relations and are truths only while these relations exist."[21] While they exist, however, they determine economic activities. A critique of political economy must therefore start with the analysis of value relations.

It is on the market that the products of labor acquire a uniform social status as commodities. This status is distinct from their varied forms of existence as objects of utility. According to Marx, this division of a product into a useful thing and a value does not stem from the labor process as the metabolism between man and nature, but is a *social accomplishment*. It gains practical importance "only when exchange has acquired such an extension that useful articles are produced for the purpose of being exchanged, and their character as value has therefore to be taken in account, beforehand, during production."[22] The private labor of each producer is socially equal to that of every other producer only because the mutual exchangeability of all kinds of labor and useful products is an established social fact. And this "equalization of the most different kinds of labor can be the result only of an abstraction from their inequalities, or of reducing them to their common denominator, viz., expenditure of human labor-power in the abstract."[23]

It is precisely the difference in the various kinds of labor which is the necessary condition for the exchange of commodities "measured" in terms of abstract labor-time. The reduction of all kinds of labor, regardless of skill and productivity, to abstract or simple labor is not only a postulate of value theory but is actually and constantly established in the exchange process. "A commodity may be the product of the most skilled labor, but its value, by equating it to the products of simple and unskilled labor, represents a defi-

20 Engels to K. Kautsky, *Aus der Frühzeit des Marxismus*, Prague, 1935, p. 145.
21 Marx to P. Annenkov, *Selected Works*, Vol. II, p. 446.
22 *Capital*, Vol. I, p. 84.
23 *Ibid.*

nite quantity of the latter alone."[24] Furthermore, it is not the
individual's productivity which determines the value of any particular commodity but the socially-necessary, or average, productivity required for its production; and it is not the individual's
particular skill which finds consideration in the exchange process
but only the social evaluation of this skill. And this evaluation, by
the nature of the thing, can only be quantitative — a multiplication
of simple labor expressed in money terms.

Capitalism is not a society of independent producers who exchange their products in accordance with the social-average labor
time incorporated in them: it is a surplus-value producing economy
engaged in the competitive pursuit of capital. Labor-power is a
commodity; its value (exchange-value) is determined by its production and reproduction requirements measured in terms of labor
time. Its use-value has the capacity to produce, besides its own
exchange-value, a surplus-value. This type of production is possible
because the workers are divorced from the means of production,
and are thus forced to sell their labor-power to the owners of
capital. Obviously, the "equal" exchange between capital and labor
in terms of value is based on the fact that part of the social labor
is not exchanged at all, but is simply appropriated by the buyers
of labor-power.

But whether appropriated or exchanged, the whole social product
enters the market in the form of commodities. Whatever part of
it cannot be sold has no value, even though labor has been expended on it. The unsold part of social labor would be a waste
of surplus-labor; there simply would be less surplus-value than
there was surplus-labor. To realize all the produced surplus-value,
it is necessary to produce commodities for which there is a sufficient demand. By trial and error individual capitalists will adjust
their production to the changing social market demand.

Labor and labor-time is every entrepreneur's preoccupation, even
if his eyes focus on market prices as he attempts to maximize his
profits. For in order to get these profits, he must first maximize
the surplus-labor in the production process. He can do so either
by lengthening the working time or by increasing the intensity and

24 *Ibid.*, p. 51.

productivity of labor during a given time. In either case, the workers' exchange-value will be at a minimum and surplus-value will therefore be at a maximum for a given total expenditure of labor-power. What holds for the individual entrepreneur holds also for society as a whole: out of total production, a minimum of wages will yield a maximum of profits.

CHAPTER IV

VALUE AND PRICE

In order to stay in business, every capitalist entrepreneur must strive for the largest possible amount of surplus-labor; for only by achieving this maximum can he maximize the profits he can realize through market prices. This profit maximum is only partly determined by his own exertions in maintaining or raising the rate of exploitation; it is *co-determined* by similar exertions on the part of all other capitalists. To increase the profitability of any particular capital, the profitability of *total social capital* must be increased, for otherwise there would be no way of realizing the increased appropriation of surplus-labor as profits in the market. Since surplus-labor in the form of commodities *falls outside the capital-labor relationship,* it must be exchanged between capitalists themselves in their efforts to preserve their capital by augmenting it.

The growth of any particular capital depends on the accumulation of total social capital. This fact sets definite limits to the expansion of all separate capitals. The owner of a growing business becomes aware of these limits when diminishing returns make it unprofitable for him to expand it further. However, capital, like labor-power in the abstract, is differentiated only quantitatively. No matter what the type of production, capital will be employed wherever there is a prospect of sufficient yields. If one avenue of expansion closes, others opening up will be invaded. It is the profitability principle which distributes investments over the different spheres and branches of production, thus allocating social labor in accordance with the surplus-value requirements of capital accumulation. And it is this competitive flow of capital which gives rise to a tendency to equalize rates of profit on capital.

Although the capital market does not differentiate between capital and labor investments, this division does affect the economy. The physical nature of the production process defines the relationship between labor and capital, and thus determines the proportion of investment falling to each factor. There is a difference, to speak in Marxian terms, between the "organic compositions" of different capitals in different spheres of production. Some production processes require great investments in means of production and relatively small investments in labor, while others need less capital investments and demand more labor. The first relationship Marx called a "high" and the second a "low" organic composition of capital. Since labor is the only source of surplus-value, or profits, and profits are measured on total investments (i.e. means of production together with labor-power), it should follow from the labor theory of value that capitals of different organic compositions, but with equal rates of surplus-value, should yield different rates of profit. In reality, there prevails a *tendency* toward their equalization.

Leaving aside such considerations as varying rates of surplus-value in different enterprises, originally diverse rates of profit point to the variety in organic compositions of various capitals. Since the differences in the organic composition of capital which industries possess are determined by their production process, they cannot be eliminated. It may be possible to a degree to average the organic composition of capital within a particular industry; but this cannot be done between totally different spheres of production. Thus the averaging of individual rates of profit must take place in circulation.

In order to understand this mechanism it is necessary to consider the "social" character of capitalist production and the dual nature of the commodity as both a use-value and an exchange-value. There exists a real need to co-ordinate production in terms of use-values. In capitalism the market fulfills this function. It can only exchange what has been produced; but what has been produced reflects the social demand of capitalism at any particular stage of its development. "Social demand" as revealed by the market is not identical with actually existing social needs but only with these needs within the frame of capital production. Still, this capitalistically-determined social demand expresses itself as a demand for use-values. The rising organic composition of capital in a particular industry implies an increasing demand for its commodities. And it is this social demand for commodities produced by industries of a high organic composition which allows them to realize prices that secure their profitability. Since the low organic composition of other industries does not by itself lend their commodities more social use-value than they actually possess, these industries will not be able to realize a greater profit than is compatible with existing social demand as determined by the economic system as a whole.

In the course of capital accumulation almost all industries will increase their investment in capital at a faster rate than their investment in labor-power. Capitals of previously low organic composition may turn into capitals of high organic composition and *vice versa*. Because of the social interdependence of the capitalist mode of production the growth and change of the total capital structure will affect all individual spheres of production and the relations between various industries. A shift from light to heavy industry, for instance, will alter the relations between the extracting and the manufacturing industries. So long as the product of any industry is necessary for the functioning of the system as a whole, it will be able to command prices that will make its existence and expansion possible.

Because all capitalists try for the highest profitability in a market where demand is predetermined by the production system as a whole, the distribution of surplus-value is a "social" affair. As such, it excludes individual considerations such as the specific organic compositions of independent capitals. The total social surplus-value comprises a definite quantity of social labor incorporated in commodities. Not only the surplus-labor but the total social product, or the great bulk of it, must go through the circulation process. The impossibility of isolating surplus-value from its commodity embodiment and the need to throw almost the whole of social production on the market divorces the realization and the division of surplus-value from its production.

If there were a value-for-value exchange, enterprises with a high organic composition of capital could not expand for lack of profitability, while those of a low organic composition could not expand for lack of additional markets. Private capital accumulation, however, implies competitive market relations which "transform" values into prices of production. Of course, the "transformation" is *only a way of saying* that although everything in the exchange process occurs in terms of prices, the latter are nevertheless determined by value relations of which the producers are not aware. This determination of price by value *cannot be established empirically;* it can only be deduced from the fact that all commodities are products of labor, of different quantities of labor, and from the necessarily proportional distribution of the whole of social labor. There is no direct way of discovering a commodity's price in its "value," or, by a reverse procedure, of discovering its "value" in its price. There is no observable "transformation" of values into prices; and the value concept has meaning only with regard to total social capital.

The "transformation" is brought about by way of competition, by the search for profits and extra-profits which constitutes the capitalist contribution and reaction to the increasing productivity of labor. As pointed out above, capital competes for the more profitable lines of business and, where possible, shifts from one type of economic activity to another. It tries to escape from spheres of production of low profitability and to enter those of high profitability. Under conditions of competitive marketing and investment, any particular capital will realize an approximately average rate of profit. Actually, of course, "the rates of profit differ from business to business and from year to year according to the different circumstances, and the general rate exists only as an average of many businesses and a number of years. . . [It is] the nature of the rate of profit and of economic laws in general, [that] none of them has any reality except as approximation, tendency, average, and not as *immediate* reality."[1] Subjected to the "equalization" of profit rates in this sense, an enterprise's share of the total social profit will depend on the size of its capital. This is a further inducement for a rapid capital accumulation. The interdependence of capitalist production, that is, the dependence of each producer on the existence of all other producers, as well as their common need to go through the market in order to turn surplus-labor into profits, pro-

---

1 Engels to C. Schmidt, Marx-Engels, *Selected Correspondence,* p. 563.

duces a kind of "capitalistic communism."[2]

According to Marx, originally different rates of profit are equalized by means of competition into a general rate of profit, which is the average of the special rates of profit. The equalization of profits "transforms" values into prices of production and divides social surplus-value equally among the individual capitals in proportion to their sizes. This world of prices is the only world for the capitalists. For them, that part of the value of the commodity which they have to pay for constitutes its cost-price, which excludes unpaid labor. Profits appear to them as the excess of the selling-price over the cost-price. Commodities can thus be sold below their value so long as they are sold above their cost-price. It is around the cost-price, or price of production, that market prices oscillate.

Cost-prices are specific but the profit added to them is not. According to Marx, while "one commodity receives too little of the surplus-value another receives too much, so that the deviations from value shown by the prices of production mutually compensate one another. In short, under capitalist production, the general law of value enforces itself merely as the prevailing tendency, in a very complicated and approximate manner, as a never ascertainable average of ceaseless fluctuations."[3] Marx thought that commodities would exchange on the basis of labor-time values only by accident. That labor time determines the production process of commodities is obvious. But this cannot find consideration in the exchange process. Already in the first volume of *Capital*, Marx, still restricted to value analysis, pointed out that a "quantitative incongruity between price and magnitude of value, or the deviation of the former from the latter, is inherent in the price-form itself. This is no defect, but, on the contrary, admirably adopts the price-form to a mode of production whose inherent laws impose themselves only as the mean of apparently lawless irregularities that compensate one another." Moreover, "the price-form is not only compatible with the possibility of a quantitative incongruity between magnitude of value and price, . . . but it may also conceal a qualitative inconsistency, so much so, that although money is nothing but the value form of commodities, prices cease altogether to express values.

---

2   Marx to Engels, *Selected Correspondence*, p. 248.
3   *Capital*, Vol. III, p. 190.

Objects that in themselves are not commodities, such as conscience, honor, etc., are capable of being offered for sale by their holders, and thus acquiring, through their prices, the form of commodities. Hence an object may have a price without having a value."[4]

According to Marx, then, commodities are not and cannot be exchanged in accordance with the socially-necessary labor time incorporated in them. Yet Marx insists that "no matter what may be the way in which prices are regulated . . . the law of value dominates the movements of prices, since a reduction or increase of the labor-time required for production causes prices of production to fall or to rise."[5] And since "the total value of the commodities regulates the total surplus-value, and this the level of the average rate of profit . . . it follows that the law of value regulates the prices of production,"[6] even though individual commodity prices do not correspond to labor-time values. Actually, of course, prices exist only individually, and their "regulation" by the law of value can only be deduced from the fact that, although there is no way of dealing with total social production in capitalism, it is nonetheless a reality which overrides all individual exchange relations.

Marx's adherence to the labor theory of value, coupled with his demonstration that commodities cannot be exchanged in accordance with their value, caused both friends and foes to accuse him of self-contradiction. To quote one of the latter, Böhm-Bawerk wrote that "either products do actually exchange in the long run in proportion to the labor attaching to them — in which case an equalization of the gains of capital is impossible; or there is an equalization of the gains of capital — in which case it is impossible that products should continue to exchange in proportion to the labor attaching to them . . . The theory of the average rate of profit and of the prices of production cannot be reconciled with the theory of value."[7]

Marx never claimed, however, that "in the long run" products exchange in accordance with their labor-time. He held that the law of value "regulates" the prices of production and the average

4   *Capital*, Vol. I, p. 115.
5   *Capital*, Vol. III, p. 211.
6   *Ibid.*, p. 212.
7   E. V. Böhm-Bawerk, *Karl Marx and the Close of his System*, New York, 1949, pp. 28-30.

rate of profit by determining whether their *levels* are high or low with respect to *total* value and surplus-value. The law of value dominates the *movements* of prices by virtue of the varying productivity of labor. There is no need for a "reconciliation" of the law of value with the prices of production and the average rate of profit. Value does not dominate the actual quantitative exchange ratios of the commodity market. But the *overall fall or rise* of the prices of production and the average rate of profit is caused by the changing value relations and the changing value content of commodities in the course of the changing productivity of labor and the structural changes in the organic composition of total capital.

Because "the rational and naturally necessary asserts itself only as a blindly working average," Marx wrote to Kugelmann, "the vulgar economist thinks he has made a great discovery when, as against the revelation of the inner interconnection, he proudly claims that in appearance things look different. In fact, he is boasting that he holds fast to appearance, and takes it for the last word. Why, then, have any science at all?"[8] For Marx, the value concept was the "science," or tool, with which he could penetrate and understand the nature and history of capitalism. But though a "concept has the essential nature of that concept and cannot *prima facie* coincide with reality, from which it must first be abstracted,"[9] Marx's "abstractions only reflect, in the form of thought, the content already reposing in the things."[10] Even if there were no chapter on value in *Capital*, Marx wrote, "the analysis of the real relationships which I gave would contain the proof and demonstration of the real value relations. All that palaver about the necessity of proving the concept of value comes from complete ignorance both of the subject dealt with and of scientific method."[11]

In order to understand the capitalist system and its dynamic it was necessary to lay bare its real social production relations and to analyse its development in its *fetishistic determination,* i.e. as a *value-expansion process.* This analysis does not require proof that the actually-given price relations between specific commodities are traceable to labor-time. It merely requires recognition of the ob-

---

8   Marx-Engels, *Selected Works*, Vol. II, p. 462.
9   Engels to C. Schmidt, *Selected Correspondence*, p. 563.
10   Engels to Kautsky, *Selected Correspondence*, p. 454.
11   Marx-Engels, *Selected Works*, Vol. II, p. 461.

vious fact that, just as in any other economic system, so also in
capitalism, social existence and development are unalterably bound
up with labor-time relations in the production process. No matter
how prices may deviate from values, they must find their explanation as well as their boundaries in labor-time relations and thus,
in *capitalistic terms,* in the law of value.

Marx took pains to demonstrate the validity of the law of value
for a system which precludes a value exchange. These efforts do
not betray any desire on his part to make the law of value "operational": he did not expect the law to verify actual exchange relations in terms of prices. Rather, his efforts relate to the theoretical
need to test the validity of the law in confrontation with a reality
which seemed to contradict it. Finding out whether or not value
relations do, in fact, underly market and price relations required
a theory of prices consistent with the theory of value. The "transformation" of values into prices of production satisfies this theoretical need. The problem of individual price determination was of
no real interest to Marx; only value relations mattered, plus the
assurance that the difference between value and price as encountered in reality would neither logically, nor actually, invalidate the
value concept as the *key* to the "essential fundamental laws" of
capital production.

Convinced that the *deviation* of price from value does not eliminate the *derivation* of price from value, even though this derivation can only be established deductively, Marx was not surprised
that the established bourgeoisie should find the value theory irrelevant to their own practical problems. Whereas the very existence
of an average rate of profit, as brought about by way of competition, turned the question of its formation and its quantitative
changes into a problem transcending the market reality and thus
the horizon of bourgeois economic interest, it served Marx as a
verification of the labor theory of value. He saw very well, of
course, that "by the transformation of value into prices of production, the basis of the determination of value is itself removed from
direct observation," and he found it only "natural that the capitalist
should lose the meaning of the term of value at this juncture."[12]
For, with regard to the average rate of profit, "the individual cap-

italists . . . justly believe that their profits are not derived solely from the labor employed in their individual spheres"; and since they saw further "that a reduction in the quantity of labor required for production . . . exerts no injurious influence on profits, . . . how, then, could living labor be the exclusive source of profit."[13]

While competition averages the various rates of profit, it does not determine the magnitude of the average rate of profit at any given time, nor does it cause the changes which occur in this rate. Competition, according to Marx, "can influence the rate of profit only to the extent that it affects the prices of commodities. It can merely make the producers within the same sphere of production sell their commodities at the same price, and make them sell their commodities in different spheres of production at prices which will give them the same profit. In order to balance unequal rates of profit, the profit as an element in the price of commodities must already exist, and competition does not create it."[14] Rather, competition is itself conditioned upon the existence of profit, and the explanation of the average rate of profit presupposes the recognition of its source, which then leads back to value and surplus-value. The average rate of profit indicates that prices are determined by the system as a whole. The system as a whole is susceptible to value analysis.

Competition leads to the division and accumulative application of surplus-value. And this competition implies a deviation of prices from values just because it takes place in a value and surplus-value producing society wherein "the distribution of social labor and the mutual supplementing and circulation of matter in the products, the subordination under the social activity and the entrance into it, are left to the accidental and mutually nullifying initiative of the individual capitalists."[15] Within the market mechanism, the actual division of the products which comprise the aggregate value of the necessary labor time, as well as the actual division of surplus-value among the capitalists and non-productive layers of society, is determined by the real activities of men in the competitive pur-

13 *Ibid.,* p. 201.
14 *Ibid.,* p. 1007.
15 *Ibid.,* p. 1026.

suit of their interests within the frame of their socially-determined but changing possibilities. And here there is nothing but the struggle of all against all, self-interest against self-interest, a general and impenetrable scramble for the amassing of wealth, or for mere existence. Market and extra-market activities intertwine and there is no room for the clear-cut exchange relations of either value or price theory. But even from a purely economic point of view, the variety of degrees of exploitation, differences in the turn-over of various capitals, differences between the spheres of production, the existence of monopolies, the effects of rent and interest upon the rate of profit, and so forth, exclude the possibility of recognizing the value base of the commodity price. This base "remains visible only in the influence of the fluctuating productivity of labor upon the rise and fall of the prices of production."[16]

Marx never intended "to descend from the general idea of value . . . by means of ever closer determinants to a direct determination of the prices of commodities."[17] What he tried to show with respect to the value-price problem is that the absence of value considerations in the market does not invalidate an analysis of capital in value terms. Beyond the statement that price relations presuppose value relations and that in this sense the latter determine and limit the former, no need exists for a "Marxian theory of prices." Marx's goal — the formulation of a theory of capital development — necessitated analysing capital in terms of labor and surplus-labor, value and surplus-value. The value-price transformation does not stand in opposition to the abstract value scheme; it merely points to its limitations. Marx saw no other way — and no other way has yet been found — to penetrate the bewildering capitalist reality and the ceaseless flux of its development except with the value concept.

The controversy around the value-price transformation problem has meanwhile abated. It is no longer doubted that it is "possible to construct an economic model in which the labor theory of value is set forth as a system of distribution but in which commodities do not exchange in proportion to the amount of labor used in their

16 *Ibid.*, p. 965.
17 K. Korsch, *Karl Marx*, London, 1939, p. 153.

respective production."[18] However, bourgeois economy is not interested in the origin but only in the making of profit. It is interested in the market, not in what sustains and determines its
mechanism and changing structure. The deviation of price from
value could not do away with the derivation of price from value
simply because social production is time spent in the laboring
process, and the quantity of products it comprises can never exceed
that number which an equivalent quantity of labor time can produce. However, the deviation of price from value, due to the
market relations which reflect social necessities *within* the system
of capital production, is not such that value is discernable in price.

Aside from being a practical impossibility, it would be a superfluous undertaking, for only in its price form, not in its value
form, does the evaluation of commodities in the exchange process
reflect the capitalistically-modified social needs which determine
the capitalist production and expansion process. The disregard
of the hidden value content of commodities through the deviation
of price from value indicates the extent of "socialization" possible
within the otherwise asocial capitalist society. So long as the
deviation of price from value secures, in one fashion or another, the
necessary and capitalistically-determined proportioning of social labor via the competitive market relations, price and market relations
are the sole concern of bourgeois theory and practice. Without
either ideological or practical applicability in capitalist society, the
labor theory of value could survive only in the Marxist critique of
bourgeois economy.

18   J. P. Henderson, "Marx, Classical Economics, and the Labor Theory of
Value," *The Centennial Review of Arts and Science*, Vol. III, 1959, p. 448.

CHAPTER V

THE LAW OF VALUE
AS "EQUILIBRIUM MECHANISM"

Marxist criticism of bourgeois society had to encompass more than proof of the exploitation of labor by capital. The idea of surplus-value was inherent in the labor theory of value, and socialists prior to Marx had utilized it in their arguments. In order to show once more that profit or surplus-value is gained in production and not in exchange, Marx found it advisable to disregard the effects of market competition on value relations. This is possible only in theory, because the production process cannot actually be divorced from the exchange process. Yet, according to Marx, the laws of capitalist production "cannot be observed in their pure state, until the effects of supply and demand are suspended, or balanced."[1] This was not meant to suggest that such an equilibrium is actually possible because, in fact, supply and demand never balance.

In bourgeois economic theory prices are determined by supply and demand. On the assumption that supply and demand discrepancies cancel one another in the "long run," it appears reasonable to abstract from them and look upon the market as an equilibrium mechanism. Even when it is admitted that extra-economic forces affect price relations, the conviction prevails that such interventions, by operating on either the supply or demand side, will finally issue into a state of equilibrium.

Bourgeois economic theory does not recognize class exploitation, for the commodities entering the market do not betray the division of labor and surplus-labor through the twofold character of labor-power as an exchange-value and as a use-value. It asserts that the

1 *Capital*, Vol. III, p. 223.

market relations assure to each and all the equivalent of their particular contributions to the production process, and that it is precisely the maximization of private self-interest which leads to the optimum of social well-being. The maximization of private self-interest, Marx pointed out, could have quite other effects, if "private interests were not already *socially-determined private interests,* whose realization depended on social conditions, and on the means provided by these conditions, as well as on their reproduction requirements."[2] Otherwise, sheer self-interest could just as well slip into the utter chaos of a struggle of all against all. It is the law of value which gives expression to the socially-determined nature of private interests, and for that reason explains whatever "order" there is in capitalism.

This "order" is itself subjected to the evolution of capital production. Marx saw no reason to deny that market competition affects price relations and the allocation of labor and capital. But this does not imply that the various actually-existing averaging and balancing processes yield the market equilibrium of bourgeois theory. It merely means that the social character of production subjects individual producers to a series of restrictions beyond their control.

This loss of "self-determination" to uncontrollable market events subordinates the whole of the economy to the dynamics of capital accumulation. To speak of a law of value is to say that the exchange relations in capitalism appear as an independent power controlling the producers instead of being controlled by them. It relates to the simple historical fact that the increasing "socialization" of production and exchange took place under the auspices of private property relations, so that individual conditions of production came under the social control of market relations. Individual successes or failures on the market lead to shifts in the sphere of production, and these shifts lead to new market situations, which then require individual producers to take still other actions in order to maintain themselves. Success, however, is simply the realization of extracted surplus-labor in the form of profits within the price mechanism, as determined by the competitive supply and

2 K. Marx, *Grundrisse*, p. 74.

demand relations which indicate the peculiar "social needs" under conditions of capital production.

Market relations derive their definite shape, at any given time, from the quantity of value and surplus-value actually produced. They are "essentially conditioned on the mutual relations of the different economic classes and their relative economic positions, that is to say, first on the proportions of the total surplus-value to the wages, and secondly, on the proportion of the various parts into which surplus-value is divided (profit, interest, rent, taxes, etc.) ."[3] Whatever takes place in the market sphere can take place only within the definite boundaries which events in the sphere of production and the peculiarities of the distribution of the social product establish.

This is not to say that supply and demand discrepancies cannot affect the economy independently; they do so constantly. But it does imply recognizing that market relations are essentially derivative, circumscribed as they are by the capacities and limitations of the production process. Because it is impossible in practice to separate the production process from the circulation process, the effects of the increasing productivity of labor upon the basic production relations as value relations appear only in the modified form of price and profit relations determined by the competitive supply and demand mechanism. But the fact that market relations can only be price relations in no way alters the primary fact that the supply and demand relations are circumscribed by social production relations and the character of social production as the accumulation of capital. In Marx's view, it is not the price system which "regulates" the capitalist economy but, rather, unknown yet capitalistically-determined necessities of production *acting through the price mechanism.* The "regulatory" competitive price mechanism is itself "regulated" by the law of value, just as the law of value may, in turn, be overruled by natural and social necessities transcending the capitalist system.

Because "society can no more cease to produce than it can cease to consume," the social production process is continuous. In capitalism, the social production process is at the same time a reproduction process on an enlarged scale. "The development of capitalist production," Marx said, "makes it constantly necessary to keep increasing the amount of capital laid out in a given industrial undertaking, and competition makes the immanent laws of capitalist production to be felt by each individual capitalist, as external laws. It compels him to keep constantly extending his capital, in order to preserve it, but extend it he cannot, except by means of progressive accumulation."[4] The need to accumulate determines the activities of all capitalists, and it is through *their* activities that the social production and reproduction process appears as the "self-expansion" of capital. The control of the producers by the market is thus simultaneously the control of the producers *and the market* by the accumulation of capital.

Since capital is appropriated surplus-value, the qualitative and quantitative nature of the social production process depends on the ability or inability to extract fresh surplus-value. Accumulation is the source and goal of capitalist production, but capitalists do not concern themselves either with total social production or with the proportional relationship of its necessary- and surplus-labor. As regards the reproduction of the working class, the capitalists leave "its fulfillment to the laborers' instinct of self-preservation and of propagation. All the capitalist cares for is to reduce the laborer's individual consumption as far as possible to what is strictly necessary."[5] The workers, on their part, may try to raise their wages at the expense of profits without regard for the accumulation requirements of capital production. Both attitudes find unknown yet yet definite limits in the conditions set by the social production relations as value relations.

The market is the stage on which all competitive activities are played out. But this stage itself is set up and bound by the class nature of the social structure. Whatever the market relations, they must fit the social production relations; surplus-value must be adequate to the value of capital for the market-play to go on. The criterion for adequacy is accumulation, for without it there may be production but no capitalistic production, i.e. *no production of capital*. The rate of accumulation or, what amounts to the same thing, the rate of surplus-value or profit, is the "ordering" element

4 *Capital,* Vol. I, p. 649.
5 *Ibid.,* p. 627.

on which the regulatory functions of the market are based.

Competition averages commodity prices and profit rates. Obviously, this averaging process presupposes individual differentiations. The sphere of production determines the social supply, and the social demand disregards individual differentiations in the sphere of production. The market demand of the laboring population cannot exceed the equivalent of the wage capital and consists, generally, of consumption goods. The surplus-value to be realized outside the capital-labor exchange is basically split up into profit, interest, and rent. Part of it is reinvested, another part consumed. Surplus-value is convertible into capital "because the surplus-product, whose value it is, already comprises the material elements of new capital."[6] Accumulation, as abstention from consuming the whole of the surplus-value, appears to the capitalists as a "saving process," and profits as the reward of this "abstinence." Actually, of course, the more "capital increases by means of successive accumulation, the more does the sum of the total value increase that is divided into consumption-fund and accumulation-fund. The capitalist can therefore live a more jolly life, and at the same time show more 'abstinence.' And, finally, all the springs of production act with greater elasticity, the more its scale extends with the mass of the capital advanced."[7] Nonetheless, the accumulation-fund cannot be any larger than what is left of the surplus-value after the consumption demands of the non-laboring population have been met. The smaller the total social consumption relative to the total social product, the larger the residue of surplus-value for purposes of accumulation.

In bourgeois theory, "postponement" of current consumption by way of "savings" is merely the way to a richer future consumption. This "postponement," however, is continuous, no matter how much has been "saved" and reinvested in new means of production. Although consumption does increase in the course of capital expansion, capital accumulation increases faster. There can be no "equilibrium" between production and consumption, at any particular time or in the long-run, because progressive capital expansion means widening the gap between the two. Market "equilibrium"

6   *Ibid.*, p. 636.
7   *Ibid.*, p. 667.

can exist only in abstract value terms: it exists when the market
demand is one that will assure the realization of surplus-value by
way of capital expansion. The semblance of a supply-and-demand
"equilibrium" exists only within the process of capital accumulation. It is only in this sense that the law of value "maintains the
social equilibrium of production in the turmoil of its accidental
fluctuations."[8]

Even so, in maintaining the "social equilibrium of production,"
the law of value asserts itself just "as the law of gravity does when a
house falls upon our ears."[9] It asserts itself by way of crises, which
restore, not a lost balance between supply and demand in terms of
production and consumption, but a temporarily lost but necessary
"equilibrium" between the material production process and the
value expansion process. It is not the market mechanism which
explains an apparent "equilibrium" of supply and demand but
the accumulation of capital which allows the market mechanism
to appear, at times, as an equilibrium mechanism.

8   *Ibid.*, Vol. III, p. 1026.
9   *Ibid.*, Vol. I, p. 86.

CHAPTER VI

ACCUMULATION AND
THE FALLING RATE OF PROFIT

Marx was not particularly interested in demonstrating the viability of anarchic capitalism. His concern with the law of value relates to his "ultimate aim to lay bare the economic laws of motion, of modern society."[1] The best points in *Capital*, Marx wrote to Engels, "are 1) the *twofold* character of labor, according to whether it is expressed in use-value or exchange-value (all understanding of the facts depends upon this); and 2) the treatment of surplus-value independently of its particular forms of profit, interest, groundrent, etc."[2] The twofold character of labor-power is, of course, the equivalent of the social relations of capital production as a production of surplus-value. And the independent treatment of surplus-value points to this basic social relationship, which lies hidden behind the various categories in which surplus-value is split up among its various appropriators.

Capitalist production is production of exchange-value by way of production of commodities. Its goal is surplus-value as additional exchange-value. Surplus-value is the difference between the exchange-value of labor power and its actual productive capacity. It is the time relation between the labor necessary to sustain and reproduce the workers and the labor that falls to the capitalists in the form of surplus-products, later realized in profits. From the standpoint of the labor theory of value, the exchange-value of a commodity decreases with the increasing productivity of labor. More use-value in commodity form finds its expression in the same

---

1   *Capital,* Vol. I, p. 14.
2   Marx-Engels, *Selected Correspondence*, p. 232.

or less exchange-value as the socially necessary labor-time incorporated in them declines.

The development of the social productivity of labor in capitalism expresses itself on the one hand in the decrease of exchange-value relative to the use-value of commodities, and on the other hand in an increase of the mass of use-values which compensates for the declining exchange-value. Viewed capitalistically, a mere increase in productivity is senseless unless it involves an increase of surplus-value in terms of exchange-value. This requires an increase in the rate of exploitation, in the "rate of surplus-value," which, in turn, involves a change in the relation between necessary and surplus-labor time. It can be accomplished either by lengthening the total working time or by shortening the work period required to cover the exchange-value of labor-power. One can assume, however, that capital expansion in a closed system will reach a point where the number of workers cannot be increased, where the working time cannot be prolonged, and where that part of the labor-time during which the workers produce their own means of existence cannot be any further shortened. At such a point capital accumulation would come to an end.

The increase of productivity, of surplus-value, and of the accumulation of capital are all one and the same process. They all imply that capital invested in the means of production grows faster than that invested in labor power. In *Capital*, Marx constructs a value-model of capital development in terms of the conceptual entity "total capital," with its social aggregates of wages, profits, and investments. Although all directly discernable connections between value and price are lost in the actual exchange process, a consideration of "society as a whole" shows that all prices together — regardless of their relations to each other — represent total value. This allows for a value analysis of capital development. The concept, "society as a whole," like the value concept itself, is justified not only as a necessary theoretical device but as a valid abstraction from reality.

In general, social development is based on the growing productive power of social labor. Increasing the productivity of labor means that more can be produced in less time. This is accomplished through the development of means and methods of production or, under capitalist conditions, by the accumulation of capital. The growth of capital changes its organic composition. To give Marx's own definition of the term, "the composition of capital is to be understood in a twofold sense. On the side of value, it is determined by the proportion in which it is divided into constant capital or the value of the means of production, and variable capital or value of labor-power, the sum total of wages. On the side of material, as it functions in the process of production, all capital is divided into means of production and living labor-power. This latter composition is determined by the relations between the mass of the means of production employed, on the one hand, and the mass of labor necessary for their employment on the other. I call the former the *value-composition,* the latter the *technical composition* of capital. Between the two there is a strict correlation. To express this, I call the value-composition of capital, in so far as it is determined by its technical composition and mirrors the changes of the latter, the organic composition of capital."[3]

It follows from this definitions that there is a difference between the rise of the value composition of capital and the rise of its material-technical composition. For instance, "if the capital-value employed . . . in spinning is $\frac{7}{8}$ constant and $\frac{1}{8}$ variable, whilst at the beginning of the 18th century it was $\frac{1}{2}$ constant and $\frac{1}{2}$ variable, . . . the mass of raw material, instruments of labor, etc., that a certain quantity of spinning labor consumes productively today, is many hundred times greater than at the beginning of the 18th century. The reason is simply that, with the increasing productivity of labor, not only does the mass of the means of production consumed by it increase, but their value compared with their mass diminishes. Their value therefore rises absolutely, but not in proportion to their mass. The increase of the difference between constant and variable capital is, therefore, much less than that of the difference between the mass of the means of production into which the constant, and the mass of the labor power into which the variable, capital is converted. The former difference increases with the latter, but in a smaller degree."[4]

The organic composition of capital reflects this particular rela-

3 *Capital,* Vol. I, p. 67.
4 *Ibid.,* p. 683.

tionship between value and material composition. The gradual change in the organic composition of capital occurs more or less in all spheres and branches of production. The average of individual compositions yields the composition of the total capital in any particular branch of production, and the average of the averages in all branches of production yields the composition of the total social capital. It is with this final average that Marx is concerned when he deals with the general law of capital accumulation.

To repeat: the rise of the organic composition of capital implies that the mass of the means of production, and production itself, rise faster than the value composition of capital; which follows, by the law of value, from the decrease of exchange-value caused by the increasing productivity of labor. By assuming a constant rate of surplus-value, the rising organic composition of capital leads to a gradual fall of the rate of profit, since it is only the variable part of capital which yields surplus-value, while the rate of profit is "measured" on total investments, i.e. constant and variable combined.

The tendency of the rate of profit to fall is compensated through the increasing productivity of labor which results from the higher organic composition of capital. Capital accumulation, according to Marx, expresses itself "on the one hand in a tendency to a progressive fall of the rate of profit, and on the other hand in a progressive increase of the absolute mass of the appropriated surplus-value, or profit; so that on the whole a relative decrease of variable capital and profits is accompanied by an absolute increase of both. This twofold effect can express itself only in the growth of the total capital at a ratio more rapid than that expressed in the fall of the rate of profit."[5]

Capital may accumulate and maintain a given rate of profit when the value of the variable capital and the value of the constant capital grow at the same pace. This would, however, imply capital formation without an increase in the productivity of labor, which contradicts the real development of capitalism, particularly its vast technological advancement. The absence of capital accumulation may not cause a fall in the rate of profit. But a non-accumulating capitalism is only a temporary possibility; it is a capitalism in crisis. For capitalist production is conceivable only in terms of

5 *Capital*, Vol. III, p. 261.

accumulation. Generally, capital formation always displaces labor and to that extent reduces the rate of profit while simultaneously increasing both the rate and the mass of surplus-value.

As long as the rate of surplus-value can be sufficiently increased, the tendency for the rate of profit to fall is only latent. To "demonstrate" a declining rate of profit one may assume a stationary rate of surplus-value in an otherwise expanding capitalist system. But a situation in which exploitation cannot be increased enough to offset the tendential fall of the rate of profit is not forseeable. Marx himself pointed out that the abstract scheme of capital development was not enough to provide any predictions about the actual world. All crises in capitalism must be explained out of the given, empirical conditions, "out of the real movement of capitalist production, competition, and credit."[6] The value analysis of capital development postulates "the possibility of crises by a mere consideration of the general nature of capital, without regard to the additional and real relations that form the conditions of the real production process."[7]

Nevertheless, the law of the falling rate of profit was for Marx, "the most important law of political economy."[8] Simple though "the law of the falling rate of profit" appears to be, the classical economists had "tried in vain to discover it."[9] They had not succeeded because they had been "tinkering with the distinction between constant and variable capital without ever defining it accurately."[10] Ricardo, for instance, "equated profit with surplus-value,"[11] but he did not observe its relation to total capital. Thus he failed to recognize the falling rate of profit as an *immanent* law of capital accumulation. Although incapable of predicting the end of capitalism in any specific sense, the recognition of the falling rate of profit as the immanent law of capital expansion destroyed the illusion that capitalism could ever reach the state of tranquility its apologists held out as the hope of the future. It implies that all the concrete contradictions encountered in reality cannot be considered accidental or remediable shortcomings. These difficulties,

6   K. Marx, *Theorien über den Mehrwert*, Stuttgart, 1905, Vol. II, p. 286.
7   *Ibid.*, p. 264.
8   K. Marx, *Grundrisse*, p. 634.
9   *Capital*, Vol. III, p. 249.
10 *Ibid.*
11 *Grundrisse*, p. 639.

singly and as a developmental pattern, are due to a trend inherent in capital production itself. When capitalism's inner connections are grasped, Marx wrote, "all theoretical belief in the permanent necessity of existing conditions breaks down before their practical collapse."[12]

In its early stages, capital formation seemed to be merely a quantitative increase in capital. Through the rising organic composition of capital, it became a qualitative change. Newly-added capital attracts fewer and fewer laborers in proportion to its magnitude, and the reproduced capital, which partakes of the changing capital composition, repels more and more of the laborers formerly employed by it. Still, accumulation implies an increase in the laboring population, since part of the surplus-value must be retransformed into additional variable capital. To do this requires an *accelerated* rate of capital expansion. According to Marx, "it is not merely that an accelerated accumulation of total capital, accelerated in constantly growing progression, is needed to absorb an additional number of workers, or even, on account of the constant metamorphosis of old capital, to keep employed those already functioning. In its turn, this increasing accumulation and centralization becomes a source of new changes in the composition of capital, of a more accelerated diminution of its variable, as compared with its constant, constituent."[13]

However, the extension of capital production brings new capital of low organic composition into the market economy. Thus the relative decline of the variable capital is mitigated by its absolute growth. Technological development reduces the capital-value of the means of production and thereby slows up the growing discrepancy between constant and variable capital. The tendency of the rate of profit to fall is compensated for by these and other "counter-tendencies." The question is, however, whether this is always possible.

As previously noted, there are two ways of increasing the rate of surplus-value for a given capital: lengthening the working-day, or shortening that part of the working-day during which the workers produce the equivalent of their exchange-value. This holds true also for the imaginary "society as a whole," i.e. the world "treated

12   K. Marx, *Letters to Dr. Kugelmann*, Moscow, 1934, p. 74.
13   *Capital*, Vol. I, p. 691.

as one nation in which capitalist production prevails everywhere, in order to examine the object of our investigation in its integrity, free from all disturbing subsidiary circumstances."[14] In this model of capital production the rate of surplus-value may be increased by increasing the total labor-time or by decreasing that part of the total labor-time which is the equivalent of variable capital. But there are definite limits beyond which the absolute labor-time cannot be extended and the necessary labor-time (the labor-time falling to the workers) cannot be reduced. This is as true for the total mass of social labor as it is for the individual worker. However, the limits which apply in the case of the individual worker are observable, while those which limit "society as a whole," or any existing society, are not. To speak in extremes: the absolute working-time during any one day cannot exceed 24 hours, and the necessary labor-time cannot be reduced to zero. The extraction of surplus-value has both natural and social boundaries.

The tendency of the rate of profit to fall is a theoretical conclusion derived by applying the labor theory of value to the capital formation process. As a result of the increasing productivity of labor, we will recall, the value of commodities declines with the reduction of the labor-time required for their production. But more commodities are now produced during the time previously needed for fewer of them. Spread over a greater mass of use-values, exchange-value is also enlarged, though to a lesser degree, and capital accumulates. A similar process affects the profitability of capital. Although the rate of profit declines with the rising organic composition of capital, the mass of surplus-value increases with the mass of the accumulated capital. For any *definite* amount of capital the rate of profit will be lower. But since the total mass of capital is larger, there is more surplus-value; and capital realizes the same, or even a higher, profitability. In Marx's words, the same causes "which bring about an absolute decrease of surplus-value and profit on a *given* capital, and consequently in the percentage of the rate of profit, produce an increase of the absolute mass of surplus-value and profit appropriated by the total capital."[15] This is so, because *"while any aliquot part, any 100 of the social capital, any 100 of average social composition, is a given*

---

14 *Ibid.*, p. 636.
15 *Capital*, Vol. III, p. 259.

magnitude, for which a fall in the rate of profit implies a fall in the absolute magnitude of profit just because the capital *which serves as a standard of measurement is a constant magnitude,* the magnitude of the social capital, on the other hand, as well as that of the capital in the hands of the individual capitalists, . . . varies inversely with the decrease of its variable portion."[16] Despite the fall in the rate of profit, "there may be an absolute increase of the number of laborers employed by capital, . . . an absolute increase of the mass of surplus-value absorbed, and consequently an absolute increase in the mass of the produced profit. And this increase may be progressive. And it may not only be so. On the basis of capitalist production, it *must be* so, aside from temporary fluctuations."[17]

The development of the social productivity of labor implies an increased production of use-values, including the means of production, and consequently requires additional labor. This labor depends not on "the value, but on the mass of these means of production (including the means of subsistence) because the laborer in the production process is not operating with the exchange-value, but with the use-value of the means of production."[18] Accumulation is therefore "accompanied by a growth of the mass of the available and appropriated surplus-labor, and consequently by a growth of the absolute mass of profit appropriated by the social capital."[19] All that is necessary is that "the multiplier indicating the growth of the total capital must be equal to the divisor indicating the fall of the rate of profit."[20] In other words, "capital must grow at a faster rate than the rate of profit falls . . . In order that the variable portion of the total capital may not only remain the same, but may also increase absolutely, although its percentage in the total capital falls, the total capital must grow at a higher rate than the percentage of the variable capital falls."[21] Thus the accumulation process itself nullifies the fall of the rate of profit. If the accumulation is large enough, the greater mass of capital of a higher organic composition will yield the same or a greater profit than that brought forth by a smaller total capital of lower organic composition.

16 *Ibid.,* p. 259.
17 *Ibid.,* p. 255.
18 *Ibid.,* p. 256.
19 *Ibid.*
20 *Ibid.,* p. 260.
21 *Ibid.,* p. 261.

Seen in the light of the labor theory of value, accumulation in terms of exchange-value is held in check by the falling rate of profit, while the simultaneous growth of use-value, in the form of additional capital, increases the mass of profit and therewith increases the *actual* profitability of capital. Nevertheless, accumulation, according to Marx, is characterized by: "First, the increase of surplus-labor, that is, the reduction of the necessary labor time required for the reproduction of labor-power; secondly, the decrease of the labor-power (the number of workers) employed in general for the purpose of setting in motion a given capital."[22] These occurrences are mutually conditioned by one another and affect the rate of profit in opposite ways. While the rate of surplus-value rises in one direction, the number of laborers falls in the opposite direction. "To the extent that the development of the productive powers reduces the paid portion of the employed labor, it raises the surplus-value by raising its rate; but to the extent that it reduces the total mass of labor employed by a certain capital, it reduces the factor of numbers with which the rate of surplus-value is multiplied in order to calculate its mass. Two laborers each working 12 hours daily, cannot produce the same mass of surplus-value as 24 laborers each working only 2 hours, even if they could live on air and did not have to work for themselves at all."[23]

Because "the relation between wage labor and capital determines the entire character of the capitalist mode of production,"[24] the fall of the rate of profit can be checked by accumulation but cannot be entirely prevented. The compensation for the relative reduction in the number of workers by means of an intensified exploitation cannot go on "forever" but must eventually find its absolute limit in the increasingly greater mass of the reproducible capital and its expansion requirements. Whatever the mass of labor-power in the real capitalist world, in relation to the progressively faster growing constant capital, it must become a relatively diminishing quantity of *surplus-value-producing* labor-power.

Carried to its "logical end," a continuously accelerating capital expansion will change the relative decline of the rate of profit into an absolute decline because of a lack of surplus-value with respect to the swollen mass of capital. When this happens, reality will correspond to Marx's model of capital expansion.

22   *Ibid.*, p. 289.
23   *Ibid.*, p. 290.
24   *Ibid.*, p. 1025.

CHAPTER VII

THE "BUSINESS CYCLE"

Marx's value model of capital development is a methodological device to "grasp its inner interconnections," which cannot be observed in immediate reality. To have a theory of capital development at all, the "force of abstraction" has to transcend the semblance of competition. The abstract value-scheme reveals that, apart from competition as the driving force of capital formation, profit production already finds a limiting element in the capital-labor relationship.

In order to forestall a decline of profitability, accumulation must never rest. More and more surplus-value must be extracted; for this purpose, production must be steadily revolutionized, and markets must be continually extended. The two-fold character of commodity production as the production of exchange-value and use-value determines that the process of accumulation, and the variations in surplus-value which follow from it, will become increasingly more detrimental to the functioning of the capitalist system.

The twofold character of the commodity — as a use-value and as an exchange-value — and their movements in opposite directions in the course of the developing productivity of labor reappears on the larger social scale of capital accumulation as a conflict between the expansion of production and the expansion of surplus-value. The conflict is resolved by an accelerated capital accumulation. According to Marx, however, the resulting growth of capital is not a smooth process. Capital has the tendency "to develop the productive forces absolutely, regardless of value and surplus-value contained in it," even though the goal of production is "the preservation of the value of the existing capital and its self-expansion to the highest limit."[1] When the expansion of production outruns its profitability, the accumulation process comes to a halt.

The interruption of the accumulation process constitutes the capitalist crisis. It appears as an overproduction of capital, which, for Marx, "never signifies anything else but overproduction of means of production — means of production and necessities of life — which may serve as capital, that is, serve for the exploitation of labor at a given degree of exploitation; for a fall in the intensity of exploitation below a certain point calls forth disturbances, . . . crises, destruction of capital."[2] In terms of Marx's abstract value analysis of capital accumulation, this would correspond to a situation in which the reduced labor-power is no longer able to reproduce and enlarge the total mass of capital. The actual accumulation process resembles the abstract value-scheme of capital development. But what in theory is the "final" outcome of an uninterrupted development appears in reality as a recurrent cycle; each cycle, so to speak, is a condensed replica of the "long-run" trend of capital expansion.

The capitalist crisis is an overproduction of capital only with respect to a given degree of exploitation. If the latter is sufficiently increased accumulation can proceed, for it was halted only because the accumulated capital proved too large in relation to the rate of profit it was able to bring forth. Because it is only by way of accumulation that the capitalists can preserve and enlarge their capital, they do so without regard to, and without the ability to regard, the necessary profitability of the total social capital, on which the profitability of all private capitals finally depends. When the rate of profit does not grow along with the mass of capital, the latter's increasing organic composition is not offset by a greater mass of surplus-value, and the decreasing profitability of capital will halt its further expansion.

Marx's descriptions of economic processes are not always the most precise, which allows for contradictory interpretations. However, as the whole of Marxian theory rests upon value theory, the validity of any particular interpretation may be judged by its fitness with regard to the law of value. Marx's statement, for instance, that capital has "the tendency to develop the productive forces abso-

1 *Capital,* Vol. III, p. 292.
2 *Ibid.,* p. 300.

lutely, regardless of the value and surplus-value contained in it,"
may easily be interpreted as meaning that it is the expansion of
the material production process itself which causes a lack of profitability. In that case, however, the fact that capitalism can overcome
crisis would be incomprehensible; for it does so precisely by developing the social productive forces still further. If the productive
forces outrun the value requirements of accumulation, they do so
only in the sense that "the expansion or contraction is determined
by the appropriation of unpaid labor, and by the proportion of this
unpaid labor to materialized labor in general, or, to speak the
language of the capitalists, is determined by profit and by the
proportion of this profit to the employed capital, by a definite rate
of profit, instead of being determined by the relations of production to social wants, to the wants of socially developed human
beings. The capitalist mode of production, for this reason, meets
the barriers at a certain scale of production which would be inadequate under different conditions. It must come to a standstill at
a point determined by the production and realization of profit,
not by the satisfaction of social wants."[3]

The relationship between the appropriated unpaid labor and the
mass of capital can be improved only by increasing the mass of
unpaid labor. This increase, in turn, leads to a further increase in
the mass of capital. From the point of view of profitability, then,
the crisis of overproduction represents a situation in which the
existing capital is *simultaneously too small and too large*: it is too
large in relation to the existing surplus-value and it is not large
enough to overcome the dearth of surplus-value. Capital accumulation is thus both the cause of crisis and the instrument that over-
comes it. The crisis sets in because the expansion of production
has lost its necessary correlation with the profitability of capital,
so that, from the point of view of the latter, capital has been
overproduced. This lack of correlation between production and
profitability can also be expressed as a discrepancy between material and value production due to the twofold character of capital
production as the production of use-value and of exchange-value.

Although subordinated to the relentless drive for exchange-value,
the use-value aspect of capital — as the material production process — continues to play a relatively independent part in capital

3 *Ibid.*, p. 303.

production. The continued existence of capitalism shows, however, that the "internal contradiction" between use- and exchange-value does not alter the dominance and control of material production by value considerations. That this dominance becomes increasingly more precarious is historically illustrated by the increasing severity and frequency of crises and, finally, by the advent of the rather permanent crisis conditions that are now oddly celebrated as the taming of the business-cycle via conscious interferences in the market mechanism.

The effect of the use-value aspect of capital production upon the accumulation of capital comes to the fore, for instance, in the determination of the mass of additional capital required for a successful capital expansion. Only a definite amount of new capital, as determined by the amount of physical capital already in existence, will suffice for an accelerated capital expansion. This definite mass of surplus-value refers to *total* social surplus-value in relation to the *total* social capital. If this definite mass of surplus-value cannot be produced under the existing conditions, there can be no profitable capital expansion. There may then exist an "abundance" of investable funds which is not large enough to serve the needs of a profitable accumulation. In the real capitalist world it cannot be known, of course, whether the mass of surplus-value is adequate for the purpose of capital expansion. The relationship between the mass of existing capital and the mass of surplus-value needed to assure its reproduction on a larger scale can only be discerned indirectly, through market and price relations which signify either an expanding or a contracting economy.

This indirect discernment is inaccurate because factors not caused by a discrepancy between material production and value production may account for a downward business trend. For, in reality, "the conversion of surplus-value into profit is determined as much by the process of circulation as it is by the process of production."[4] Discrepancies in the supply and demand relations may hinder the realization of surplus-value even though — under different market conditions — the actually-produced surplus-value may have proved adequate for the requirements of capital formation. Be this as it may, the point is that even on the assumption that *no realization problem exists,* it is possible that a discrepancy

4 *Ibid.,* p. 964.

between material production and value production will arise which will have to be overcome before accumulation can go on.

On the assumption that no difficulties arise in the circulation process, a sufficient mass of surplus-value would lead to the simultaneous expansion of material and value production, and an insufficient mass of surplus-value would not. The arrest of the accumulation process is, of course, the capitalist crisis, which manifests itself in a sudden decline of profitability. Once in crisis, capitalism can only resume its expansion through changes in the sphere of production which increase the surplus-value relative to the value of the existing capital. Such changes require a "starting-point" different from that which constituted the "endpoint" of the previous phase of capital expansion, for this "endpoint" proved to be a crisis-point. In other words, the new upswing presupposes both the crisis and the destruction and devaluation of capital which it brings.

The crisis leaves the use-value side of capital largely unaffected, except when the material means of production are actually destroyed, as in times of war. But it affects the value of the total constant capital through the destruction of capital-values during the crisis and ensuing period of depression. The same quantity of use-value now represents a smaller exchange-value; and the surplus-value, determined by the unaltered use-value of capital, relates itself to a smaller total value of capital. With regard to its material side, the organic composition of capital remains the same, but as regards its value side, it has been lowered. This adjustment raises the profitability of the surviving capitals.

Capital stagnation cannot have physical causes, for the existing material forces of production, as both means of production and labor power, are not altered by the crisis. Nor can it find its cause in a material overproduction of the means of production, for in this respect the world is obviously under-capitalized; not enough means of production exist to satisfy even the minimal needs of the world's population. The turn from prosperity to depression can only be explained as a shift in value relations, that is, as a shift from a sufficient to an insufficient profitability of capital. As profits are only another name for surplus-value, or surplus-labor, the crises-cycle finds its explanation in the loss and restoration of an adequate rate of exploitation. As there was apparently no lack of surplus-value during the phase of accumulation preceding the depression, the accumulation process itself, by altering the organic composition of capital, must have led to a relative dearth of surplus-value and produced the crisis. The resumption of the accumulation process indicates that ways have been found to increase the production of surplus-value in a measure great enough to neutralize the effects of the rising organic composition of capital on the rate of profit.

The rising organic composition of capital, the law of the progressive increase of the constant capital in proportion to the variable, Marx found "confirmed at every step by the comparative analysis of the prices of commodities, whether we compare different economic epochs or different nations in the same epoch."[5] The height of the organic composition of capital at any particular time says nothing, of course, about the further prospects of capital production. Capital can accumulate with a high as well as a low organic composition of capital, so long as its rate of exploitation is correspondingly accelerated. Over-accumulation of capital relative to the exploitability of labor reduces the rate of accumulation or stops it altogether; yet the resulting crisis conditions provide opportunities for the reorganization of the total capital structure which allows for a new phase of capital expansion. The devaluation of capital relates a given mass of surplus-value to a smaller total capital. And the capital concentration which it aids plays this surplus-value into the hands of relatively fewer entrepreneurs. Less-productive capital disappears to make room for more-productive capital, and the sharper competition between remaining capital hastens the search for capital-saving and labor-saving innovations, until the increase of surplus-value makes expansion possible once more. This increase must be large enough, however, to enlarge total capital beyond the highest point of expansion it previously reached.

Although no actual crisis is predictable as to the time of its arrival and the extent of its devastation, the state of crisis can be awaited as the certain result of an enhanced accumulation process unable to maintain its necessary profitability. Because the decline of profitability, associated with a scale of production signifying an

5 *Capital*, Vol. I, p. 682.

overproduction of capital, becomes apparent in the market sphere, it appears as a mere market problem, as a temporary disequilibrium of supply and demand. No capitalist can admit more, for to trace the crisis to the underlying value relations of capital production means to accept responsibility for the crisis as an economic expression of the exploitative capital-labor relations.

CHAPTER VIII

THE REALIZATION OF SURPLUS-VALUE

According to Marx, "the contradictions inherent in the move-ments of capitalist society impress themselves upon the practical bourgeois most strikingly in the changes of the periodic cycle through which modern industry runs, and whose crowning point is the universal crisis."[1] Throughout the nineteenth century, crisis followed crisis in intervals of roughly ten years. The periodicity of crises, according to Marx, stems simply from capitalism's ability to overcome the overproduction of capital through changes in conditions of production which increase the mass of surplus-value relative to the existing capital. The *definite* crisis-cycle of the last century is, however, an empirical fact not directly related to Marx-ian theory. It is true that Marx tried to connect the definite per-iodicity of the crises with the turn-over of capital. But he did not insist on the validity of this explanation. In any case, his theory does not depend on any particular periodicity of crises. It only maintains that crises are bound to arise as an expression of a temporary overproduction of capital and as the medium for the resumption of the accumulation process.

In Marx's abstract value-scheme, an absolute overproduction or over-accumulation of capital sets in as soon as a further enlargement of the total capital would yield a mass of surplus-value smaller than that previously realized. Although the conditions which the value-scheme of development assumes do not exist in the real world of capital production, it is nevertheless clear that individual capitals, and capitalism as a whole, exist in situations which set limits to their growth. If these limits are transcended, crisis sets in; this leads to activities that remove these borders by reorgan-

1 *Capital,* Vol. I, p. 26.

izing the total capital structure. Yet this reorganization sets up conditions which contain specific limits of their own.

At any given time the actual borders of capital expansion are determined by general social conditions, which include the level of technology, the size of the already accumulated capital, the availability of wage-labor, the possible degree of exploitation, the extent of the market, political relations, recognized natural resources, and so forth. It is not the market alone but the whole social situation in all its ramifications which allows for, or set limits to, the accumulation of capital. Because it is not possible to calculate when the expansion of one or all capitals reaches its limits in actual social conditions, limiting conditions have to be assumed in order to reveal the meaning of the process here involved.

The capitalist economy is an entity of production and exchange. The great bulk of the commodities produced must be sold; for if commodities cannot be sold, the capital and surplus-value they contain cannot be realized, and the increased exploitation that produced them may not be able to prevent reduced profits. The discrepancy between the creation of surplus-value and its realization appears as a glut on the market, as an over-production of commodities. Seen from the angle of productive development rather than from that of its results, the over-production of commodities is an over-production of capital. For Marx, the over-production of capital always implies the over-production of commodities, but the distinction between them is still important. For the over-production of capital and commodities, instead of leading to a curtailment of productivity, only accelerates the latter, thereby indicating that the discrepancy between the production of surplus-value and its realization arises because of a decline in the rate of accumulation. With a sufficient rate of capital expansion there would be no over-production, and as soon as the accumulation process is resumed, the market becomes once more what is considered "normal," despite the even larger quantity of commodities now offered for sale. What is involved here, then, is not an over-production of commodities in relation either to the absolute consuming power of society or to the relative consuming power of capitalism, but an over-production of commodities in relation to the capitalistically-limited demand under the particular conditions of relative capital stagnation.

Over-production of capital is always the "end-point" of a period of successful capital formation wherein the extension of production parallels the expansion of the existing capital. To prevent this point from arriving, the conditions of production must be altered. These change, of course, in the very process of accumulation. There is, however, no reason to assume that the conditions of production will always change so as to accomodate the need for capital expansion, the less so because the former are the general social conditions of production and the latter a particular need bound only to the exploitative capital-labor relationship. And though it is true that social demand, by affecting the distribution of social surplus-value via the competitive establishment of an average rate of profit, sets or removes limits to particular capitals, this social demand does not represent the realities of social conditions but is itself largely determined by the production of capital.

At any rate, a crisis is an interruption of the accumulation process. Whatever specific crisis theories have been brought forth since Marx, these things are generally acknowledged — that a rate of expansion sufficient to forestall stagnation and decline depends on the profitability of capital; that it becomes increasingly more difficult to maintain such a profitability in view of the size of capital already reached; that economic stagnation can be ended only by an improvement in profitability. These constitute the content of all business-cycle theory.

All crises have been preceded by a speculatively-enhanced expansion of production and credit. This does not mean, however, that overproduction results from speculation and the extension of credit; for "the extension of the credit system is only the form which hides the overproduction of capital."[2] Overproduction is already inherent in competitive capital accumulation because of the two-fold character of value production and the single-minded drive for exchange-value. "The expansion and contraction of credit is a mere symptom of the periodic changes of the industrial cycle."[3] The decline of profitability contracts the credit structure just as the increase of profitability enlarges it. Similarly, while it is true that competition enhances capital expansion regardless of the profitability of total capital, this is so only because the tendency for

2 Engels to Marx, *Briefe über das Kapital*, Berlin, 1954, p. 74.
3 *Capital*, Vol. I., p. 695.

the rate of profit to fall exists in the production process, independent of the competitive mechanism.

Aside from windfalls of colonial robbery, early capital formation proceeded at a relatively even pace because of the still placid course of technological development and because of social barriers to the creation of a vast industrial proletariat. The non-capitalist aspects of the economy were still strong enough to give the total social process of development the general appearance of production for consumption. The same backwardness accounts, of course, for the horrors of early capitalism and the extraordinary greed for surplus-value that found its expression in the pauperization of the working population. It also explains the classical economists' pessimism about the capitalist future, and their own, inadequate, concern with the problem of the falling rate of profit.* Only with the rise of modern industry, the opening of the world market and the preponderance of capital-labor relations in production, did capital expansion itself become the major determining factor of social development. Until then, human physical necessities under less complex social conditions gave the early capitalist development an element of "order" not its own.

Although predetermined by the division of labor into necessary labor and surplus labor, social demand in early capitalism was in large measure a demand for the means of consumption. Hence the idea that the market equilibrium of supply and demand is determined by the social requirements of production for consumption. As capitalism became the dominant mode of production and the tempo of accumulation increased, "social demand" became in always greater measure a demand for capital. Supply and demand in the traditional sense ceased to determine the production process; the production of capital, *as capital,* determined the size and nature of the market demand.

Commodity production creates its own market in so far as it is able to convert surplus-value into new capital. The market demand is a demand for consumption goods and capital goods. Accumula-

---

* For instance, Adam Smith thought that capital accumulation lowered the general rate of profit in the same sense in which the competitive expansion of particular trades lowered the profit for these trades; and David Ricardo held that the general rate of profit was bound to decline because capital accumulation, while raising the productivity of industry, diminished the productivity of agriculture through the increasing inferiority of natural resources.

tion can only be the accumulation of capital goods, for what is consumed is not accumulated but simply gone. It is the growth of capital in its physical form which allows for the realization of surplus-value outside the capital-labor exchange relations. So long as there exists an adequate and continuous demand for capital goods, there is no reason why commodities entering the market should not be sold.

According to Marx, a market "equilibrium" in terms of prices implies an "equilibrium" in terms of values and presupposes the full realization of surplus-value. For a given time period, total social labor is accounted for only when the unconsumable part of surplus-value is converted from commodities into fresh capital. Only then is the circulation process in "harmony" with the production process. Without this accumulation, prices will fall not only because of the increased productivity of labor but also because the supply of commodities will exceed the demand. On the other hand, if the demand for capital exceeds the supply, prices will rise despite the increasing productivity of labor. Prices rise or fall with variations in the productivity of labor *and* in supply and demand. These latter variations, however, depend on the rate of capital expansion; and this rate depends in turn on the productivity (profitability) of labor relative to the existing mass of capital. In other words, price changes due to supply and demand relations derive from the value and surplus-value relations which determine the rate of accumulation.

Whatever the price movements that accompany the accumulation process, and whatever their particular fluctuations in times of crisis, at no time do they tend toward an equation of supply and demand which gears social production to social consumption. Price changes always relate themselves to the expansion or contraction of capital accumulation. A low rate of capital expansion will appear as an excessive market supply of commodities and depress prices. A high rate of accumulation will reverse the market situation and raise commodity prices.

There can be surplus-labor production without capital accumulation. In that case, "surplus-value" would comprise no more than the consumption fund of the non-working population. But capital production excludes this state of simple reproduction. Coerced by competition, the individual capitalists must accumulate, if only to preserve the capital already their own. Capital is used up in the production process as a cost-of-production item, and is recovered in the circulation process as part of the price of commodities. Generally, any particular capital which does not increase its productivity by expanding will disappear, for capital can only realize its surplus-value on the market, and the market averages prices according to the changing productivity of labor.

An entrepreneur may invest in new and more productive capital equipment even when his profit on current production makes this a questionable undertaking, because the additional investment may promise a greater competitive ability and enable him to enlarge his market at the expense of other capitalists. All additional investments are so many attempts to partake of an expected larger market demand, or to get a larger share of an existing stable, or even declining, demand at the expense of other enterprisers.

A larger market presupposes a larger production, even though a larger production may not find an adequate market demand. In the attempt to safeguard capital by augmenting it, the capitalists accelerate the accumulation process. There is no certainty that the expansion of production will extend the market in equal measure. However, this very acceleration is itself a market extension in that it increases the demand for the means of production. If, in consequence, the market demand increases generally and affects all spheres and branches of production, a period of "prosperity" ensues and will appear as an "equilibrium" of supply and demand. On the assumption that capital accumulation has this effect, the only possible reason why it should suddenly be halted is a lack of surplus-value; and this lack must have arisen within and despite the accumulation process.

In reality, of course, it seems to be the other way around; it appears that the surplus-value is unrealizable due to an abundance of use-values (commodities). And to the individual capitalist it is indeed lack of demand which hinders the sale of his commodities and which induces him not to increase production by additional investments. But this apparent dependency of accumulation on market demand merely reveals the individual capitalists' reactions to the social dearth of surplus-value, or surplus-labor, i.e. to the insufficiency of the *laborers' use-value* (their working capacity) that falls to the capitalists in exchange for the laborers' exchange-value (wages), or, what is the same, to the decrease of the exploitability of labor in comparison with the profit requirements of a progressive capital accumulation.

Hidden in the sphere of production, this situation is not contradicted by a glut in the commodity market. It must always be kept in mind that capitalist production is for profit and capital. The production of commodities as concrete use-values is merely the medium for the production of capital as abstract exchange-value. It must also be remembered that, with respect to profitability, the decline of the exchange-value element of commodity production is immunized by the increasing productivity of use-value production. Likewise, the decline in profitability that a definite amount of capital experiences finds its compensation in the growth of the total capital. In this manner, an increase in the quantity of unpaid labor — expressed as a greater mass of commodities — sets aside the tendential fall of the rate of profit. Thus, the actual glut on the commodity market must be caused by the fact that labor is not productive enough to satisfy the profit needs of capital accumulation. Because *not enough* has been produced, capital cannot expand at a rate which would allow for the full realization of *what has been* produced. The relative scarcity of surplus-labor in the production process appears as an absolute abundance of commodities in the circulation process and as the overproduction of capital. This is made evident by the fact that periods of overproduction are always terminated by an increase, not a decrease, in production and in the means of production made possible by improving the conditions of exploitation.

Although the expansion of capital depends on the realization of surplus-value in circulation and sporadically comes to a halt through market limitations, capital accumulation is not a realization problem. It is that too, of course, but the realization problem derives from the fact that capital production is a value-expansion process. Even assuming the non-existence of the realization problem, Marx saw the accumulation process as historically limited because it destroyed its own source of existence and secret of development through the fall of the rate of profit in the course of the rising organic composition of capital.

This process, to be sure, can also be described in the less abstract form of surplus-value realization. The results would be the same, however. The sphere of circulation grows with the growth of capital. But the capital expansion process is also a capital concentration and centralization process. This hampers the spatial extension of capital production, for capitalists become increasingly unable and unwilling to capitalize world production. The increasing difficulty of maintaining a rate of profit sufficient for the expansion of existing capital diminishes the desire to extend capital into non- or under-developed regions. Instead these regions are largely maintained as cheap raw material bases in exchange for commodities produced in capitalistically-developed territories.

Accumulation did imply the constant extension of capitalist production through the transformation of more primitive modes of production into commodity production. This is one way of arresting the rise of the organic composition of capital and of stabilizing the rate of profit. But accumulation also brings centralization and concentration which depress the formation of new capital, and thus gradually diminish the "beneficial" effects new capital can have on the average rate of profit. According to Marx, "the concept of capital contains the tendency to create the world market";[4] but capitalist development simultaneously hinders the capitalist development of world production by its immanent tendency to monopolize the capital accumulation process.

This is not to say that capitalism is responsible for the existence of underdeveloped countries. But it is to say that a full industrialization of world production cannot be accomplished through the accumulation of private capital. The growth and monopolization of private wealth hampers and distorts the formation of social wealth. To be sure, there is nothing in the capitalist system which prevents it from searching for profits all over the globe, and there is no place capital will not enter if it is profitable to do so. Yet the concentration of wealth based on private-property divides the world into capital-rich and capital-poor regions, just as it polarizes each particular nation into capitalists and wage-workers.

Capitalism found it more profitable to restrict industrial development to its own part of the world. Once this monopolistic position was reached and consolidated, it could not be given up without seriously disturbing the whole fabric of Western capitalism. To preserve the nonindustrial nations as markets for their

4 K. Marx, *Grundrisse*, p. 311.

manufacturing industries was then the commercial policy of all developed nations, and it was politically enforced in countries under their control. Nature itself, it was asserted, destined some countries to be producers of industrial commodities and others to be producers of primary products. More than a "natural fact," this division was also an economic convenience, as elucidated by the theory of comparative costs, i.e. the notion that it was more "economical" to produce primary products in primary-producing countries and more "economical" to produce industrial commodities in industrial nations. In this way, supposedly, everyone gained by the "international division of labor," that is, by the division of the world into industrial and nonindustrial nations. Actually, however, the exchange between these countries was always advantageous to the developed ones and disadvantageous to the underdeveloped.

This is one way in which capital concretely hinders the unfolding of the social forces of production. But while this procedure hastens the expansion of the monopolized capital for some time, it later becomes an additional cause of capital's stagnation. And this is so because in relation to the rising accumulation requirements of the existing concentrated capitals less and less surplus-value can be extracted out of the productively-stagnating underdeveloped territories. For their own part, these territories cannot capitalize production in competition with the already highly-monopolized capitals; and the rise of new independent capitals is possible only in relative isolation from the capitalist world market.

Designed and built up with a view toward an expanding world market, the productive capacity of capitalistically-advanced nations exceeds the scope of their national markets. As this is more or less true for all industrial countries, their combined production exceeds the scope of the world market, unless a *general* rapid capital formation expands the world market as fast as it does production. Although this is seldom the case, it is not impossible. Marx's model of capital accumulation assumes that this is possible and therefore restricts the tendential fall of the rate of profit to events in the sphere of production. In reality, of course, the widening productivity-gap between the capitalistically-developed and underdeveloped regions impairs the realization of surplus-value through the latter's increasing impoverishment. By fostering only the exploitation of primary goods production, by transferring profits made in these areas to the industrially-advanced nations, and by imposing terms of trade favoring the developed capitalist countries, the advanced nations reduce the underdeveloped area's ability to buy manufactured goods. The poorer the underdeveloped nations become, the less a market they offer for the products of the industrially-advanced countries, and the less able they are to capitalize themselves and thus to increase the general demand. This lacking demand is actually a lack of surplus-value in territories unable to buy. What appears as a *realization problem* in advanced capitalist systems is a *production problem* in less developed nations. The total effect, however, is a shortage of surplus-value, which hinders the advance of the *general* accumulation process.

Whether one looks at the production of surplus-value, or its realization, when seen from the position of total capital, the real problem of capitalism is a shortage, not an abundance, of surplus-value. Only by looking at a particular capitalist nation in isolation, or by separating the developed capitalist world from the world as a whole, does an actual lack of surplus-value appear as an overproduction of commodities. Similarly, it is only from the standpoint of the individual producer in any capitalist nation that an actual shortage of socially-produced surplus-value appears as a declining market demand. But in the world at large and in each nation separately, there is overproduction only because the level of exploitation is insufficient. For this reason, overproduction is overcome by an increase in exploitation — provided, of course, that the increase is large enough to expand and extend capital and thereby increase the market demand.

CHAPTER IX

CAPITALISM IN CRISIS

Because of the fetishistic character of capital production, the capitalist system in all its phases and in all its details may in a way be considered to be in a "permanent" condition of crisis. Depression is a precondition for prosperity; prosperity comes to an end in a new depression. They are, so to speak, two sides of the same coin. Since capitalists operate as individual concerns in a social production of world-wide scope, and are not able to comprehend the real possibilities and limitations of the "system as a whole," over-expansion in some spheres of production, or in some nations, may lead to over-expansion in other industries and nations and may finally affect the world at large. Both the force of competition and the desire to profit by a boom turn an upward trend in business into a self-propelling expansion which can drive investments to a point where the profits demanded of them are no longer forthcoming.

Over-production of capital demands a fairly well developed capitalism. It is not a real issue in the early stages but becomes an increasingly greater problem as capital accumulates. In a certain sense, each crisis is more severe than the one preceding it because of the growing interdependence of production and of social life generally. In another sense, each successive crisis faces greater opportunities because the breadth of structural changes required for capitalism's further expansion becomes ever greater. Past a certain point, however, capital expansion's need to extend geographically runs into the national barriers within which capitalism developed. The nations in crisis attempt to bridge these difficulties at the expense of other nations. Economic opportunities shift from one country to another, from one continent to another; and the economy now requires not only the rationalization of industry but a general reorganization of the economic, social and political structure of world economy.

The crisis lays bare the discrepancy between material and value production: its approach is signalled by a slackening rate of accumulation, an over-production of commodities, and an increase in unemployment. So the way out of the depression is effected by closing the gap between expansion and profitability, by new investments and the "normalizing" of the commodity and labor markets. A crisis does not just start. It starts in specific industries, even though it is caused by the total situation. Like the crisis, the upswing, too, starts in specific industries and cumulatively affects the whole of the economy. Because capital accumulation is the enlarged reproduction of the means of production, the upswing and decline, although general, are first and foremost noticeable in the manufacture of production goods.

The crisis does not, however, reflect the real situation. Just as the upswing exaggerates profit expectations, so the crisis exaggerates declining profitability. To speak in Keynes' subjective terms, the unrealistic "optimism" of prosperity leads to the unrealistic "pessimism" of depression. In either direction, the competitive process tends to extremes: it hastens both the over-production of capital and the reorganization of the capital structure. A depression may "sneak" into existence by a gradual slowing down of economic activity, or it may be initiated by a dramatic "crash" with sudden bank failures and the collapse of the stock market. The crisis itself is merely the point at which the reversal of business conditions is publicly recognized.

Whatever the circumstances surrounding the reversal of the economic trend, it is accompanied by an over-production of commodities. Even the last phases of the boom preceding the crisis are, viewed in retrospect, already unprofitable; but recognition of this fact has to await the verdict of the market. Commitments made on the assumption of a continuous upward trend cannot be met. The conversion of capital from commodity to money form becomes increasingly more difficult. The crisis of production is at the same time a financial crisis. The need for liquid funds and the attempt to avoid losses intensify the fall of securities and commodity prices. Competition becomes cut-throat competition and for some businesses prices are forced down to the point of ruin. Capital values are rapidly depreciated, fortunes are lost, incomes are wiped out. Social demand declines further as the number of unemployed grows: the commodity-glut is checked only by the still faster decline of production. The crisis extends into all spheres and branches of production. Its general form reveals the social interdependence of the capitalist mode of production despite the private property relations which control it.

After a period of panic, however, the capitalist economy reorients itself towards a new stability under changed conditions. The ensuing stagnation or depression, while destroying many businesses, improves the profitability of the survivors by presenting them with larger markets. A more concentrated capital now commands a larger sphere of business operations. It defends and consolidates its newly-won position, cutting labor-costs by investing anew in technological innovations. To a greater or lesser degree competition forces all surviving capitals to do the same, and a new wave of investments, altering the relationship between profit and wages, initiates a new period of capital production. The problems of capitalism, coming to the fore on the market, find their solution in the sphere of production, though the solution is not complete until it also affects market relations.

Not only the conditions of capital production but also its circulation improve and ease the realization of surplus-value. As the upward trend gains momentum, demand increases and the oversupply of commodities diminishes. Prices begin to rise under conditions of a greater volume of business, for the concentration process affects the sphere of circulation, too. To be sure, wages also begin to rise and the average rate of productivity of labor declines because of the greater number of workers employed, including less productive workers laid off during the depression. But as long as profitability can be raised through new methods and means of production faster than it falls due to the improvement of labor conditions, the rate of accumulation remains unaffected.

Despite intermittent periods of depression, each upswing brings capital production to a higher point and wider extension than its previous level of development. There are fewer capitalists relative to the increased capital but more in absolute numbers. There are fewer workers employed relative to the accumulated capital but more in absolute numbers. Capital develops in a manner that may be described as three steps forward and two steps backward. This type of locomotion does not hinder the general advance; it only slows it. When capitalist development is seen as a continuous and

steady process, quite apart from the hectic fluctuations of expansion
and contraction, the rate of capital accumulation is quite moderate
and gives no indication of the many upheavals and social struggles
it involves.

To speak, then, of the capitalist crisis or the business-cycle is
merely to refer to the specific manner in which capital accumulates under competitive market conditions where the interrelations
of capitalist production as a whole are left to enforce themselves by
way of crisis. Any mechanism in capitalism which regulates anything at all must first regulate the relationship between production
and profitability. With the self-expansion of capital as the determining developmental factor, the "law of value" asserts itself less and
less in terms of price changes in everyday market activity; it requires, instead, an all-embracing economic crisis. The "equilibrium
tendencies" of the competitive market come to the fore not in their
actualization but in the expansion and concentration of capital.
And just because it requires a crisis to re-establish the type of pro-
portionality necessary for a further capital formation. the various
crisis-elements accumulate undetected and unchallenged in each
expansion period.

For Marx, each period of crisis and depression is a manifestation
of the workings of the "law of value," a "healing-process" on which
the continued life of capital depends. The "equilibrium" forces
of the market operate within a mechanism which "equates" the
rate of accumulation with the rate of profit and to this end demands recurrent crises. The type of market equilibrium of which
bourgeois economy speaks cannot be brought about. The only
equilibrium possible is a "dynamic equilibrium" which implies a
successful accumulation of capital and, therewith, a steady increase
of the disequilibrium between "social demand" and actual social
needs, between the profit-determined expansion of production and
the expansion and organization required for the satisfaction of
social needs.

The capitalist crisis validates the general theory of capital accumulation, as it is here that Marx's abstract value analysis of capital
production finds its *observable* verification. The rise of the organic
composition of capital is an incontestable development. The fall
of the rate of profit as a consequence of the rising organic composition of capital is, however, experienced only in periods of crisis

and capital stagnation, as expanding capitalism compensates for the fall of the rate of profit by a rise in the mass of profits on the larger total capital.

No specific data exist for the organic composition of total capital. According to the state of industrialization, it is high in some nations and low in others. Even for a particular nation, the organic composition of capital can only be vaguely calculated from insufficient, unsuitable, and largely unreliable data, which yield not much more than the obvious; namely, that the increasing productivity of labor manifests itself in the continuous expansion of capital. A hundred years after the writing of *Capital,* it must still be said that not even for a single country, America in this instance, can "past performances with respect to capital formation and financing be studied in adequate detail, because of lack of data."[1] However, what data exist do verify Marx's expectations as to the course of capital development.

As regards capital formation in America, Simon Kuznets relates that during the period 1869 to 1955 "there was a marked growth of capital per person and per number of the labor force. Net capital stock per head rose, over the period as a whole, to about four times its initial level . . . at a rate of about 17 per cent per decade."[2] To be sure, capital formation per head of population and even per head of labor force is not related to the rise of the organic composition of capital in the Marxian sense. It shows nonetheless that capital increased constantly and, for the period under consideration, rose four times faster than population. Kuznets summarizes the growth in the volume of capital formation in terms of dollar values in constant (1929) prices. He distinguishes between gross- and net-capital formation, the latter being the actual additions to the existing capital after the deductions of the "consumed" fixed capital are made. "The annual value of gross capital formation rose from $3.5 billion in 1869-1888 to $19 billion in 1929-1955, and to $30 billion in 1946-1955. This long-term rise over some three quarters of a century was thus about nine times the original level. Capital consumption (depreciation) charges . . . also rose rapidly, from an annual level of about $1.5 billion in 1869-1888 to over $14 billion in 1929-1955 and slightly over $19

1 S. Kuznets, *Capital in the American Economy,* New York, 1961, p. 33.
2 *Ibid.,* p. 66.

billion in 1946-1955. The rise here was, therefore, to about thirteen times the initial level. Net capital formation also grew appreciably, from $2 billion per year in 1869-1888 to $4.7 billion in 1929-1955, and to about $10.5 billion in 1946-1955. The rise was over five times the initial level."[3]

Data somewhat more relevant to the organic composition of capital exist for selected industries. For instance, for America's 100 largest firms, employing 5 million persons and having combined assets of $126 billion, the average amount of assets per worker grew from $12,200 in 1949 to $20,900 in 1959 and to $24,000 in 1962.[4] There were wide variations between different industries, as the following table shows:[5]

Average Total Assets per Employee, by Industry,
of the largest Manufacturing Corporations in 1959

NUMBER OF COMPANIES	INDUSTRY	AVERAGE INVESTMENT PER EMPLOYEE
21	Petroleum Products	$62,000
3	Distilling	53,400
3	Tobacco Products	50,700
8	Nonferrous Metals	28,200
8	Chemical Products	24,700
9	Iron and Steel	21,200
3	Pulp and Paper	18,800
3	Autos and Trucks	14,800
11	Machinery and Equipment	13,000
6	Food Products	10,500
4	Tires, Rubber Products	10,300
5	Electrical Equipment	10,100
7	Aircraft	7,600
9	Other Manufacturing	17,700
100		20,900

With all their imperfections, including their failure to distinguish between capitalistically-productive and unproductive labor in the amalgam "head of labor," Kuznets' figures suggest nonetheless that capital formation does proceed in accordance with the value character of capital production, which requires a faster increase of the constant than of the variable part of capital. Leaving periods of depression aside, the overall rate of capital formation indicates a sufficient rate of profit by the very fact of the accumulated capital. Only a decline of the rate of accumulation causes the

3 *Ibid.,* p. 394.
4 First National City Bank, *Economic Letter,* New York, June, 1963.
5 *Ibid.,* August, 1960.

latent tendency of the rate of profit to fall to manifest itself. This can also be expressed in reverse: a decline of profitability comes to the fore as a reduced rate of capital formation which, in turn, arrests the rise of the organic composition of capital.

Now, one of Marx's "countertendencies" to the fall of the rate of profit is precisely a slowing down of the rise of the organic composition of capital through cheapening the elements of constant capital. It is made possible by technological changes increasing the productivity of labor so that relatively less surplus-value is converted into additional capital. While labor-saving devices foster the more rapid increase of capital investments relative to wages, capital-saving devices diminish to some extent the widening gap between the money invested in labor and that invested in capital. This could not be otherwise because the increasing productivity of labor also affects the production of the means of production. Capital-saving and labor-saving innovations are actually one and the same, meaning that, relative to the quantities of commodities produced, less and less labor is employed in all branches of production and thus also in the manufacture of capital goods.

To accumulate capital, the mass of capital must increase despite and because of the cheapening of the means of production. The cheapening of constant capital is thus a "countertendency" to the fall of the rate of profit only in so far as it allows for a more rapid capital accumulation. This is already made obvious by the fact that crises and depressions accompanied capitalist development under conditions of a low as well as a high organic composition of capital. Since only conditions of rapid capital formation bring forth a social demand large enough to employ all, or nearly all, productive resources, capital must accumulate irrespective of the state of its organic composition. Because capital is not only a production relation but also a value relation, the mass of capital in any one cycle of production must be larger in value terms than it was in a previous cycle.

Returning to Kuznets' observations, we learn that during the last three decades the organic composition of American capital has not risen as it did previously. Over some sixty years, prior to 1920, capital stock per worker grew at high rates; from then on, however, capital stock per worker declines drastically. It is true, Kuznets writes, "that the period beginning in 1929 includes the

Great Depression; on the other hand, it includes also the expansion years of World War II and a decade of a particularly high level of capital formation following the conclusion of the war. If we view the average in 1929-1955 as an approximation of long-term secular levels, we can hardly escape the conclusion that substantial changes have occurred in the factors that determine capital formation."[6]

The lowering of the rate of capital formation in the United States, in Kuznets' view, appears to be the result of a growing rate of capital depreciation and capital-saving inventions. Whereas in the period from 1869-1888 "it took $1.7 of gross capital formation to provide $1 of net capital formation," in the decade between 1946-1955, "it took almost $3 of gross capital formation to do so." Gross capital formation itself, relative to gross national product (in constant prices), declined from "22.6 per cent in 1869-1888 to 21.5 per cent in 1909-1928 and to 17.6 per cent in 1946-1955." With gross capital formation declining in proportion to gross national product, and with "the rate of capital consumption to gross capital formation rising appreciably, the ratio of net capital formation to national income (or national net product) shows a distinct downward trend. Its share declined from 14.6 per cent in 1869-1888 to 11.2 per cent in 1909-1928 and to 7.0 per cent in 1946-1955."[7]

The rise of capital "consumption," with its depressing effect upon net capital formation is explained not by a quicker physical deterioration of capital but by the quickening of its competitive obsolescence. On the other hand, the more productive capital replacements tend to be of a capital-saving type, combining higher efficiency with a lower supply of capital per worker. The growing "wealth" of America expresses itself as a growing wealth of marketable commodities rather than of capital investments. Whereas in times past the net effect of technological changes was an increase in both output and capital, in more recent times real production per capita has grown with a declining rate of capital formation.

Not infrequently, then, it is said that "capitalism is in crisis . . . because it produces too much surplus-value for its ultimate realization in the progressive accumulation of capital."[8] Qualitative changes in the technology have supposedly brought forth the "pos-

---

6 *Capital in the American Economy*, p. 68.
7 *Ibid.*, p. 395.
8 J. M. Gillman, *The Falling Rate of Profit*, New York, 1963, p. 126.

sibility of producing additional surplus-value without corresponding additions to the invested capital, [and] the chief form of rela-
ization, that of its conversion into capital, becomes [therewith]
impaired."[9] The result is that the national product grows faster
than does capital.

This is not, however, a novel situation. According to Marx, as
we have seen, production and the productivity of labor always
grow faster than the value of capital. At all times and by all means,
capitalists try to trim capital-costs and labor-costs in their search
for the greatest amount of profit possible. Throughout every economic depression, moreover, surplus-value in the form of unsalable
commodities cannot be converted into additional capital, and gluts
the market as an apparent abundance of surplus-value. To go back
once again to fundamentals: the rising organic composition of
capital does not reduce the *actual* rate of profit on capital so long as
capital accumulates faster than the rate of profit falls. If capital
accumulates without a corresponding rise in the organic composition of capital, that is, if new capital of low organic composition
constantly enters the market economy through the spread of the
capitalist mode of production and thereby lowers the *average* composition of capital, the mass of surplus-value and the rate of profit
will rise. Capital-saving innovations which lower the organic composition of capital should have the same effect; indeed, according to
Gillman, in twentieth century capitalism they have led to a super-
abundance of surplus-value. In Gillman's view this surplus-value
cannot be realized as *new* capital, and also cannot be realized in
the form of consumption because of capitalism's antagonistic system of distribution. Capitalism's difficulties are here shifted from
the sphere of production into the sphere of distribution. Not production but realization of surplus-value accounts for the capitalist
crisis. This is a flat rejection of Marx's theory of capital accumulation and, by implication, of the labor theory of value itself. Furthermore, this "shift" has nothing to do with the social conditions
peculiar to twentieth century capitalism, because the production
problem of capital could at all times be *read* as a realization problem. Even in the nineteenth century, Malthus, for instance, saw
the crux of the capitalist dilemma in the realization problem. And
at the turn of the century, the Marxist Rosa Luxemburg saw in

9 *Ibid.,* p. 61.

the difficulties of surplus-value realization the objective reasons for crises and wars and for capitalism's eventual demise.

All this has little to do with Marx, who saw that the actual world of capitalism was at once a production and a circulation process, to be sure, but who held nevertheless that nothing circulates unless it is first produced, and for that reason gave priority to the problems of the production process. If the production of surplus-value is adequate to assure an accelerated capital expansion, there is little reason to assume that capitalism will falter in the sphere of circulation.

Because of the tendential fall of the rate of profit there can never be an abundance of surplus-value in relation to the accumulation needs of capitalism. Of course, due to market disproportionalities, particular industries may experience a realization problem; however, these same disproportionalities will overcome the problem by re-allocating labor and capital in accordance with the principle of profitability. A general overproduction of capital and commodities, affecting all spheres and branches of production at once, cannot be explained by market disproportionalities. It impairs the realization of surplus-value for total capital, affecting individual capitals to varying degrees; and this general impairment cannot be resolved by a mere reallocation of the existing labor and capital.

In theory, according to Marx, a sufficient increase of surplus-value will change a period of capital stagnation into one of expansion. The relative stagnation of the American economy, for instance, could be considered a prolonged crisis situation which, in fact, it is. There is nothing in Marxian theory which excludes the resumption of an enhanced capital expansion, though the *actual situation* in which American capitalism finds itself may preclude such an event. Capital stagnation is a crisis situation. Within this crisis situation attempts are made to increase the profitability of capital. If these attempts do not result in accelerated accumulation, this does not indicate that there is too much surplus-value for purposes of capitalization; rather it indicates that *for this end* the surplus-value is not sufficient, whatever it may be. If this particular situation continues for long, it would point to the insolubility of crisis conditions, for a *continuous increase of production without capital accumulation* is no longer true capitalist production. An increasing part of surplus-labor would lose its value character and to that extent decrease the profitability of capital. In that case, one could speak of a "permanent crisis" of capital production, which is to say that the crisis mechanism fails to restore the conditions for an expanding capitalist economy.

Marx did not concern himself with the individual firm or country save in so far as a description of either would throw light upon the character of the capitalist system as such. He used England for demonstrative purposes, and pointed out that the "country that is more developed industrially only shows, to the less developed, the image of its own future";[10] but this image relates only to the capitalist conditions of production and exchange, and does not exclude variations between nations in other respects. British capitalism substantiated Marx's general theory of capital accumulation, but this theory, once evolved, was independent of any particular country. Just as the fortunes of individual capitals vary in the general competitive accumulation process, so do the fortunes of individual nations. But for the world as a whole, the capitalist accumulation process remains determined by the increase or decrease of surplus-value relative to the growing mass of total capital. Stagnation of capital in one nation may allow for a more rapid accumulation in another. But it is the unknown quantity of total capital and its relation to total surplus-value which determine the fortunes of capitalism as a whole. This implies that some nations will experience a *general* shortage of surplus-value in the *particular* form of a shortage of investment funds, while other nations may experience the same situation as an "abundance" of unrealizable surplus-value. But the peculiarities of the distribution of surplus-value do not affect its quantitative relations to total capital. In any case, unrealizable surplus-value ceases to be surplus-value, so that the lack of profitability becomes a general phenomenon.

It is not that a disproportionality of the market supply and demand issues in the simultaneous inability to sell and buy. An actual shortage of surplus-value *creates this disproportionality*. If capitalism as a whole could develop faster than it actually does, surplus-value would possibly be convertible into additional capital. Yet even if the unsalable part of the surplus-labor could be fully realized in additional capital, the rate of profit would nevertheless fall with the rising organic composition of capital, which would

10 *Capital,* Vol. I, p. 13.

lead once more to overproduction and the transformation of a production problem into a realization problem.

From a Marxian point of view, the various existing theories of crises which categorize the problem as either underconsumption or the overproduction of commodities — the one implying the other and both involving the realization problem — only describe the externals of the capitalist crisis mechanism. The periodic overproduction of the means of production and of commodities which prevents the realization of surplus-value is, in Marx's view, only an overproduction of means of production that cannot serve as capital, that is, cannot serve for the exploitation of labor at a given degree of exploitation. And though the overproduction of commodities is an obvious fact, Marx's theory is not a theory of underconsumption. According to Marx, capitalist production is, and must always be, at variance with the consuming power it brings forth — in periods of prosperity as well as in periods of depression.

It is not a "consuming power" growing in proportion to production which explains the increasing social demand for consumption goods in the upswing period of capital development; it is merely the greater number of workers now employed. In periods of expansion, prices rise faster than wages and reduce individual workers' incomes while enlarging the income of the class, or increase individual incomes only in so far as they are based on steady and prolonged work. Furthermore, it is not the rising consumption of the non-working population which narrows the gap between social production and social consumption, since the increasing surplus-value is now largely reinvested. It is the rapidly increasing demand for production goods which explains the increasing demand for consumption goods and allocates social labor accordingly. At the beginning of a depression, prices fall faster than wages, and the individual worker's lot improves while that of his class, which embraces the unemployed, worsens. With the development of a new stability within the depression, the situation changes and even the employed worker's wages decrease in terms of buying power. But this is already an aspect of a new upward trend. Similarly, at the height of prosperity, wage-increases which keep pace with, or even outrun, the rise in prices, are largely a sign of the approaching crisis. In short, the business-cycle is not caused by variations in social consuming power, particularly not in that of the workers; rather the cycle determines these variations.

Aside from these considerations, however, the ultimate cause of all real crises "remains the poverty and restricted consumption of the masses as compared to the tendency of capitalist production to develop the productive forces in such a way that only the absolute power of consumption of the entire society would be their limit."[11] For in view of actual productive capacity and the restricted consuming power of the broad masses, the *observable* cause of crisis is the obvious inability to consume what has been produced. That this is a condition of capitalist existence does not alter the fact that it is also a contradiction between production and consumption. In the real crisis, apart from the hidden crisis-mechanism of capital production, the mass of unsalable commodities faces a steadily declining buying-power and a productive capacity designed for an increasing demand. In capitalist theory, this means that demand does not equal supply in terms of prices, which will lead to market changes in price relations that will eventually close the gap. For Marx, however, the gap can only be temporarily closed by an enhanced capital accumulation, which then enlarges the permanent gap between production and consumption. In his view, the crisis cannot be eliminated by a reduction of production, or by an increase of consumption, or by the co-ordination of both. To do the last would be equivalent to ending the capitalist system itself. Neither underconsumption nor overproduction are self-explanatory. They can be understood only in the context of capital production.

11   *Capital*, Vol. III, p. 568.

CHAPTER X

THE EXPROPRIATION OF CAPITAL

Capitalist production must progress, for standing still means retrogression. It cannot cease accumulating without disrupting the whole social fabric on which it rests. Any static analysis of its relationships is purely fictitious, and is excusable only as a possible medium for grasping its real dynamics. In order to secure a continuous production of surplus-value adequate to the continuous need to accumulate capital (which is the capitalistically-necessary precondition for a more or less satisfactory social production in real terms — such as sustains social existence) capitalism must unceasingly revolutionize the sphere of production in its search for ever more surplus-value, and must consistently expand its markets in order to transform surplus-value into additional capital. Yet the realization of surplus-value depends not simply on a larger market, but on one which allows for the expansion of capital in the form of new means of production, for the realization of surplus-value as *capital*.

Accumulation proceeds by way of competition. This is not to say that capitalism depends on competition. Just the same, competition is its true mode of motion. "So long as capital is still weak," Marx wrote, "it supports itself by leaning on the crutches of past, or disappearing, modes of production. As soon as it begins to feel itself strong, it throws away these crutches and moves about in accordance with its own laws of motion. But as soon as it begins to feel itself as a hindrance to further development and is recognized as such, it adapts forms of behavior through the harnessing of competition which seemingly indicate its absolute rule but actually point to its decay and dissolution."[1] In other words, a

1   K. Marx, *Grundrisse*, p. 544.

"healthy" capitalism is a strictly competitive capitalism, and the imperfections of competition in the early and late stages of its development must be regarded as the ailments of an infantile and of a senile capitalism. For a capitalism which restricts competition cannot find its indirect "regulation" in the price and market movements which derive from the value relations in the production process.

Marx was concerned with the competitively-expanding private-property capitalism of his time, which either advances by way of accumulation or suffers crisis and depression. When he speaks of the "self-expansion" of capital, of "accumulation for the sake of accumulation," he speaks of the compulsive and never-resting drive for exchange-value. This drive, while making capitalism the hitherto most productive social system of production, also accounts for all its social and economic difficulties and, finally, for its tendency to freeze the social forces of production when and wherever their further development collides with the specific capitalist relations of production. The principle of accumulation accounts for both the rise and the decline of capitalism. The contradictions of capital formation — all traceable to the value character of capital production — both foster and retard the general development of the productive powers of society. But at some point in the accumulation process "the development of the social productive power turns into an obstacle to capital, or, what is the same, the capitalist relations of production become obstacles to the further development of the productive power of social labor. At this point, capital and wage-labor stand in the same relation to the development of social production and social wealth as did, previously, the guild-system, serfdom, and slavery. The fetters of capital production must now be shed. Contradictions, crises, social convulsions point to the incompatibility of the social productive development with the capitalist relations of production. In the violent destruction of capital, not by external circumstances, but as a condition of its self-preservation, it becomes evident that capitalism's time is done and that it must be replaced by a higher state of social production."[2]

By contemplating the effect of the increasing productivity of labor upon the capitalist relations as economic value relations, Marx was able to predict the major trend of capital expansion, even

2 *Ibid.,* p. 635.

though these predictions relate to no more than the broad "*histor-ical tendency* of capitalist accumulation."[3] His highly abstract model of capital expansion can explain only why capital moves by way of expansion and contraction, and why this kind of locomo-tion finds increasingly more obstacles put in its way by the always growing mass of capital, its concentration and centralization, its rising organic composition, and the latter's detrimental effect upon its profitability. But these findings are logical conclusions drawn from a model bound to a limited set of economic assumptions, which, though basic to the capitalist system, do not exhaust the concrete capitalist world.

Although there is no real understanding of given reality without a theory of development, such a theory tells only *where to look* in the attempt to comprehend the unfolding real world of capital production. The logical end-consequence of capital development as a value expansion process need not become a practical reality; yet, at any particular time, the theory provides a point of orienta-tion for a narrower, more concrete analysis of the *actual movements* of capital production. If capitalism could get out of its own skin, so to speak, and suddenly become something other than itself, then, of course, the value analysis of capital expansion would be quite superfluous. As it is, however, any particular mode of production rests on definite social production relations which remain unaltered no matter how much the mode of production may be modified. So long as social relations are economic value relations and determine the general development as such, capitalist accumulation will have the *historical tendency* detected by Marx.

Marx's value theory of capital development is *at once* a general theory of accumulation and a special crisis theory; that is to say, neither the one nor the other can be dealt with separately. Assum-ing an uninterrupted capital expansion in a closed system, the general theory reveals the fall of the rate of profit as a consequence of the rising organic composition of capital. However, this general tendency comes to the fore only in periods of crisis, with the over-production of capital. Only through these *actual* occurrences does the general theory gain its *practical* importance. The *real* limita-tions of the capitalist system are not given by the abstract tenden-tial fall of the rate of profit as elucidated in the value model, but

3 *Capital*, Vol. I, p. 834.

reveal themselves in the *concrete conditions* of the crisis of over-accumulation.

The only relevant crisis-point in the general theory of capital accumulation is that point at which surplus-value can no longer be sufficiently increased to overcome the tendential fall of the rate of profit by permitting an accelerated capital expansion. In the real world there is no way whatsoever to determine when such a point will be reached. The actual capital accumulation process can be slowed down and is, in fact, constantly slowed down by non-productive, i.e. non-profitable, capital expenditures, by the outright destruction of capital (as in times of war), and by political interventions in the economy. The average rate of capital expansion, calculated over a period of time, is quite moderate and does not seem to justify the expectation that capital will find its end in the tendential fall of the rate of profit as depicted in Marx's model of capital accumulation. The distinction between the model and reality must always be kept in mind.

However, it is not the average rate of accumulation over long periods of time which determines social activities, but the actual state of capital production at *any given time* — during periods of prosperity or periods of depression. Marx's general theory of accumulation makes clear "that *the real barrier to capitalist production is capital itself.* It is the fact that capital and its self-expansion appear as the starting and the closing point, as the motive and aim of production; that production is merely production for *capital,* and not vice versa, the means of production mere means for an ever-expanding system of the life process for the benefit of the *society* of producers."[4] Yet because capital production has this character, it can for a time overcome the barriers it sets in its own way. It is not until this mode of production actually and permanently becomes a hindrance to a further unfolding of the social productive powers that its immanent barriers appear as absolute barriers in the concrete world of capital production.

Although the general law of accumulation points to the historical limits of capitalism, there is no way of telling when these limits will be reached — that is, what particular conditions in the fluctuations of capital production will constitute that crisis point which the system will not be able to overcome. But since capitalism is

4 *Capital,* Vol. III, p. 293.

beset with crises of always greater destructiveness, the social convulsions released by any crisis could — with luck — lead to social
actions that could end the capitalist system. With the rise of capitalism there also arose the new class of industrial workers. If
these workers become conscious of their class position and of the
historical obsolescence of capitalism, it is not inconceivable that
they would elect to abolish their own conditions of exploitation
and deprivation by ending the capitalist system through political
means.

This not only was conceivable but in some measure actually
occurred, finding its expression in the rise of an anti-capitalist
labor movement. There was also the historical evidence that prev-
iously-existing class relations, based on other modes of production,
had actually been ended by political means, and there was no reason to assume that this pattern of historical development had come
to a close with capitalism. In brief, Marx did not await an "automatic" or "economic" collapse of capitalism. Whether any particular crisis situation would prove to be capitalism's "final crisis"
was determinable only by the probing force of revolutionary
actions.

We are not here concerned with the question of whether Marx
relied too much upon historical precedent as regards social development, or proved to be over-optimistic or even the victim of
illusion in his expectation of the rise of a revolutionary proletariat
— which seems to be the case in view of the actual unfolding political conditions of twentieth century capitalism. What concerns us
here is merely the limited predictive power of a value analysis of
capital development. Marx was aware of this "shortcoming," as is
indicated by his refusal to predict the end of capitalism in other
than general historical terms. But however limited his theory may
be, due to its high level of abstraction, it is the only theory of capital accumulation which has found verification in the actual course
of capitalism's development. Whether we consider the rising organic composition of captial; the tendentially falling rate of profit
as actualized in the capitalist crisis; the increasing severity of crises;
the production of an industrial reserve army; the unrelieved misery
of the great bulk of the world's population despite increasing
wealth as capital; the elimination of competition through competition (or concentration, centralization, and monopolization of cap-

ital) — we cannot fail to notice the pattern of development projected by Marx.

Capital monopolization, concentration, and centralization are generally recognized and widely publicized facts. To quote just one example: at the present time "approximately 50 per cent of American manufacturing — that is, everything other than financial and transportation — is held by 150 corporations, reckoned, at least, by assets value. If finance and transportation are included, the total increases. If a rather large group is taken, the statistics would probably show that about two-thirds of the economically productive assets of the United States, excluding agriculture, are owned by a group of not more than 500 corporations. This is actual asset ownership. In terms of power, without regard to asset positions, not only do 500 corporations control two-thirds of the non-farm economy but within each of the 500 a still smaller group, has the ultimate decision-making power. This is . . . the highest concentration of economic power in recorded history. Since the United States carries on not quite half of the manufacturing production of the entire world today, these 500 groupings . . . represent a concentration of power over economics beyond anything we have yet seen."[5]

However, Marx's general law of capitalist accumulation derives its *real* importance not so much from the transformations of the capitalist system in the course of accumulation as from the effect of these changes upon the lot of the laboring population. To re-iterate: Competition forces all enterprises to enlarge their capital, and to enlarge it faster than the labor it employs. As the larger capital beats the smaller, the minimum amount of capital required to engage in business increases. While the growth of the total social capital implies the emergence and growth of many individual capitals, it also increases the concentration of accumulated capital. Competition is thus a centralization process, transforming many small into fewer, larger capitals. As it requires no more than a change in the distribution of the available capital, it takes place whether capital accumulates or not, in periods of prosperity as well as in periods of depression. Concentration is greatly enhanced by the credit system, which becomes a "formidable weapon in the

5   A. A. Berle, *Economic Power and the Free Society*, New York, 1957, p. 14.

competitive struggle, and finally transforms itself into an immense social mechanism for the centralization of capital."[6]

According to Marx, centralization supplements the work of capital expansion. Accumulation alone, i.e., "the gradual propagation of capital by a reproduction passing from a circular into a spiral form, is a very slow process as compared with centralization, which needs but alter the quantitative grouping of the integral parts of the social capital."[7] The centralization process in any particular "line of industry would reach its extreme limit, if all the individual capitals invested in it would have been amalgamated into one single capital. This limit would not be reached in any particular society until the entire social capital would be united, either in the hands of one single capitalist, or in those of one single corporation."[8] Meanwhile, however, the centralization tendency adds to the exploitation of labor the expropriation of capital by capital, pointing to its final destruction. The whole process is summed up by Marx in the well-known statement that the expropriation of capital follows directly from the immanent laws of capitalist production. "One capitalist always kills many," Marx wrote, "hand in hand with this centralization, or this expropriation of many capitalists by a few, develops, on an ever extending scale, the co-operative form of the labor-process, the conscious technical application of science, the methodical cultivation of the soil, the transformation of the instruments of labor into instruments of labor only usable in common, the economizing of all means of production by their use as the means of production of combined, socialized labor, the entanglement of all peoples in the net of the world-market, and with this, the international character of the capitalist regime. Along with the constantly diminishing number of magnates of capital, who usurp and monopolize all advantages of this process of transformation, grows up the mass of misery, oppression, slavery, degradation, exploitation; but with this too grows the revolt of the working-class, a class always increasing in numbers, and disciplined, united, organized by the very mechanism of the process of capitalist production itself. The monopoly of capital becomes a fetter upon the mode of production, which has sprung up and flourished along with it, and under it. Centralization of the means

6 *Capital,* Vol. I, p. 687.
7 *Ibid.,* p. 688.
8 *Ibid.*

of production and socialization of labor at last reach a point where they become incompatible with their capitalist integument. This integument is burst asunder. The expropriators are expropriated."[9]

We are here only concerned with the underlying general tendencies of value production and capital accumulation. Capital accumulation increases the number of both capitalists and workers absolutely, while reducing their number relative to the growing mass of capital. With a decreasing rate of accumulation, this relative decline tends toward an absolute decline. Workers cease to produce surplus-value and capitalists cease to appropriate it, thereby ceasing to be capitalists. The decrease in the number of capitalists merely increases the number of proletarians, employed and unemployed. Thus, the accumulation and centralization of capital polarizes society into a diminishing number of owners of capital and a growing number of propertyless people who can exist only through the sale of their labor-power, or not at all.

The twofold character of capitalist production, expressed in the single commodity in its double nature as both exchange- and use-value, and in society at large in the contradiction between material and capital production, reappears and determines capital development in its various manifestations and in its manner of motion by way of expansion and contraction. The life conditions of the propertyless masses are dependent on the movements of capital as determined by its profitability; and the more capital accumulates, the more precarious their dependence becomes. While the accumulation of capital increases the proletariat, it also decreases the demand for labor relative to the growing capital. It produces a surplus population of laborers, both as a result and as a condition of capital accumulation, since the changing needs of capital expansion require now a larger, now a smaller, mass of exploitable labor-power. "The whole form of the *movement* of modern industry depends upon the constant transformation of a part of the laboring population into unemployed or half-employed."[10] The accumulation of capital is thus simultaneously an accumulation of misery. According to Marx: "The greater the social wealth, the functioning capital, the extent and energy of its growth, and, therefore, also the absolute mass of the proletariat and the productiveness of its

9   *Ibid.*, pp. 836-37.
10   *Ibid.*, p. 695.

labor, the greater the industrial reserve army. The same causes which develop the expansive power of capital, develop also the labor-power at its disposal. The relative mass of the industrial reserve army increases therefore with the potential energy of wealth. But the greater this reserve army, the greater is the mass of the consolidated surplus-population, whose misery is in inverse ratio to its torment of labor. The more extensive, finally, the Lazarus-layer of the working class, and the industrial reserve army, the greater is official pauperism. *This is the absolute general law of capitalist accumulation.* Like all other laws it is modified in its working by many circumstances, the analysis of which does not concern us here."[11]

The increasing misery accompanying the accumulation process is here seen as a *general tendency* which underlies the actual movements of labor and capital, but which may be modified in the same sense in which the accumulation process itself is modified by the *specific nature* of its contraction and expansion at *any particular time.* Marx does not expect that increasing misery will always be an empirical reality, just as the fall of the rate of profit is not always an observable fact. In the same way in which a sufficient capital expansion will compensate the fall of the rate of profit through an increase in the mass of capital, so the tendency of misery to increase will be suspended in periods of capital expansion which increase the demand for labor and raise the price of labor through the reduction or elimination of the industrial reserve army. To be a socially significant fact, the increasing misery must be accompanied by an actual and steady decline in the demand for labor. It can become an ever-present social reality only under conditions of crisis, depression, and capital stagnation. However, the absence of wide-spread and increasing misery during periods of capital expansion is also only a temporary condition and can never gain permanence under conditions of capital production. With the increasing frequency of crises, the lengthening of periods of depression, the increasing difficulty of accelerating capital accumulation — taking "good" times and "bad" times together — increasing misery will be revealed both as a social fact and as the "absolute general law of capitalist accumulation."

Increasing misery follows from the law of value only in so far

11 *Ibid.,* p. 707.

as the accumulation of capital decreases the demand for labor relative to the growing mass of capital and thereby produces an industrial reserve army. Employment fluctuates with the expansion and contraction of capital production. A steadily decreasing rate of accumulation — as a permanent condition — would increase the industrial reserve army constantly, and, therewith, the mass of pauperized people living on the offal of society. But as long as an accelerated capital expansion is actually possible, the industrial reserve army lives up to its name and provides the accumulation process with the required exploitable human material. To expect an absolute impoverishment of an always greater portion of the proletariat is to expect a steadily declining rate of accumulation. Marx did expect this to be the final outcome of the accumulation process, even though the time of its actual arrival was unpredictable.

Marx's value theory of capital accumulation assumes that employed labor-power always receives its full exchange-value, i.e., its production and reproduction costs. On the basis of this assumption, there is no increasing misery but merely the misery of wage-labor. But there is displacement of labor and consequently the production of misery, because "labor power is only saleable so far as it preserves the means of production in their capacity as capital, reproduces its own capital, and yields in unpaid labor a source of additional capital."[12] All other labor-power, without either use-value or exchange-value, ceases to be part of the social production process and, consequently, of society itself. But even on the assumption that those who work receive the value of their labor-power, accumulation finds its "logical end" in the falling rate of profit.

In theory the value of labor-power is determined by its production and reproduction costs. But these labor-costs themselves are variable within definite limits. The price of labor-power may be higher or lower than its value. With a large surplus population, for instance, there may be no need to reproduce the whole of the working population and for some workers at least wages may be lowered without consideration for their reproduction needs. Under different conditions, the wages of many workers may exceed the value of their labor-power, particularly when the demand for labor

12 *Ibid.*, p. 678.

exhausts the industrial reserve army. Wages may be raised by way of wage struggles; or fluctuations in wages due to supply and demand, may be offset by the monopolization of certain types of labor or by political interventions in the labor market. Under competitive conditions, however, and considering the working class as a whole, "the general movements of wages are exclusively regulated by the expansion and contraction of the industrial reserve army, and these again correspond to the periodic changes of the industrial cycle."[13] Whatever the circumstances, a rise of wages, or "the diminution of unpaid labor, can never reach the point at which it would threaten the system itself. . . Accumulation is the independent, not the dependent, variable; the rate of wages, the dependent, not the independent, variable."[14]

The wages of the *working* population may not decrease, or may even increase, in the course of accumulation, but this will not end the misery for the expendable part of the population. According to Marx, the actual value of labor-power, moreover, is not identical with the physical minimum of existence; "it differs according to climate and conditions of social development; it depends not merely upon the physical but also upon the historically developed social needs, which become *second nature*. But in every country and at a given period the regulating average wage is a given magnitude."[15] This average wage, no matter what kind of living standard it may imply, constitutes the necessary labor, or the value of labor-power. The capitalists may see no need, or may not find a way, to lower it. And if the productivity of labor is high enough and yields sufficient surplus-value to satisfy the requirements of accumulation, it does not matter what the quantity or quality of the commodities that express the equivalent of the value of labor-power, or constitute the social average wage-rate. It is only that such a situation, i.e., one of high profits and high wages, requires a high productivity of labor and, therefore, a high organic composition of capital and a rapid rate of accumulation. But just as wages reach their highest point shortly before the onset of a particular crisis, so Marx expected that the general trend of capital accumulation, though accompanied by rising wages, was bound to reach a point where the available surplus-value would not suffice

13   *Ibid.*, p. 699.
14   *Ibid.*, p. 679.
15   *Capital*, Vol. III, p. 1000.

to sustain the customary profits and further capital expansion. At this point accumulation could only proceed at the expense of necessary labor, through a reduction of wages below their historically-established value. The continuing accumulation process would then be quite literally an increasing misery of the proletariat.

At this point we must remember that *Capital* was written a hundred years ago. Under the social and technological conditions then prevailing a projection of capital development based on the labor theory of value could easily lead to an underestimation of the resilience of capitalism through an overestimation of its difficulties. The lot of the working class was at that time deplorable, and under conditions of cut-throat competition the extraordinary greed for surplus-value accelerated capital expansion from one crisis into another, with only a slow improvement in the general social conditions of existence. The future of capitalism did not look too bright. In any case, Marx desired its early demise.

Although Marx's theory does not really require the rise of conditions such as those depicted in his foreshortened view of development, there is no point in denying that he did expect that the actual accumulation process would increase the social misery far more rapidly and extensively than was actually the case. However, capitalism's ability to better instead of worsening the living conditions of the large bulk of the industrial proletariat in the advanced capitalist nations would have forced Marx, had he experienced it, to revise only his time-conditioned subjective estimation of the concrete aspects of capital expansion, not his general theory of accumulation. This theory is not committed to a specified timespan; so long as capital moves along as predicted by Marx, the social consequences of this development cannot be set aside.

Marx's theory of development offers various "counter-tendencies" which interrupt capital's "self-destructive" course as determined by its inherent contradictions. The "counter-tendencies" substantiate the general trend, for they are merely reactions to it. They are historically conditioned, as is the whole of capitalism, but they are of greater consequence at one time than at another. Their effect upon the general development of capitalism cannot be estimated in advance; their actual force can only be observed and adjudged with reference to the actual course of capital accumulation.

Marx mentioned only a few such countertendencies: raising the intensity of exploitation, depressing wages below their value, cheapening the elements of constant capital, relative overpopulation, increase of stock capital, and foreign trade. All these countertendencies fall *outside* the general law of accumulation as established for a closed system operating strictly in accordance with the value principle. In the same sense, the capitalist crisis is a countertendency, or for that matter any *concrete phenomenon* which either raises the surplus-value for the operating capitals or reduces the value of the operating capitals relative to the available surplus-value. It is thus not possible to appraise the capitalist system with respect to its durability or fragility, except by having recourse to actual occurrences and their specific weights upon the general scheme of capital expansion, or, *vice versa,* by looking upon the latter from the position of the real capitalist world.

Although capital accumulation implies an increase in the productivity of labor, the actual extent of this increase is not forseeable, as it depends on both the evolution of technology and its recurrent revolutions, with their specific effects upon the accumulation process. The effect of the widening world market upon the production and realization of surplus-value, and therewith upon the tempo and viability of capital expansion, must be gauged not merely by the spread of commodity production but also by the capitalistic "international division of labor" and the exploitation of extra-capitalist territories.

While Marx saw the destructive aspects of industrial crises, which arrested the growing discrepancy between profitability and accumulation, he could not envision the destruction of capital on a scale such as was achieved during the two world wars. Nor did he envision the possible end of capitalism in an atomic holocaust. Marx also did not concern himself sufficiently with the possible internal modifications of the capitalist structure through persistent state interventions, because he was interested in the abolition of capitalism, and not in its modification. Furthermore, he was fully convinced that no reform of capitalism could alter its essential capital-labor relationship or the value character of its social production. Any reformed capitalism was therefore bound to suffer the same fate that he predicted for the conventional *laissez-faire* system of his own time.

CHAPTER XI

SAVING CAPITALISM

Despite its highly abstract character, Marx's capital analysis has proved to have great predictive power. The actual course of capital accumulation followed its general outline of development. Indeed, the course of capital development as predicted by Marx has never been denied; other explanations merely state the reason for this trend differently. Keynes offers one of these explanations. He explains the "long-run" trend of capital production differently, but his description of the trend itself and of observable crisis conditions differs from Marx's only in the terminology employed. It boils down to the simple statement that investments depend on profitability, current and expected, and that investments tend to decline with a declining profitability.

In contradistinction to latter-day Keynesians, Keynes himself discerned a direction and a goal for capitalism. He described the "end" towards which capital formation was tending as the loss of its "scarcity-value," and he thought this goal attainable within one or two generations. "I feel sure," he wrote, "that the demand for capital is strictly limited in the sense that it would not be difficult to increase the stock of capital up to a point where its marginal efficiency had fallen to a very low figure. This would not mean that the use of capital instruments would cost almost nothing, but only that the return from them would have to cover little more than their exhaustion by wastage and obsolescence together with some margin to cover risk and the exercise of skill and judgment. In short, as in the case of short-lived goods, just cover their labor-costs of production plus an allowance for risk and the costs of skill and supervision."[1]

1 *The General Theory*, p. 375.

Keynes did not like to think of capital as being "productive." He held that the "only reason why an asset offers a prospect of yielding during its life services having an aggregate value greater than its initial supply price is because it is *scarce;* and it is scarce because of the competition of the rate of interest on money. If capital becomes less scarce, the excess yield will diminish, without it having become less productive — at least in the physical sense."[2] Keynes' reluctance to speak of capital as "productive" and his expectation and acceptance of a declining profitability in the course of the diminishing scarcity of capital could hardly please unsophisticated capitalists; it has even disturbed some of his disciples.[3] The notion of profit as a yield from scarcity is, however, only another form of the doctrine of the "productivity" of capital: neither concept provides an explanation of the origin of profit, and both serve as apologies for the fact of exploitation.

According to Marx, the "demand for capital" is a demand for profits. And this demand for the exploitation of labor increases constantly, increasing the faster the more rapidly capital accumulates. From this point of view, Keynes' statement that "the demand for capital reaches its limits with the increase of the stock of capital to a point where its marginal efficiency has fallen to a very low figure," makes no sense. For the increasing supply of capital is not identical with a falling demand for capital, i.e., for profits. To assume that the demand for capital is limited by the increasing stock of capital is to assume that capitalism is not capitalism but a system of production employing the profit-motive solely for the purpose of increasing the means of production so as to bring profit-production to an end. In reality, of course, the means of production are increased in order to raise or maintain a given profitability.

2 *Ibid.,* p. 213.
3 Joan Robinson, for instance, remarks that Keynes' idea "that labor is the sole factor of production," cannot be justified by the fact "that he found it possible to reckon output in terms of wage-units." Keynes could do so, she says, "because he was chiefly interested in analyzing short-run situations, in which capital equipment is given, so that real output is correlated with employment." However, "as soon as output per man, at a given level of employment begins to alter, the wage-unit ceases to measure real output." Though she agrees with Keynes that "the owning of capital is not a productive activity," she thinks it more cogent to say "that capital, and the application of science to industry, are immensely productive." *An Essay on Marxian Economics,* pp. 21-27.

Assuming with Keynes that capital abundance abolishes "excess yields" such as interest, it follows that this abundance also reduces investments. What at first was the capitalist dilemma — the lack of investments — becomes the great blessing of capital abundance. In Keynes' view, this merely means that "the demand for capital has reached its limits." A period of mere reproduction replaces one of accumulation; in short, that system of production with which economic theory concerned itself from Marx to Keynes has ended.

In order, then, to lead his theory to its "logical conclusions," Keynes boldly accepts the implications of the marginal theory for the "long-run" trend of capital production, and forces his theory beyond the boundaries of capitalism. That this vision of a productive apparatus large enough to satisfy social needs to the extent that no further significant capital expansion seems desirable lies beyond the horizon of capitalism is borne out by Keynes' own statement that "if capital becomes less scarce, the excess yields will diminish without it having become less productive — at least in the physical sense." The physical side of capitalism, however, is just that aspect of this mode of production which contradicts its motivation, the drive for exchange-value, profit, and accumulation.

Whether capital is scarce or abundant, in Marx's view, capital production must be profitable in order to be carried on. A persistent decline of profitability implies a slowing rate of accumulation, a crisis condition which can be overcome only through the resumption of an accelerated rate of capital expansion. The disappearance of "excess-yields" — whatever that may mean — spells not the end of capital scarcity but the end of capitalism. The relatively stationary state of capital abundance projected by Keynes, where the "demand" for capital does not exceed the production requirements of waste and obsolescence and where the profits square with the consumption needs of entrepreneurial skill and supervision, cannot be reached within the frame of private capital formation. The capitalist reproduction process is always an accumulation process. This does not exclude periods of "simple reproduction," or even of temporary decline; but a stationary and simultaneously prospering capitalism did not enter Marx's vision.

Although Keynes considered it his "practical judgment and not a theoretical imperative" that even in "mature" capitalism the emphasis should be on capital formation instead of on consumption, he saw the reversed emphasis as a possibility for the not too distant future. And because of this possibility, he thought it a "sheer lack of intelligence" to presume that it required radical solutions to end the disparity between the actual and the potential performance of the economy. Socialism, which in his definition meant state-ownershsip of the means of production, he thought quite superfluous; for ownership itself is of no importance once it is possible to control the rate of investment. He was convinced that "a somewhat comprehensive socialization of investments will prove the only means of securing an approximation of full employment," but "this need not exclude all manner of compromise and of devices by which public authority will co-operate with private initiative."[4] Only experience would show, he thought, "how far the common will, embodied in the state, ought to be directed to increasing and supplementing the inducement to invest; and how far it is safe to stimulate the average propensity to consume."[5]

Dogmatic proponents of the private enterprise system not only view Keynesianism as the theory of the transformation of a "free" into a partly controlled capitalism, but look upon this transformation as the beginning of the end of capitalism itself. They see a radical return to a market-determined economy, at whatever social cost, as the only way of escaping the emerging "new serfdom" of the totalitarian society. They may be right, but totalitarianism was the last thing that Keynes was willing to support. Though he admired the Nazi State for having devised a means of producing and maintaining full employment, he thought that the same thing could be achieved under existing British institutions, since he saw no necessary connection between a society's economic policy and its political structure. As regards the Russian system, he "did not think that it contains, or is likely to contain, any piece of useful economic technique which we could not apply, if we chose, with equal or greater success in a society which retained all the marks . . . of British bourgeois ideals."[6] All that Russia contributed to economics is a demonstration that centralistic control can bring about a balanced growth of the economy. This did not depend on bolshevism, but on centralistic controls, which could be made even more effec-

4 *The General Theory*, p. 378.
5 *Ibid.*, p. 377.
6 J. M. Keynes, *Laissez-Faire and Communism*, p. 130.

tive under the auspices of the more advanced economic techniques of the Western world.

Keynesianism, in its liberalistic interpretation, reflects the degree of *laissez-faire* still possible in "mature" capitalism. It represents a "type of hybrid system," in which "the essentials of capitalism — consumers' sovereignty, freedom to invest, and liberty to choose occupations — can be preserved."[7] For Keynes the choice between a controlled and a "free" economy no longer existed; there was only the choice between different sets of controllers. As one of Keynes' disciples expressed this, "fascism is the form that our capitalist society will acquire, unless we are successful in bringing about Keynesian reforms or a socialist economy."[8] Keynes realized, of course, that an appeal to reason was not enough to make all capitalists fit themselves cheerfully into the new situation and he considered it the duty of government to save the reluctant ones from their own folly. He thought that the government's usurpation of the regulatory function would not affect the entrepreneurial role. In his view there was nothing wrong in the sphere of production; but communal savings were better collected and invested by the government than by private capital. Centralizing control of the amount of economic activity in the hands of the government was the only way to overcome capitalist inertia.

Bourgeois economic theory saw in the economy's lack of conscious organization a specific form of "order" — the automatic by-product of market exchange, a "law of value" which regulated the economic aspects of life. And, indeed, for periods of time, relatively stable market situations induced economic behavior to follow conventional patterns and the law of the market seemed to produce a definite kind of order. During periods of steadily-advancing capital formation the market mechanism functioned without serious difficulties. Periods of crisis were overcome with relative ease, and as the profits of the capitalists were largely re-invested, their number — small compared to the laboring population — turned their possibly luxurious life into an economically uninteresting fact. From a capitalist point of view, the situation could well appear to be directed by an ordering, though invisible, hand.

War and long-term depression ended this idyllic belief and led

7   S. E. Harris, *Saving Amerian Capitalism*, New York, 1950, p. 369.
8   L. R. Klein, *The Keynesian Revolution*, p. 167.

to increased government control of the economy. And what at first appeared to be a special situation, an emergency, became the general situation, so that the partial subordination of private to national and governmental interests took on a rather permanent character. With this the economists' functions began to change. They could now suggest practical policies and speculate about the effects of various government interventions upon one or another or all of the aspects of the economy. However, "social experiments" are rather hasty answers to the pressing political problems which themselves determine the kind of actions taken. The form of their execution may vary in the test of experience, but the problems that arise in capitalism and the "solutions" for these problems are generally clear and obvious. This is why no economic policy has thus far been suggested which did not make its debut before the "theory behind it" was formulated. All the monetary and fiscal policies suggested by Keynes had already been employed at different times by various governments to safeguard themselves and the society over which they presided. By bringing the changed capitalist practice of his day into the frame of economic theory, Keynes supported the expanding governmental control both practically and ideologically.

Under *laissez-faire* conditions, capitalists feel no need to accept responsibility for the social consequences of their activities, and they have no way of discerning whether they affect the whole of society negatively or positively. To them "applied economics" signifies no more than the desire to buy cheap and sell dear. The actions of workers, too, are conditioned by their desire to sell their labor-power at the highest possible price. For them "applied economics" exhausts itself in the wage-struggle. Nevertheless, the struggle between capital and labor performs "regulatory" functions by determining the degree of exploitation and thus affecting the rate of capital expansion. The fetishistic "self-adjustibility" of the economy is here partly lost to the simple, open struggle between men and men. With the extension and intensification of this struggle, the economically-manipulated part of the economy grows. But as the "manipulation" serves particular interests, the increasing organization implied therein only enlarges social disorganization. And this growing disorganization can be immunized only by a still faster rate of accumulation, so that a weakening of the market-fetishism on the one hand strengthens the fetishistic attitudes with regard to accumulation on the other.

From the point of view of capitalist society as a whole, market-distribution is always a class-distribution of commodities. Labor and surplus-labor, whatever its productivity, are finally reducible to lengths of time. So much time in terms of products, or products in terms of time, falls to the individual worker or to the individual capitalist; so much to social capital or to the working class as a whole. What falls to the individual worker need not be enough to reproduce his labor power; what falls to the individual capitalist need not be enough to sustain him in his social position. What falls to the working population, however, must be enough to reproduce it, and what falls to the capitalist class must be enough to reproduce the social structure. As regards the social reproduction process, a certain quantity of social labor that enters the market in commodity-form enters it, so to speak, "unnecessarily," since the market can only complicate the inescapable and proportionally definite requirements of the reproduction process. Because the reproduction process controls the production process, it is only surplus-labor time — incorporated in commodities beyond the need of simple reproduction — which is not "predetermined" by the material requirements of a social production that secures the maintenance of a once-established level of production under given, definite social relationships.

In the course of capital concentration, more surplus-value comes to be divided among relatively fewer enterprises, a process by which the market loses some of its functions. When the market mechanism ceases to "square" supply and demand by way of capital expansion, it complicates the formation of an average rate of profit, which is needed to secure the simultaneous existence of all necessary industries regardless of their individual profit rates. The average rate of profit, as will be recalled, implies the "pooling" of surplus-value so as to satisfy the physical needs of social production which assert themselves by way of social demand. Capital stagnation, expressed as it is in a defective demand, hinders an increasing number of capital entities from partaking of the social "pool" of surplus-value in sufficient measure. If their continued existence is a social necessity, they must be maintained by government subsidies. And if the number of unemployed constitutes a danger to social stability, they, too, must be fed out of the declining "pool" of surplus-value. Control of surplus-value becomes essential for the security of capitalism, and the distribution of profits becomes a governmental concern.

From a theoretical point of view it is a matter of indifference whether the necessary division of value and surplus-value and the necessary distribution of the latter occur on a "free" market or on a market manipulated by government authority. In practice, of course, it makes all the difference to those capitalists who stand to lose by the "proper" functioning of the "system as a whole." For government concern with profit distribution interferes with the profitability of specific enterprises; extra-profits may be taxed away and some businesses may be ruined while others are aided by governmental favoritism. So long as it is not clear which capital entities will be favorably affected by governmental control, all tend to object to controls as such. But as soon as it is evident that governmental controls mean security and expansion for some capital entities at the expense of others, the capitalist front against governmental controls is broken.

Although there is no necessary connection between Keynes' theoretical reasoning and the "applied economics" of today, the "mixed economy" is a fact and demands justification in economic terms. Government interventions in the depressed economy were at first merely supposed to act as "pump-primers" for renewing the flow of private economic activity. Public work expenditures and welfare-payments were supposed to create new income which would, in turn, generate additional economic activity. The idea was formalized in the so-called "multiplier effect" introduced by R. F. Kahn. Estimates were made as to the repercussions to be expected from an increase in "effective demand" due to government-financing; they varied from a doubling to a five-fold increase in the initial investment in the form of new income. These assumptions, however, elude factual verification. In theory, which discounts the indiscernable counteracting influences of capitalism's private sector, they appear convincing. Actually, these estimates are based on too many "ifs" to say anything definite about the effects of governmental spending. It was then freely admitted that the notion of the "multiplier is no magic formula which will enable us to predict with any degree of accuracy just what the influence of public investment will be. By assigning different weights to various factors, one might conclude either that public investment will have tremendous income-creating effect or that it will have, on balance, a negative effect on employment and income."[9]

However, as government depression policy did increase employment to some extent, it may be said that the Keynesian theory proved itself in a general way wherever it was employed and to the degree in which it was applied. The American New Deal is a case in point, even though Keynes himself expressed dissatisfaction with Roosevelt's vacillating policies. Bourgeois supporters of Keynesian economics hope to see them so "developed and applied as to involve only a slight and safe and useful departure from strict *laissez-faire,* or use of governmental power to influence total spending and demand in the economy and keep it in better balance with the total, potential output of all goods and services."[10] In this view, it is the function of government to secure the existence and welfare of private enterprise. Aside from the overall effect of governmental money and fiscal policies, depressed industries are to be helped along with special credit facilities. Public works are to be constructed with an eye to the needs of private capital — roads for the automobile industry, airports for the aircraft industry, and so forth. Along with preferential treatment for new investments there should also go an increase in the propensity to consume by way of social security legislation as an instrument of economic stability.

A mixed economy presupposes that a substantial portion of its total productive capacity is owned and controlled by private capital. Since government funds proper can come only from taxation or from possible profits out of government-owned industries, additional funds must be borrowed from private capital. Debt-financing is supposed to bring forth a general increase in "effective demand." This is not "effective demand" in a capitalist sense, for the capitalist market has no demand for public works, welfare, and armaments. It has of course a demand for the various intermediary commodities used in government-induced production. But this demand would be non-existent were it not for government purchases. The costs of government-induced production, as well as the profits accruing to private capitalist suppliers, are paid out of taxes or borrowed money, i.e., out of funds from capitalism's private

9 D. Dillard, *The Economics of John Maynard Keynes,* p. 12.
10 O. H. Taylor, *The Classical Liberalism, Marxism, and the Twentieth Century,* Cambridge, 1960, p. 118.

sector. This simply means that the government avails itself of means of production that belong to private capital and supports workers from privately owned resources. The borrowed funds are only monetary expressions of the government's power to set unemployed resources to work. The rising national debt indicates that this power has only temporarily been granted and for a price, i.e., interest paid to the bondholders.

While the "end-product" of capital production is an enlarged capital, the "end-product" of government-fostered production is only an enlarged production. The productive apparatus which government-induced production calls into being can function only on the government's behalf. Though it is nominally in the hands of private capital, it can be fully used only at government command. And from the point of view of private enterprise, any production which the government commands, whether in the form of public works, welfare, or armaments, falls in the sphere of consumption. In effect, then, government-fostered production reverses the usual procedure of capital accumulation. Instead of expanding production at the expense of consumption, in a process where consumption increases more slowly than capital accumulates, it expands production with the help of consumption, though it is "consumption" in the form of public works and armaments.

Up to now government-induced expansion of production in the mixed economy has led to full employment only by increasing the "effective demand" for products not directly consumable, whose value cannot be "realized" through the capitalist circulation process. Insofar as this has been accomplished by way of deficit-financing, it has led to a steady increase in the national debt. Monetary inflation diminished and often repudiated the debt at the expense of private capital. But even under non-inflationary conditions, the interest paid on the national debt and its final redemption has to come out of private production. As the funds spent by government yield no profits they also cannot yield interest. Of course, since the "nation as a whole" stands behind the national debt, it is possible that interest will be paid and bonds redeemed if the national income rises faster than the national debt. All this means is that sufficient new wealth must be created by new and additional production to take care of old obligations.

CHAPTER XII

KEYNESIANISM IN REVERSE

Keynesian interventions in the economy were at first rather ineffective. Keynes explained this by saying that "the medicine he recommended was too niggardly applied." The unemployment problem remained unsolved until the approaching Second World War forced the various governments to do for the purpose of waging war what they had been unwilling or unable to do during the preceding depression. With the beginning of war production, however, Keynes was finally convinced that his theory would find confirmation, for now it would be seen "what level of consumption is needed to bring a free, modern community . . . within the sight of the optimum employment of its resources."[1]

War-policies, however, were quite independent of the developing Keynesian ideology. They did not differ from those employed in the First World War; nor did they differ between various nations, not all of which adhered to the "Keynesian revolution." Already "in the first world war it proved possible to devote almost half of the total resources of the community to fighting;" and the "moulding of industry into the shape for war needs," was "helped forward by direct government coercion of industry."[2] All the innovations associated with the commandeered economy of the Second World War, such as forced savings, controls on money, credit, prices and labor, priorities, rationing, government-borrowings, and so forth, had been employed in the first conflict despite the "orthodox" approach to economics which prevailed at that time.

While rather unsuccessful in increasing the "propensity to consume" during the long depression, Keynesian theory was celebrated

1 *The New Republic,* New York, July 29, 1940.
2 A. C. Pigou, *The Political Economy of War,* London, 1940, pp. 43, 71.

as a "brilliant success" in cutting it down during the war by way of compulsory savings. Though not able to increase investments toward full employment, it led to labor-shortages by the destruction of capital. To put a theory in reverse can only mean to put it out of commission; yet, strangely enough, the sacrifice of the theory was seen as a sign of the "flexibility and the fruitfulness for practical actions of the kind of thinking that went into the general theory of employment, interest and money. There is nothing in Keynes' plan for preventing inflation in war," it has been said, "that contradicts his explanation of unemployment in peace. The plan for war finance suggests the need for compulsory savings, whereas the emphasis in the *General Theory* is upon the social disadvantages of thrift. The reversal of circumstances from peace to war calls for a reversal of emphasis."[3]

But this can hardly be considered a "reversal of emphasis." After all, Keynesian theory was based on the concept of a "mature" capitalism unable on its own account to bring forth investments large enough to assure full employment. The purpose and meaning of Keynes' theory was: to provide a way to have full employment in the *absence* of war or prosperity; and to overcome depression *not* in the orthodox fashions of waging war or passively awaiting the destructive results of the crisis, but through the new and "rational" method of government-induced demand. It is more accurate to say that Keynes suspended his theory "for the duration." In fact, his celebrated "plan" for financing the war was merely a suggestion to do dictatorially what was done at first by persuasion.

Because of the "stickiness" of wages, Keynes at one time opposed deflationary policies; he now opposed price inflation for the same reason. In both cases he was not intent on changing an existing practice, but wanted only to make it more effective by making it more palatable. Just as he once thought that a decrease in real wages would be more acceptable when carried out under stationary or increasing money-wages, so he now thought that "it makes all the difference in the world to each individual personally whether the excess of his income over his consumption is taken from him by tax or loan. To him personally government stock is an addition to his wealth, to his security, and to his comfort in facing the future. It gives him a claim over the future resources of the com-

---

3 D. Dillard, *The Economics of John Maynard Keynes*, p. 242.

munity. Someone will have to meet his claim. But this someone is not necessarily himself, and, even if it were, it may suit him better and involve less sacrifice to part in installments with his personal resources and to possess meanwhile a title to wealth which he can realize in case of need."[4]

It is clear that "wealth" used up during the war cannot be drawn upon in the future. A "claim over future resources" merely means additional future work: enough work must be done in the future to produce the commodity-equivalent for the then-existing wage-rates plus the commodity-equivalent of war-savings. It is true, of course, that people only cash their war-bonds gradually, which spreads the surplus-labor necessary to redeem them over a longer time. But this does not alter the fact that any increased consumption stemming from the purchase of war-bonds can come only out of new production. The individual's claim over future resources is an illusion he maintains by not looking at society as a whole. If "someone else will have to meet his claim" at some time, then, of course, at some other time, he will have to meet somebody else's claim. Keynes was at one time convinced that the individual must be taught to see the problem of society as a whole. But for the sake of victory he suspended that conviction, and now hoped that the workers, at least, would retain all those illusions which helped reconcile them to the increased exploitation necessitated by war.

Keynes thought of the future in still another respect while making his proposals for financing the war. He feared that the post-war situation would look much like the pre-war, with a lack of "effective demand" and its consequent unemployment. In distinction to the pre-war situation, however, there would be a backlog of postponed effective demand, which could serve to bolster industrial activity by increasing the "propensity to consume." Though suspended during the war, his theory would hold good as soon as "normalcy" had been restored.

The war itself only proved to Keynes that any economic system could have full employment if it so wished; it did not occur to him that under present conditions war and preparation for war may be the only way to full employment. It occurred to others, however, and some of his disciples viewed war "as a great new industry whose colossal demands stimulate economic activity in every nook

4 J. M. Keynes, "Paying for the War," *London Times*, November 14, 1939.

and cranny of the economic system," even though "the expected yields which raise the marginal efficiency of government investments are mainly in terms of social and military advantages rather than pecuniary profits."[5] Generally, however, the Keynesian "spirit" was better represented by those who emphasized the "socialistic" aspects of government control. Near the end of the Second World War, for instance, William Beveridge proposed a program of full employment based on the "socialization of demand without the socialization of production."[6] Built on Keynesian principles and choosing fiscal means for its realization, such a program was to carry the full employment policy of war into the conditions of peace.

The fear that there might be a return of persistent widespread unemployment in the wake of the war proved to be exaggerated. In the defeated nations it once more became a problem for a time, but if a distinction is made between economics and politics, this was not a "strictly economic" problem. Unemployment here was clearly caused by the devastation and dislocations of war and was maintained for some time by occupation policies that restricted economic activities. For the victorious powers, however, large-scale unemployment did not recur in the immediate post-war era because of the need to consolidate national gains, to renew used-up means of production, to try to regain lost markets, and to prepare for the eventuality of a Third World War. These economies remained in part war-economies and thus retained a high level of employment. As the distinction between war-time production and peace-time production ceased to exist, there was no need to adapt the Beveridge or any other plan for the full utilization of national resources.

Whereas a decade of depression and government intervention had failed to create the conditions of a prosperous capital accumulation, the actual capital expansion after the war kept the "government in business." Full use of productive resources, where and when it came about, was accomplished by extending government-induced "non-profitable" production. Part of this increase resulted from public welfare and foreign-aid measures; most of it was gen-

5   D. Dillard, *The Economics of John Maynard Keynes*, p. 243.
6   W. H. Beveridge, *Full Employment in a Free Society*, New York, 1945, p. 29.

erated by military expenditures.[7]   At various times attempts were
made to operate with balanced budgets and to gain surpluses for
debt retirements. But ensuing business recessions reversed these
policies quickly. It was by way of inflation, debt-accumulation,
government-induced production, war preparation and actual warfare that the dominant capitalist nations reached an approximation
of full employment. This experience strengthened Keynesianism
and led to the wide-spread belief that a government-maintained
"quasi-boom" could be indefinitely continued.

Keynes' untimely death in 1946 deprived him of the opportunity
to witness the "validation" of his theories in government-manipulated post-war economies. That this had been achieved largely by
way of war and preparation for war was to be regretted; yet "logically" it should have been possible just as well under conditions
of peace. Indeed, it had been Keynes' interest in international
peace and general social welfare which had led him to advocate
a government-regulated investment policy in the first place. Such
a policy, Keynes felt, would remove the pressing economic motives
for war, since no country would need "to force its wares any longer
on another, or to repulse the offering of its neighbors. . . International trade could cease to be what it is, namely, a desperate
expedient to maintain employment at home by forcing sales on
foreign markets and restricting purchases, which, if successful, will
merely shift the problem of unemployment to the neighbor which
is worsted in the struggle." Instead it would become a "willing and
unimpeded exchange of goods and services in condition of mutual
advantage."[8]

While still adhering to neo-classical doctrine, Keynes had been
undogmatic enough to advocate protectionism whenever British

---

7   During the first seven-year period of the North Atlantic Treaty Organization, a total of about $312 billion was expended for military purposes, of
which the United States contributed $252 billion. From 1946 to 1955 Amer-
ica's expenditures for national security amounted to $309 billion — the
equivalent of the entire national income for the year 1955. Since then,
national defense has absorbed roughly 10 per cent of the total national
product, leaving aside that part of the total which private capital used
on its own account to increase its capacity for arms production. The United
States government budget for 1960 exceeded $80 billion, of which roughly
$48 billion constituted military expenditures. America's national debt by
1960 amounted to about $290 billion and interest charges to about $9.5
billion.

8   *The General Theory*, p. 383.

interests made this advisable. During the Great Depression he
went beyond this to rediscover an "element of scientific truth in
mercantilist doctrine,"[9] in the mercantilist's disregard for the world
at large. At that time, it was the gold standard which, in Keynes'
view, was largely responsible for the prevalence of unemployment;
for under its rule, there was no "orthodox means open to the
authorities for countering unemployment at home except by struggling for an export surplus and an import of the monetary metal
at the expense of their neighbors."[10]

Keynes favored economic policies "unimpeded by international
preoccupations" and directed to attaining an optimum level of
domestic employment. In his view, it was the "simultaneous pursuit of these policies by all countries together which is capable of
restoring economic health and strength internationally, whether
we measure it by the level of domestic employment or by the
volume of international trade."[11] Recognizing the limitations and
dangers of such a policy, Keynes tried to overcome them by taking
part of the national economy out of the process of international
competition. If all countries would do likewise, there could be full
employment everywhere.

With or without the gold standard, a full-employment policy
implies different things for different nations and for the different
classes within these nations. Its success or failure depends on the
nation's relative strength in terms of natural resources, on its position within the given "international division of labor," and on the
degree to which it is dependent on a certain level of international
trade. For some nations full employment is a lesser consideration
than the extent and terms of international trade. They cannot
exist, let alone achieve full employment, save by an extraordinary
"preoccupation" with the international economy. However, Keynes
regretted "international preoccupations" only insofar as they
were based on the gold standard, which did not have the "equilibrating" power it was supposed to posssess. He wanted to replace
it with agreements reached by conscious considerations of international economic needs. Just as Keynes thought it possible to devise
state interventions in the national economy which did not come

 9 *Ibid.*
10 *Ibid.*
11 *Ibid.*, p. 349.

in conflict with private enterprise, so he thought that international bodies could regulate the world economy without violating the special interests of any particular country. Additional data and instrumentalities of control would be required, of course; but Keynes saw no insurmountable difficulties in applying his suggestions for the domestic economy to the world.

In the midst of the Second World War, and in anticipation of the coming peace, Keynes proposed the establishment of an international currency and credit system designed to remove the reason for war by alleviating international depressions and guaranteeing the necessary international trade. An International Clearing Union and a new international form of money called "bancor" were to serve as instruments for the revival of a multilateral trade and payments system which would stress the positive and avoid the negative aspects of the defunct gold standard. In an emasculated form it became, in Bretton Woods, the International Bank for Reconstruction and Development and the International Monetary Fund.

Although the desirability of and the necessity for international economic cooperation have been generally recognized, little has actually been done in this respect. After World War II, Keynes himself began to realize the enormous difficulties in the way of making the capitalist system work more efficiently. "No one can be certain of anything in this age of flux and change," he wrote now; "decaying standards of life at a time when our command over the production of material satisfaction is the greatest ever, and a diminishing scope for individual decisions at a time when more than before we should be able to afford these satisfactions, are sufficient to indicate an underlying contradiction in every department of our economy. No plan will work for certain in such an epoch."[12] He hastened to add that "if all plans should fail, we and everyone else will try something different." We should "act on the optimistic hypothesis until it has been proved wrong." The optimism Keynes suggests was to nourish itself on no more than the "permanent truth of classical theory," on the "undercurrent of a law of value," which, like a "natural force" or Adam Smith's "invisible hand," will restore the disturbed ceonomic order. But

---

12 J. M. Keynes, "The Balance of Payments of the United States," *The Economic Journal*, June, 1946, p. 85.

Keynes still held that there was no need to wait passively for the "natural forces" to take their course. The process could be eased and hastened along by rational implementations in support of the naturally-given equilibrium tendencies.

In view of the war's vast devastation of both Europe and Asia, the revival of the disturbed world economy became, in the Keynesian view, America's responsibility. The Americans would have "to discover ways of life, which, compared with the ways of life of the less fortunate regions of the world, must tend toward and not away from, external equilibrium."[13] What this would imply in practical terms Keynes was spared the necessity of relating. His disciples, however, approached the problem either in strictly business terms or as a question of philanthropy. Because private foreign loans and investments were not sufficient to revive and develop extra-American economies, government loans and grants would have to fill the gap. If the United States "enters into international co-operation on international monetary and financial arrangements," it was said, "and if the foreign loans are invested in productive and useful projects, then it is reasonable to suppose that over a long-run period the interests and amortization charges can be paid. They will be relatively small in proportion to total international transactions and can quite easily be managed in a reasonably stable and prosperous world."[14] More radical Keynesians suggested some form of peace-time lend-lease, with a periodic cancellation of international credit balances; for "surplus output should never be considered a problem as long as people in any part of the world are underfed and living in subnormal conditions, until, as Keynes has been quoted as saying, 'the last Hottentot owns a Rolls-Royce car.' "[15]

From a Keynesian point of view, foreign aid by way of grants, like public works and armaments, may be regarded an instrument for domestic full employment. At any rate, it is easier to get rid of surplus commodities than surplus populations. As wages are "costs of production," the profitability of private enterprise would suffer if surplus products were distributed as higher wages. The wage-system itself precludes any significant "free distribution;" for

---

13 *Ibid.*
14 A. H. Hansen, *America's Role in the World Economy*, New York, 1945. p. 136.
15 S. MacBride, *The Statist*, London, December 19, 1949.

under this system, people work only if they must. In any case, a large part of surplus production consists of products which cannot be directly consumed at all. Eliminating overproduction through foreign aid thus appears almost irresistible, for it seems to leave the socio-economic conditions at home undisturbed.

But "sharing the wealth" with other nations will not benefit domestic business. While it helps some enterprises which could not function properly without a steady demand, foreign aid has to be paid for out of the whole of domestic production. And the disposal of surpluses by way of foreign aid, like their distribution via the wage-system, is limited for both the giving and the receiving countries. Insofar as it involves free distribution, or disposal at unrealistic prices, it cuts down the "effective demand" still enjoyed by private producers, if not in the aid-dispensing country then in other nations. Though unavoidable, it thus does not always suit private interests in the aid-receiving nations. Shortages yield extra profits and the distribution of free, or low-priced, commodities does affect internal price relations to some extent. Trade instead of aid is then preferred by both aid-dispensing and aid-receiving nations in which private property relations dominate. Aid, particularly in the form of loans, is regarded a necessary medium for the creation of future trade relations and future profitable capital investments. The "external equilibrium" to be achieved is thus still a market equilibrium.

CHAPTER XIII

THE "TRANSFORMATION"
OF CAPITALISM

Evaluating the work of Keynes, economists came to "distinguish the problems he opened up from the particular solutions he suggested. These solutions might all be altered, or discarded and replaced," it was said, "and his work would still be revolutionary in the opening up of problems and the admission of the possibility of *some* solution different from the one that had previously been accepted and had foreclosed fresh inquiry."[1] In this, Keynes "succeeded where previous heretics had failed, partly because he came at a time that was ripe to receive his ideas."[2] Although Keynes' "theory of stagnation gave modern expression to some indigenous elements stressed in Marx's 'break-down' theory, such as chronic underconsumption, general overproduction, and the secularly declining rate of profit, the important practical difference between them, though, is that Keynes sought the remedy in the modification of *laissez-faire* capitalism through 'deliberate State action'; whereas Marx dogmatically dismissed any and all such State actions as inevitably and invariably benefitting only 'the capitalist class' instead of the economy as a whole."[3] Possibly it was for this reason "that Keynes was adopted by some economists in recoil from what may have seemed like possible Marxian implications in the great depression"; Marxists they could not become, even though "Marx anticipated Keynes," because of Marxism's "misanthropic bent with regard to Western culture which does not represent a very good career line for economists of the West."[4]

1 J. M. Clark, *Alternative to Serfdom*, New York, 1960, p. 98.
2 *Ibid.*
3 K. K. Kurihara, *The Keynesian Theory of Economic Development*, New York, 1959, p. 20.
4 J. McDonald, *Fortune*, New York, December 1950, p. 134.

It is the state-organized, or "Keynesian" aspect of present-day capitalism which, by serving as a belated but unavoidable critique of the capitalism of old, simultaneously serves as a refutation of Marxism. Even if it is admitted that "the laws of motion which Marx's model of capitalism revealed may still be visible in American capitalism," it is maintained that these laws are now "faced with a set of remedies which spring from social attitudes quite beyond his imagination."[5] Not only Americans but Europeans too refer to a changed capitalism; although "we still commonly speak of England and France as capitalist countries," it is said, "they are no longer capitalist in the sense understood by Marx and his contemporaries."[6] In this view, it was Keynes who assisted the capitalist metamorphosis and who made "the greatest single contribution to the techniques of democratic transition. In so doing he helped to show the peoples of the West a way forward which did not lead across the bourne of total class war — a bourne from which the wage earners of the West recoil, now that they have seen its raging waters."[7] Keynesianism is thus celebrated not only as the savior of capital but as the savior of labor as well.

It is of course true that contemporary capitalism differs from the capitalism analyzed by Marx. He did not foresee all the actual changes. Capitalism's transformation was not only the economic but also the social and political result of international competitive capital accumulation which, by issuing into two world wars and revolutions, led to a rapidly increasing, or even total, state control of national economies. This course of events, however, even if Marx had expected it, would not have affected his economic theory; for these events relate to political reactions to economic crisis situations. Aware of the basic contradictions of capital production and convinced that its expansion and extension could only enlarge and sharpen them, Marx was interested not so much in speculating about the possible staying-powers of capitalism as in developing a revolutionary force to put an end to it.

The celebrated "failure" of Marxism is a failure not of economic theory, but rather of the social and political expectations based on

5 R. L. Heilbroner, *The Worldly Philosophers*, New York, 1953, p. 159.
6 J. Plamenatz, *German Marxism and Russian Communism*, London, 1954, p. 303.
7 J. Strachey, *Contemporary Capitalism*, New York, 1956, p. 312.

it. Of course, it is also a "failure" of economic theory insofar as its application to reality led to an underestimation of capitalism's susceptibility to change. However, no reasonable person would demand that Marx should foresee actual social and economic development in all its concrete manifestations. And to the extent that socio-economic development is predictable with some degree of certainty, Marx did rather well, as is demonstrated by the rise of Keynesianism. In the Keynesian formulation, Marx's findings are silently accepted and simultaneously "remedied" by conscious interventions in the market mechanism.

Marx was not a social reformer interested in the amelioration and perpetuation of existing production relations. For him capitalism had no future because its transformation was already an observable phenomenon. Its expansion was at the same its decay when regarded from a revolutionary instead of from a conservative point of view. With regard to theory, he saw his function not so much as providing the rationale for the ever-changing political actions of his time as in discerning the general trend of capital development at the very start of its international ascendancy.

Future events may be anticipated only on the basis of present knowledge, and predictions are possible only on the assumption that a known pattern of past development will also hold for the future. It may not; yet existing knowledge warrants some expectations and thus allows for actions whose results will confirm or refute these expectations. In view of the past pattern of historical development and on the basis of his own experience, Marx was certainly convinced that the development of capitalism, by giving rise to a revolutionary proletariat, would lead to its abolition. He did not contemplate the possibility of a "second life" for capitalism by way of governmental activities. Nor could he imagine that "Marxism" itself could be transformed into an ideology serving state-capitalism, which accelerates the concentration and centralization tendencies inherent in competitive capital accumulation by political means. Marx's political expectations have not as yet been realized. The very existence of a modified capitalism and the absence of a revolutionary working class seem to disprove his political theories.

The turn of the century witnessed two parallel trends — the progressive objective "socialization" of bourgeois society and the progressive subjective "bourgeoisification" of the labor movement. When it proved possible to better workers' conditions within the confines of capitalism, the once radical labor movement turned into an institution providing additional support for the social *status quo*. Out of the experiences of the labor movement itself arose the idea that it was possible to transform capitalism into some kind of "socialism" gradually, by way of reforms. Although less sophisticated, Fabianism and Marxian Revisionism anticipated the Keynesian theory; now it is this theory which serves as the ideology of the reformist labor movement. In more senses than one, it was said, the political importance of Keynes' book "is that at every point, without a single exception, it is in full agreement with Labour policy in this country [England], and what is even more significant, expresses in proper economic form what has been implicit in the Labour Movement's attitude all along."[8] Although running counter to Marx's revolutionary expectations, all this is in conformity with his idea that existing socio-economic conditions determine the ruling ideology.

Although Marx did not concern himself with possible modifications of the capitalist system by way of government controls, his economic theory does not deny the feasibility of such endeavors. It is of course possible to intervene in economic processes by political means. War itself illustrates this as well as Marx's theory of social revolution. What was important to Marx was the analysis of capital development on the assumption that there were no interventions in the fetishistic accumulation process. Only thus was it possible to detect capitalism's inherent contradictions and limitations. Marx's theory does not deny the fact that full employment can and may be created either by government-induced investments or by an increase in the propensity to consume. It simply does not discuss such maneouvers. They are, of course, possibilities, provided that neither policy seriously infringes upon the prevailing social class relations.

Of this Keynes was also fully aware. "Apart from the necessity of central controls to bring about an adjustment between the propensity to consume and the inducement to invest," he wrote, "there is no more reason to socialize life than there was before."[9] Favor-

---

8 A. L., Rowse, *Mr. Keynes and the Labour Movement*, London, 1936, p. 12.
9 *The General Theory*, p. 379.

ing the prevailing social relations, he saw no "reason to suppose that the existing system seriously misemploys the factors of production"; the system had failed only in "determining the *volume*, not the *direction*, of actual employment."[10] By affecting only the volume of production, Keynesian interventions in the economy nceessarily "adjust" production and consumption in favor of "investments." Such "adjustments" cannot end the "paradox of poverty in the midst of plenty," and are not designed to do so. It is precisely for this reason that they are "operational," as they are still in line with the general tendency of capitalist production to "accumulate capital for the sake of accumulation."

In contrast with Keynes, Marx saw in capitalism an irrational social mode of production. But as there are no economic processes independent of human activities he called the capitalist irrationality fetishistic behavior. It is the fetishistic self-expansion of capital which determines both the volume and the direction of production. Social control of the economy would imply the conscious determination of both the volume and the direction of production. This would, however, constitute a radical change in existing social relations, based as they are on the subjugation of the working population by way of value production. By insisting that only the volume, not the direction, of production should be subject to government planning, Keynes indicated that he was not concerned with altering the existing class relations but only with removing its dangerous proclivities in times of crisis.

Interventions in the economy have been forced on capitalist governments by circumstances beyond their control. These interventions do not point to a reformative tendency in capitalism. What they do reveal is that the system finds it more and more difficult to solve capitalist problems by strictly capitalistic means. In a consistent capitalist ideology the "new economics" spell not success, but failure. To be sure, government interventions may postpone or mitigate a crisis; but the need for such intervention only bears witness to the depth of the crisis situation.

With the power to side-track depression goes the power to control the boom, and the "business-cycle" may now appear as the expansion and contraction of government-induced production. Since a slackening rate of private capital expansion may be com-

10   *Ibid.*

pensated for by government-induced production, the latter may be pared down when private investment increases. Government-induced production may even bolster the rate of economic growth. Conditions of "prosperity" more impressive than those brought forth under *laissez-faire* conditions may arise, and neither capital nor government show any interest in changing this state of affairs so long as it lasts. At any rate, recent economic history has demonstrated the possibility of a "prosperous" development of the mixed economies.

An unbridled private capital accumulation by way of competition presupposes what has been called a free world market and the free movement of labor and capital between all nations as well as within each of them. Although there never were such conditions, some semblance of them existed in capitalism's *laissez-faire* stage. This stage was then celebrated as the capitalist condition *per se*. In reality, however, it was the case merely of a temporary monopolization of industrial production and of the world market by a few nations, allowing them a vast and rapid accumulation of capital. Their monopolistic positions were often broken by extra-market means, such as state-subsidies, national protection, and warfare. Because it is not capital in the abstract which competes for the markets of the world, but definite national capitals, their economic rivalries take on the form of struggles for political power. "Strictly" economic competition was only nationally possible, and even here it was never "pure."

Capital accumulation expands the world market and determines its character. But the accumulation process is interrupted or slowed down by insufficient profitability. This lack of profitability has *concrete reasons*, and with capitalism a world-market system, the concrete reasons will be determined by the structure of the world economy as well as by that of each capitalist nation. The anarchy and national character of capital production prevents the detection of any definite set of concrete reasons for the conditions of capital stagnation. What appears as the "reason" for the depression is only the result of empirically undetectable causes. The individual capitalist experiences the depression as a decline in the demand for his commodities. The individual nation feels it as a decline of production caused by a lack of markets, and defends itself against foreign competition by trying to secure and enlarge its own market at the expense of other nations.

The rise of "big business" in any particular nation is an expression of a successful reproduction of its capital structure. To achieve an international reorganization, although this is also necessary for continuous capital formation, is far more difficult. Big business, outgrowing the frame of the national economy, expanded in all capitalist countries and led to the export of capital and to all manner of international trustification and cartellization. But the "internationalization" thus achieved was less a true internationalization of the market-determined capitalist concentration and centralization process than an attempt to cope with the internationalization of the capitalist production and exchange process without giving up its earlier-developed national form. It also expressed the difficulty of bringing "accumulation for the sake of accumulation" into conformity with the consistently more stable social institutions that developed within the separate national states. No really effective way has been found to repeat on an international scale the competitive accumulation and concentration process that took place in each country individually.

Because the "self-expansion" of capital disregards the particular needs of national states, governments have seldom been in favor of a strict *laissez-faire* policy in their international economic relations. The "automatic self-expansion" was strongly opposed by all social layers whose interests were vested in the national state as an entity relatively independent of the general development of capital. Not satisfied with the monopolistic "internationalization" of big business, which *tended* to arrest rather than promote general capital expansion, governments, representing national capitals, expressed their own "internationalism" in a policy of national expansion. The "internationalism" of capitalism thus comes to the fore as an imperialistic nationalism. This presupposed a certain unity between government and capital, brought about by way of collaboration, compromise, or force, which delimited and finally terminated the earlier forms of individualistic competition. To fulfill their new — or rather added — functions, governments entered the arena of international competition with most or all of the national power at their disposal. The earlier system, a state-supported economic competition that might carry through into war, was replaced by a war-like competition, or actual warfare, supported by the national economy.

As long as crises and depressions were effective enough to alter the conditions of production and the structure of capital and thus bring about a resumption of capital expansion, a state of over-accumulation at one level of capital production led to a state of over-accumulation on a higher level of capital production. Under nineteenth-century conditions it was relatively easy to overcome over-accumulation by means of crisis that more or less affected all capital entities on an international scale. But at the turn of the century a point had been reached where the destruction of capital through crisis and competition was no longer sufficient to change the total capital structure towards a greater profitability. The business-cycle as an instrument of accumulation had apparently come to an end; or rather, the business-cycle became a "cycle" of world wars. Although this situation may be explained politically, it was also a consequence of the capitalist accumulation process.

Capital was now "accumulated" in growing measure in the form of armaments. The armaments-race led to an expansion of industry not because it was "profitable" in the regular sense of the term, but because an increasing part of profits could now be "realized" through government purchases. To be sure, the "extra-economic" recourse to war-production was not adopted solely to avoid a business decline; it found its rationalization in political and ideological objectives as well. Wars are not unique to capitalism; but the objectives for which capitalist wars are fought are. Aside from all imaginary reasons, the main objective, made patent by the policies of the victorious powers, is the destruction of the competitor nation or bloc of nations. In its results, then, war is a form of international competition. It is not so much a question of competition by "extra-economic" means as an unmasking of economic competition for a bloody and primitive struggle between men and men.

The resumption of the accumulation process in the wake of a "strictly" economic crisis increases the general scale of production. War, too, results in the revival and increase of economic activity. In either case capital emerges more concentrated and more centralized. And this both in spite and because of the destruction of capital. In a world of internationally-competing capital entities, this implies changes in economic and therewith political power positions. While this is true throughout the capital accumulation process, it is accelerated in times of war and thus becomes quite obvious. Despite the losses of some nations, the gains of others are large enough to initiate a new period of capital expansion soon to excel, in terms of world production, the pre-war level of economic activtiy.

The general process of capital accumulation, which occurred within a world economy dominated by Great Britain, slowly shifted the locus of economic power. Long before the outbreak of World War I, Germany and the United States had taken over Britain's power position. While this was one of the reasons for war, the war itself shifted the controlling economic power from Europe to America. The relative stagnation of European capital prior to the First World War was mitigated by a government-fostered armaments race; while America's slowing rate of capital expansion was reversed with the outbreak of war. Her recovery of 1915 "was generated by the demand for war supplies emanating from European governments." Expansion of production "was derived in part from taxation and in part from the sale of securities to individuals and banking interests," so that the process of American recovery "was generated by an outpouring of purchasing power by way of government treasuries. It did not begin with an expansion of ordinary consumption demand or an increase in the production of private capital goods."[11]

Although the increase in production was set in motion by the policies of governments engaged in or profiting by war, total world production rose to unprecedented heights. For the warring nations of Europe the post-war period was a time not of real prosperity, but of a slow return to, and an insufficient enlargement of, their pre-war level of production. This was, moreover, at the price of an increasing indebtedness to America and an intensified exploitation of the workers, manifesting itself in lowered living standards. But America prospered, and in 1929 her wealth was two-and-a-half times as great as in 1914. Measured by world production, economic activity had increased and capital had accumulated. Its seat of strength had shifted from Europe to America. Like previous depression periods, the war had touched off a new expansion of capital and had concentrated it in the strongest capitalist nation. This is further illustrated by America's foreign financial relations. While in 1914 "American investors held foreign securities amount-

11   H. G. Moulton, *The Formation of Capital*, Washington, 1935, p. 65.

ing to less than 1 billion dollars, in 1924 such private holdings amounted to almost 4.6 billions — or roughly to 5.4 billions, if short-term credits are included. In addition, the government of the United States held foreign government obligations aggregating 11.8 billion dollars. Thus, within the space of ten years, the foreign securities acquired by the government and the people of the United States were more than fifteen times as great as the amount that had accumulated during the preceding 130 years of the nation's existence."[12]

Though American production grew and her "national wealth increased, that portion utilized directly for the reproduction process of wealth continued to decline."[13] In other words, there was a slackening of the rate of accumulation; the percentage of productive capital in relation to non-productive wealth became less instead of more. This was no longer the type of capital production which characterized the nineteenth century. The expansion of production initiated by war and carried over into peace was not enough to lead to a general expansion of capital production under the conditions of the market-determined economy. After a decade of limited prosperity, restricted largely to the United States, a new collapse of the market system led to new state interventions. These, however, succeeded only in stabilizing depression conditions; the full utilization and further expansion of productive resources had to await another war.[14]

War-production was then, in its effects, not really "waste-production" but a medium for the resumption of the accumulation process. In this sense, it was not only a subsidy to armaments produ-

---

12 *America's Stake in International Investments*, The Brookings Institution, Washington, D.C., 1938, p. 375.
13 R. R. Doane, *The Measurement of American Wealth*, New York, 1933, p. 16.
14 According to S. Kuznets the ratio of net investments to national income in the United States rose until the turn of the century and declined from then on to nearly nothing in the 1929-1938 period.

Net Capital Formation in Percentages of National Income (1929 Prices)

Decade	Net Capital Formation	Decade	Net Capital Formation
1869-78	13.7	1904-13	13.1
1874-83	14.4	1909-18	13.0
1879-88	14.6	1914-23	11.4
1884-93	16.1	1919-28	10.2
1889-98	16.2	1924-33	6.0
1894-03	14.8	1929-38	1.4
1899-08	13.6		

(*National Income—A Summary of Findings* National Bureau of Economics Research, New York, 1946, p. 53.)

cers but a condition for a better profitability of post-war capitalism. This is an additional reason why, generally, capitalists will object to useful public works and welfare spending but not to the extension of "defense" expenditures. Aside from ideological considerations, experience shows that the possibility of war is intrinsic to capital accumulation and that wars must be won to hasten the expansion process.

The First World War and its aftermath required an enormous extension of governmental controls over the whole of the economy — the so-called "war-socialism." After the war, some countries returned quickly to what was considered the "normal" state of capital production, characterized by a minimum of government control. Other nations could not achieve "normalcy," but carried decisive governmental controls from war into peace in order to cope with their internal difficulties and with the changed world situation. The Bolshevik regime adopted the conditions of war-socialism — in a more consistent form — as the model for reconstructing the Russian economy and for transforming private into state-controlled capital production.

Government controls were extended during and after the Second World War, first to wage war more efficiently, and later to maintain social stability in the post-war world. Although the Second World War, like the first, led to a world production higher than the pre-war level, this increase was not enough to sustain more than the American post-war "boom." In the beginning of 1950, unemployment became once more a dominant issue. With the sole exception of Great Britain, in all Western nations and particularly in the United States the Keynesian anti-slump suggestions were revived. The United Nations Organization saw the need for drawing up a "master-plan" for combating unemployment through world-wide actions. But all the deliberations in this respect came to nothing; they always returned to the general demand that the "creditor nations," i.e., the United States, extend further credits to the debtor nations. By 1949, however, America found herself in a business depression which had immediate repercussions all over the world. "The fall of 5 per cent in the American national product caused a 30 per cent fall in American imports, and, for a time, in the summer of 1949, threatened to cancel all the progress made in the first year of Marshall Plan aid."[15]

15 *The Economist*, London, February 11, 1950.

The Korean War altered the situation once more. The conditions created by the Second World War and the resumption of armaments production for the Korean War do not explain all aspects of the American post-war "boom." However, the depression which preceded the Korean war and its end by way of the war were obviously connected with the decline and the resumption of government spending. Prior to the Korean War, and despite 20 billion dollars' worth of American aid to Europe, government expenditures in America dropped considerably from their wartime height. Bank holdings of government securities diminished by 25 billion dollars. With the reversal of the post-war "disarmament" trend caused by the new war, economic activity increased not only in America but throughout the Western world. But despite an increasing rate of government defense spending under the ensuing cold-war conditions, there was no full employment. Only under conditions of actual large-scale warfare, then, in which nearly half of the Gross National Product served the needs of war, was there a full use of productive resources.

Conditions after World War II made it clear that the war had failed to provide the impetus for a market-determined private capital accumulation on a scale sufficient to allow for the retraction of government-induced demand. Any decrease in government spending led to a contraction of economic activity which could be altered only by the resumption of government spending. The best that could be hoped for was a stable relationship between private production and government spending. But even this presupposed a definite rate of economic growth to keep the economy competitive and to prevent the steady growth of unemployment. It has been possible in some measure to stabilize government expenditures but, in the long run, this stabilization itself depends on an increasing rate of capital formation. Without such a rate, government expenditures must increase to compensate for a lack of fixed capital formation. "Between 1947 and 1953," for instance, in the United States, "real output increased 4.6% a year, whereas the rise averaged only 2.9% annually from 1953 to 1963."[16] The following gives the percentage distribution of components of Gross

---

16 B. G. Hickman, *Investment Demand and U.S. Economic Growth,* Washington, 1965, p. 123.

National Product at business cycle peaks, in current dollars, from
1948 to 1963.[17]

Component	1948	1953	1957	1960	1963
Government purchases	13.3	22.7	19.5	19.8	21.4
Gross private domestic investment	16.6	13.8	14.9	14.3	14.1
Personal consumption	68.7	63.7	64.4	65.3	63.8
Net exports	1.3	0.1	1.1	0.6	0.7
Total	100.0	100.0	100.0	100.0	100.0.

While capitalist governments will try with all the means at their
disposal to foster private capital accumulation, lack of success will
force these same governments to increase their own part in the
economy and therewith to increase the difficulties in the way of
private capital expansion. At times both policies are tried, or are
suggested; namely, to improve the earnings of capital by way of
tax reductions, and simultaneously increase government expenditures through deficit-financing. But as the deficit must be covered
by private production, this amounts to no more than giving with
one hand what the other hand takes, even though the process is
stretched out over a long period of time.

There is now general agreement that the conditions of nineteenth
century capitalism — the relatively unhampered and market-determined accumulation of private capital — cannot be recaptured.
"It is no longer a matter of serious controversy whether government
should play a positive role in helping to maintain a high level
of economic activity; what we debate nowadays is not the need
for controlling business cycles; but rather the nature of government action, its timing and its extent."[18] Particularly its extent;
for if the growth of government control changed the *laissez-faire*
into the "mixed" economy, its further extension is bound to change
the latter into something else. While the process that led to the
mixed economy is now recognized as irreversible, it is held that the
mixed economy itself is permanent, in order to secure that degree
of private initiative and private capital production still possible
within it.

The traditional form of capital production was once also held
to be unalterable, and changed nonetheless. The changes were
brought about by political interventions in the apparently self-

17 *Ibid.*, p. 135.
18 A. F. Burns, *The New York Times*, October 19, 1954.

sufficient market mechanism. They ranged from reform to revolution, from protectionism to imperialism, and they created new social institutions and new vested interests which affected both the character and the direction of capital development. These new institutions and the interests vested in them assure the irreversibility of the process that created them. It seems unlikely, for instance, that the institutional changes brought about by the Russian Revolution and the Russian victory in World War II will be undone. But neither is it feasible to undo the usurption of economic controls by government bodies in the nominally private capitalism of the West. Quite aside from whether or not it should prove economically possible to reduce the "public sector" of the economy, the interests vested in the "public sector" will not abdicate on their own, but will use their institutional power to perpetuate themselves. All that can be expected in this respect is the attempt to arrest the growth of the "public sector" by speeding up the expansion of private capital.

A strictly capitalist private-enterprise economy has never existed; the private property economy was always accompanied by a public sector, whose relative importance varied according to the specific historical conditions of developing capitalist nations. But the public sector was not regarded as autonomous; it was considered an unavoidable expense for assuring the proper functioning of the market economy. This was so even where the public sector included — besides the "military capital" — the transportation system, utilities, and other special industries. All in all, whether more or less extensive, the public sector has always accounted for a part of the national economy.

With respect to public enterprises no two countries are exactly alike, even though the general trend towards increasing government control is visible in all. The United States was (and is) the country least affected by the nationalization of industries. The difference between America and Europe in this respect occasioned the notion "that few European economies — perhaps none — can be called capitalistic in the sense given to that word in the United States and Canada, where noncapitalist elements play only a secondary role."[19] But even in America the direct utilization of human and material resources by government has grown persis-

19 M. Salvadori, *Europe's Needs and Resources*, New York, 1961, p. 737.

tently. Between 1900 and 1949, for instance, while "private employment in the United States doubled, the combined employment of state and local government quadrupled, while federal employment increased twelvefold. One out of twenty-four workers was on some government payroll in 1900; the proportion rose to one out of fifteen in 1920, one out of eleven in 1940, one out of eight in 1949. In 1920, one out of every fourteen dollars of capital assets (excluding military equipment) was government property; in 1946 the proportion became one out of four."[20] The trend towards bigger government continues still. "Whereas in 1929 less than one dollar in ten of national production owed its origin to government purchasing, today about one dollar in five of all goods and services produced is sold to some branch of government."[21] The growing role of government in the economy is too obvious to be enlarged upon. It is visible not only in the direct employment of labor and capital, but also in the growth of the armed forces, in foreign financial relations, in trade and exchange arrangements, in the public debt and in the fact "that about half of the economists in the United States are on the Federal Payroll."[22]

Whereas in theory — no matter what the actual practice — government control in authoritarian countries serves the whole of society and not a particular class, in most Western nations, and particularly in the United States, government control is subordinated even in theory to the specific property relations of capitalism and therewith to the interests of big business. What real redistribution of income exists in the United States is to a large extent a shifting of tax-money from nonsubsidized to subsidized sections of the economy; taxation and deficit-financing, i.e., deferred taxation, "has been turned into a vehicle for assuring the economic potency of private enterprise."[23] The economy is thus co-determined by government and big business to such a degree that, for all practical purposes, government is big business and big business government.

Capital concentration has been much aided by government sub-

---

20 A. F. Burns, *The Frontiers of Economic Knowledge*, Princeton, 1954, p. 40.
21 R. L. Heilbroner, *The Making of Economic Society*, Englewood Cliffs, 1962, p. 175.
22 *The New York Times*, February 25, 1953.
23 P. K. Crosser, *State Capitalism in the Economy of the United States*, New York, 1960, p. 97.

sidization favoring the big producers which supply the great bulk
of government-created demand. "In 1962 just under three-quarters
of all prime contracts were let to 100 large corporations. Small businesses, which are defined as those having less than 500 employees,
received somewhat less than one-fifth of all prime contracts
awarded. Even when allowance is made for the fact that small
business receives a substantial number of subcontracts, the extent
to which defense work is concentrated in large organizations is
pronounced."[24] In newly-opening spheres of production, enterprises are often launched with government money and supported
by steady government contracts and other forms of aid.

American capital has reached a degree of concentration which
makes the existence of the whole of the economy dependent on
the preservation and growth of its big corporations. An economic
failure of this highly concentrated capital, which employs the great
bulk of the laboring population, would be nothing short of national
disaster. Its power is enormous; but if its power were less, or were
endangered, it would have to be shored-up by the government to
avoid economic collapse. Tax money is poured into private industry through government contracts and private enterprise becomes
"in its most significant phase — the phase of capital formation —
state-financed enterprise."[25] It has been estimated, for example,
that "tax money poured annually since the end of World War II
into private industry, that is, defense contracts, is about equal to
the amount of net capital formation in all United States industry,
as represented by the rate of United States annual industrial
expansion."[26]

Governments, of course, cannot subsidize anything; they can only
see to it that one part of the economy subsidizes another part, that
socially-available profits are distributed in such a manner as to
enable the prevailing society to function. In a way this has always
been the case, through the workings of competition as well as
through monopolization. But what previosuly occurred "automatically" through the market mechanism is now, under conditions
of capital stagnation, done consciously by way of government-
created demand, which is only another name for subsidization.

24   E. Ginzberg, *The Pluralistic Economy*, New York, 1965, p. 151.
25   P. K. Crosser, *State Capitalism in the United States*, p. 28.
26   *Ibid.*, p. 27.

It is then not surprising to find economists lumping together market-determined and government-induced production to deduce from this total production the state of the economy, as if the mere quantity of production and not its profitability was indicative of the good or bad health of the national economy. Still, the rising national product must find a definite limitation in the associated relative decline of non-subsidized capital and in the further course of capital concentration.

There is more outright nationalization of industries and services in Western Europe, although with wide variations between different countries and with regard to industries affected. The main industries either completely or partially under government control are railways, coal, oil, utilities, and metals. In Austria, basic industries are a complete government monopoly due to institutional changes brought about by the Russian occupation following the Second World War. With the exception of Switzerland, all Central Banks are government controlled, and so are most of the national railways. In some nations, Norway for instance, substantial state participation in private companies takes the place of outright government ownership. But nationalized industries play a substantial role in all West-European countries. In 1955, for example, "public treasuries of various sorts in Western Europe spent an estimated $62 billion (excluding operating expenditures and publicly owned corporations). This represented 28 per cent of Western Europe's total gross national product, which approached $221 billion that year."[27]

A "mixed economy" can be a mixture in which private capital dominates, as presently in Western Europe and, to a greater extent, in the United States. Or it can be one in which state-ownership is predominant, such as existed in the early years of the Bolshevik regime in Russia. State ownership and private enterprise may co-exist without encroaching upon each other, as has been more or less true in many nations for some time. In this case, the operational sphere of private capital production by-passes that of government production; it merely operates, so to speak, in a smaller economic world. Where government production monopolizes certain industries there is no competition between private and government production. This may affect private enterprise fav-

27   J. O. Coppeck, *Europe's Needs and Resources*, p. 404.

orably or unfavorably, as government pricing policies may be designed to provide a medium of taxation and to support a policy of selective subsidization.

With a smaller economic world to operate in, private capital will reach its limits of expansion sooner than otherwise. It must thus try to hold the extension of government-controlled production and capital in check. Governments, representing the interests of private capital, will on their own accord check their extensions into the sphere of private production. The choice of monetary and fiscal policies and the emphasis on waste-production illustrate the efforts of governments to avoid the nationalization of industries. Where nationalization has occurred, it has been largely the result of political activities on the part of movements opposed to private enterprise or to its monopolistic practices. In France, enterprises were nationalized after the Second World War because their owners had been collaborating with the enemy. The British Labour Party, reaching the government after the war, nationalized the coal and transport industries, not so much because nationalization was part of the Party program, but because these industries found themselves in a moribund state. Whatever the reasons for a particular act of nationalization, the mixed economy was conceived not as a partial transformation of private enterprise into state-enterprise, but as a full employment program realized through government initiative in order to increase production within the private-enterprise system. Aside from the degree necessary to any capitalistic system, nationalization of industry was not the Keynesian but a socialist program, which considered all partial nationalizations as so many steps towards total nationalization.

The mixed economy in the Keynesian sense is seen as an alternative to socialization (or nationalization), and as the only alternative. Progressive nationalization of capital implies a steady decline of private enterprise and this decline, in turn, speeds up the nationalization process. With state-ownership the dominant form of ownership, private enterprise would slowly disappear, not only by way of competition but also through political activities issuing from the state-capitalist part of the economy and the new institutions connected with it. To avoid the transformation of private capital production into state-capitalism, the state-controlled part of the national economy must be kept at a minimum. It is for this reason, that social movements which lost their early socialist inclinations, such as the British Labour Party, avoid the comprehensive nationalization of industry even when it appears possible. The nationalization *goal* of the Labour Party, for instance, was set at between 20 and 30 per cent of all industry. It was not carried out to that extent. "The nationalized sector of the British economy," it was said, "will always remain a minority of the whole. Total national ownership of all the means of production and distribution once advocated in most early socialist doctrines does not come within the modern socialist concept as it exists in Britain."[28]

Because socialism is no longer the goal of "socialist organizations," these organizations have no choice but to accept the Keynesian concept of the mixed economy as their own. The mixed economy appears now as an expression of the evolution from *laissez-faire* capitalism to the modern welfare-state, and the latter as the realization of the *modern* concept of socialism, i.e., *socialism based* on private property or, in crude American terms, "people's capitalism." Insofar as greater equality of incomes is thought desirable and necessary for full employment, monetary and fiscal manipulations are regarded as sufficient to bring this about. The program depends upon the character of the government, for which reason it is necessary to have a "socialist government" to assure the effective working of "modern private-property socialism."

Like the British Labour Party, all Western socialist parties no longer attach importance to public ownership and operation of industry. Such parties in West Germany, France, and Italy have even programmatically dropped their calls for public ownership of the means of production. In the Scandinavian countries, they are content with the prevailing partnership between government and private enterprise. Except as an empty Communist Party slogan, nationalization plays no political role in the Netherlands, Belgium, Switzerland, and so forth. The problem of ownership is seen as irrelevant with regard to social and economic needs, which now appear solvable within the *status quo* of the mixed economy. Of course, this ruling attitude has its cause not only in the changed character of the labor movement, whose very existence is bound to the *status quo,* but also to the relatively prosperous conditions due to the reconstruction of the war-devastated European economies.

28 F. Williams, *Socialist Britain,* New York, 1949, p. 91.

"By 1955 Western Europe was spending $45 billion on investments — more than one-fifth of its total gross product; two thirds of it in plant, machinery and equipment. During the period 1949-1959 fixed capital formation increased more than national product. In 1959 Gross National Product was 48 per cent above the 1949-1959 average, and fixed capital formation 69 per cent higher."[29] Conditions of economic expansion will not call forth demands for nationalization; nationalization is an answer to the failure, not the success, of capitalism, even if this success is temporary and partly illusory.

A great part of this investment was a result of political decisions rather than individual initiative. Governments arranged for compulsory, or near-compulsory, institutional savings, and for the retention of a large share of corporate profits for reinvestment purposes. Expansion was achieved by way of deficit-financing and "under almost universal inflation to a degree never before so widely experienced in peace time. Prices in Western Europe rose by 66 per cent between 1947 and 1957. This was a compound rate of increase of more than 5 per cent per year, a rate roughly equal to the yield of government bonds (before taxes) ."[30] These methods made investments possible by cutting down consumption in favor of "savings," i.e., capital accumulation. Aided by government, capital could now expand as in times of old.

Not to be misled by this success story, it must be pointed out that the forced capitalization of Western Europe was not the result of the application of "modern economics." Rather, the "application" worked in this particular way because of the conditions in which Europe found herself after the war. The enormous destruction of capital, not only in value terms but in material, physical terms, and the obsolescence of a large part of the surviving productive apparatus, allowed for — and demanded — a rapid capital formation to avoid a total collapse of the private property system. Both capital and labor accepted the demands of government not to work for more consumption but for capital formation. And, as in times past, more consumption became a by-product of the accelerated capital expansion.

The same "economics" did not have the same results in the

29 J. O. Coppock, *Europe's Needs and Resources,* p. 450.
30 *Ibid.,* p. 461.

United States. At the end of World War II America's productive capacity exceeded the available market demand. While the European economies began again to accumulate capital at the expense of consumption, a further rapid expansion of the American economy would have led only to more unused capacity. Not even the peace-time simulation of war-time conditions by way of defense expenditures enabled America's productive resources to be fully used. Where European governments applied fiscal and monetary policies to further the accumulation of productive capital, the United States used these policies to subsidize waste production. Real capitalistic prosperity depends on an accelerated rate of capital formation, for it is only such a rate which creates an aggregate market demand large enough to employ the productive resources. "A review of the principal components of aggregate demand strongly suggests that the sluggishness of business fixed investments was at the heart of the demand lag after 1957."[31] This sluggishness reflects a low rate of profit relative to the stock of fixed capital and inventories. "The profit rate in the United States fell steadily in the 1950s. There was not even an upward trend in the absolute level of profits in spite of a cumulative manufacturing investment of about $125 billion over the decade."[32] In contrast, in Germany, "the absolute level of profits rose by 1960 to about three and a half times the 1950 level"; and the return on capital during the same period "averaged in Germany about 28 per cent and in the United States about 18 per cent."[33]

Government interventions in the American economy did not break the relative stagnation of capital formation. In despair, a symposium of twenty prominent American economists called for a "new Keynes."[34] The standard Keynesian categories were now recognized as "inadequate to diagnose the trends in the economy since the mid-fifties. What is needed is a meta-Keynesian approach."[35] With the demand for business capital in a long-term relative decline, the question was no longer, it was said, "whether fiscal policy can offset a temporary gap in demand, but how we can restructure

31 B. G. Hickman, *Investment Demand and U.S. Economic Growth*, p. 9.
32 A. Maddison, *Economic Growth in the West*, New York, 1964, p. 54.
33 *Ibid.*
34 *The New Republic*, October 20, 1962.
35 B. Caplan and H. Malmgreen "More than Keynes," *The New Republic* December 1, 1962.

our economy so that new *permanent* sources of demand may be found."[36] Although the answer to the query should be obvious, with two-thirds of the world population near or at starvation, and with the underdeveloped countries' urgent need for all kinds of means of production to overcome their miserable conditions, the "obvious" is not an answer, not even for alleviating misery in the developed nations where tens of millions of people cannot satisfy their most immediate needs. What prosperity there has been, has been largely a by-product of the Cold War, which "has not proved that recessions can be avoided except by armaments expenditures, and since to justify armaments international tension has to be kept up, it appears that the cure is a good deal worse than the disease."[37]

36 *Ibid.*
37 J. Robinson, *Latter Day Capitalism,* New Left Review, London, July-August. 1962, p. 43.

CHAPTER XIV

THE MIXED ECONOMY

As far as *laissez-faire* capitalism is concerned, Marx's prediction of its decline and eventual demise is obviously still supported by the actual course of development. The prevalence of the "mixed economy" is an admission that capitalism would find itself in a depression were it not for the expanding government-determined sector of the economy. What does this government intervention imply as regards the private-enterprise economy?

No doubt, State intervention increases production and thus expands the productive apparatus. But if the goal of such intervention is the stabilization of the market economy, government-induced production must be non-competitive. Were the government to purchase consumption goods and durables in order to give them away it would reduce the private market demand for these commodities. If the government owned enterprises were to produce such commodities and offered them for sale, it would increase the difficulties of its private competitors by reducing their shares of a limited market demand. Government purchases must fall out of the market system; the production entailed must be supplementary to market production. The government is therefore predominantly concerned with goods and services that have no place in the market, that is, with public works and public expenditures of all descriptions.

The division between private and public production is, of course, not absolute. Political exigencies induce governments to enter the sphere of private market production, for instance, by subsidizing certain commodities and by purchasing surplus products to be utilized in foreign and domestic aid projects. There is some overlapping of private and public business activities in various branches of production as well as in their marketing and financing. Generally, however, one can speak of the division of the economy into a profit-determined private sector, and a smaller, non-profitable, public sector. The private sector must realize its profits through market transactions. The public sector operates independently of the market; though its existence and its activities affect the private sector's market relations.

The government increases the "effective demand" through purchases from private industry, financed either with tax money or by borrowings on the capital market. Insofar as it finances its expenditures with tax money, it merely transfers money made in the private sector to the public sector, which may change the character of production but does not necessarily enlarge it. Production will, however, be enlarged through government borrowings and deficit-financing. Capital exists either in "liquid" form, i.e., as money, or in fixed form, i.e., as means and materials of production. The money borrowed by government puts productive resources to work. These resources are private property, which, in order to function as *capital,* must be reproduced and enlarged. Depreciation charges and profits gained in the course of government-contracted production — not being realizable on the market — are "realized" out of the money borrowed by the government. But this money, too, is private property — on loan to the government at a certain rate of interest. While production is thus increased, its expense piles up as government indebtedness.

To pay off its debts and the attendant interest, the government has to use tax money, or make new borrowings. In other words, the products which the government "purchases" are not really purchased, but given to the government free; for the government has nothing to give in return but its credit standing, which, in turn, has no other base than the government's taxing-power and ability to increase the supply of credit-money. However the credit expansion is brought about, and however it is dealt with in the course of an expanding government-induced production, one thing is clear — that the national debt, and the interest on it, can be honored only as a reduction of current and future income generated in the private sector of the economy. Although unused productive capacities are put to use by government contracts, "profits" made in this way, and "capital accumulated" in this manner are mere bookkeeping data relating to the national debt. They are not actual *profit-yielding* new means of production, even where the physical productive apparatus grows with the increase in production. A relatively faster increase in government-induced production than in total social production implies the relative decline of private capital formation. The decline is covered up by the increase in production to government account, the "profits" of which take on the form of claims on the government. In the United States, for instance, "the not-for-profit sector expanded relatively rapidly in the 1930s in response to the multiple problems created by the Great Depression and very rapidly in the first half of the 1940s in response to the challenge of war. While the late 1940s saw a dynamic expansion of the profit sector, at the end of the decade the not-for-profit sector had grown relatively more over the ten-year period than the profit sector. The 1950s saw more of the same: the not-for-profit sector grew much more rapidly than the profit sector . . . It is clear that since 1929 the not-for-profit sector has grown relatively more rapidly than the profit sector in terms of the labor force directly employed and in terms of the national income produced."[1]

The claims on the government that make up the national debt can be repudiated, of course; in this case, the "profits" made via government-induced production are revealed for what they actually are, namely, imaginary. Though this may perhaps be unavoidable some day, governments, representing private capital, will postpone this day as long as possible; particularly because the repudiation of debts does not by itself guarantee the resumption of a profitable capital accumulation. Meanwhile, there is a slow but steady depreciation of incomes and debts due to inflation, a process necessary in connection with the expansion of government-induced production by way of deficit-financing.

Notwithstanding the long duration of rather "prosperous" conditions in the industrially-advanced countries, there is no ground for the assumption that capital production has overcome its inherent contradictions through state interventions in the economy. The interventions themselves point to the persistence of the crisis of capital production, and the growth of government-determined production is a sure sign of the continuing decay of the private-enterprise economy. To arrest this decay would mean to halt the vast expansion of government-induced production and to restore the

---

1   E. Ginzberg, *The Pluralistic Economy*, p. 195.

self-expansive powers of capital production; in short, it implies a reversal of the general developmental trend of twentieth-century capitalism. As this is highly improbable, the state will be forced to extend its economic inroads into the private sector of the economy and thus threaten to become itself the vehicle for the destruction of the market economy. Where the government represents private capital, it will do this only with great hesitation and against growing opposition on the part of private capital. This hesitation may be enough to change the conditions of an apparent "prosperity" into conditions of economic crisis.

There was always opposition to government controls as exemplified in *laissez-faire* ideology, yet the present objective conflict between government and business is of a different character because of the relatively faster growth of the government-determined production in the course of the general expansion of capital. The quantitative change points to an undesired yet inescapable qualitative change, for extensive state control of the economy forecasts the end of private enterprise. This objective opposition between state-control and private capital is still clouded and appears as the subjective cooperation of business and government in the nominally market-determined economy. The "cooperation" is possible only because it still subordinates government policies to the specific needs of big business. But the specific needs of big business contradict the general needs of society, and the social conflicts thereby relased will turn into conflicts about the role of government in economic affairs, that is, will be political struggles for the control of government in order either to restrict or to extend its interventions in the economy.

Although the economic role of government seems to divide the whole of the economy into a "public sector" and a "private sector," actually there is of course just one economy, in which the government intervenes; for it is not government ownership but government control which characterizes the mixed economy. There is in addition, to be sure, a great and growing amount of direct government ownership, just as there was government ownership in *laissez-faire* capitalism. But no matter how self-supporting, self-liquidating, or even profitable some government undertakings are, governments still require an increasingly larger portion of privately-produced wealth.

The "mixed" character of present-day capitalism is thus only an appearance, due to the fact that government-induced production stimulates the whole of the economy. It is obvious that public works and waste-production employ machinery, materials, and labor. Production is generally increased as the government's initiative creates additional markets for all capitals involved in producing goods that enter into government-induced production, including the consumption goods of the laborers employed therein. However, the *final product* of government-induced production, resulting from a long chain of intermediary production processes, does not have the form of a *commodity* which could profitably be sold on the market. Whatever entered into its production counts as its production cost and cannot be recovered in a sales price, for there are no buyers of public works and waste-production.

Nonetheless, the dual-economy, with its public and private sectors, will appear as a "mixed" economy benefitting both private capital and society at large. Although each sector goes its separate way, in that the one is profitable and the other not, they are nevertheless inseparably intertwined in the actual production and marketing process. For all *practical* reasons, then, the economy is a "mixed" economy, even though government-induced production cannot add but can only subtract from the total profit of total social production.

In *laissez-faire* capitalism the social character of various individual labor processes came to light only awkwardly and indirectly in the supply-and-demand fluctuations of the market. The growth of the banking and credit system, as well as the growth of the stock-company, reflected in a similar awkward and indirect fashion an increasing "de-privatization" of capital. However, it made possible an expansion of production beyond the limitations of dispersed privately-owned enterprises, and beyond the limitations which the market mechanism placed on the expansion of particular capital entities. The modern system of finance has, among other things, centralized the control of capital so that the need for immediate profits can be overruled in favor of policies which provide for larger future profits. Even here, of course, profits must finally be shown. They are then "measured" on the invested capital: if its profit-claims cannot be met, the investment is deemed "unproductive," even though it has created new productive apparatus.

What is called capital formation is this "anticipatory" expansion of production. It was the slackening rate of capital formation which induced Keynes and the Keynesians to recommend government interventions: the government should step into the picture as soon as private capital endangered the present by neglecting the future. Since government was not bound to specific sub-groups of capital, which were expected to yield customary profits, Keynes thought it could command a production limited by nothing but existing productive resources. In doing so, it would only carry on where private capital left off; it would not really encroach upon private interests whose limitations had already been revealed by the declining rate of investments.

Employment can be increased when the government pays out more money for its expenditures than it receives by way of taxes. This is deficit-financing, or the expansion of production by way of credits. There is really no need, it is said, for a regularly balanced government budget. In times of depression, the government should run a budgetary deficit; and in times of prosperity it should try for a surplus by taxing more money out of the system. This surplus would retire the government debt. In this manner there would still be a budgetary balance, but it would be spread over a longer period of time. Meanwhile, the business-cycle would be flattened out, neither deflation nor inflation would become excessive, and current depressions could be halted at the expense of future prosperities. Instead of the violent fluctuations of the business-cycle there would be a steady and balanced growth of the economy.

This argument overlooks the fact that only an accelerated capital formation creates conditions such as are designated by the name prosperity, and that these conditions require — as a precondition — severe depressions bringing a vast destruction of capital values. Keynes himself envisioned a stationary state of capital production in "mature" capitalism, wherein there is neither depression nor prosperity in the traditional sense but a continuing government-created "quasi-boom" with a declining rate of capital formation. Most of his disciples, however, deny the stationary tendencies of capital production. But they do suggest that the rate of capital accumulation should not be "maximized" but "optimized," i.e., kept in bounds most suitable to economic and social stability. Despite the theory, however, experiences with deficit-financing have shown that intervening in the course of depression hinders the return of a state of capitalist prosperity rich enough to yield a budgetary surplus. There has been, then, no alternation between deficits and surpluses but merely an accumulation of the national debt.

The national debt, Marx pointed out, "finds its support in the public revenue, which must cover the payments for interests. The modern system of taxation was the necessary complement of the system of national loans. These loans enable the government to meet extraordinary expenses without the taxpayers feeling it immediately, but they necessitate, as a consequence, increased taxes. On the other hand, the raising of taxation caused by the accumulation of debts contracted one after another, compels the government to have recourse to new loans for extraordinary expenses. Modern fiscality, whose pivot is formed by taxes on the most necessary means of subsistence, thus contains within itself the germ of automatic progression."[2] Under conditions of enhanced private capital accumulation, however, deficit-financing of government activities may "benefit" the "national economy." This will be the case if the activities in question serve to create or improve the conditions for expanding and extending the national private capital. The extraordinary government expenses contracted for international loans, colonization, or war exemplify this situation, as they are devoted to undertakings outside the proper realm of private capital production but to its ultimate benefit.

Capital will object to government deficit-financing if it violates the principle of profitability in favor of a larger national production which does not serve the specific needs of capital. The Keynesians argue, of course, that the "test of profitability," decisive in the case of private investments, is not adequate when applied to public investments. "An investment may be highly remunerative from the social point of view," it is said, "even if its direct return is nil; if, in consequence of the investment, the real income of the community is increased."[3] In addition, it is supposed that "whenever the government spends money, income is created for the producers of what is bought. The income thus created results in more spending by those who have received it and this in turn creates extra income for still others so that the total income is increasesd by several times the initial increase in spending. The two hundred

2 *Capital*, Vol. I, p. 829.
3 W. H. Beveridge, *Full Employment in a Free Society*, p. 401.

and ninety billion dollars of government spending (in the United States) — which was financed by borrowing that built the national debt to its present size — has thus resulted in contributing several times that amount to our total national income up to date — perhaps a thousand billion dollars."[4]

This is the notion, already mentioned, of the "multiplier," i.e., the idea that an increased income resulting from government expenditures will have subsequent income effects, which will add up to a sum greater than the original spending. The multiple repercussions of investments result from the fact that the employment thus provided will increase income and thus consumption. The suppliers of consumption goods are in this way also provided with additional income, with which they can increase their own consumption; and their suppliers, in turn, can repeat the procedure. Thus a chain reaction of income creations is released by the initial spending. However, people will not spend all their income on consumption. What they do spend is supposedly determined by the prevailing "propensity to consume." If the latter is low, that is, if a relatively small part of the new income is spent on consumption, the multiplier ratio between changes in income and investments will also be low; and if the propensity to consume is high, the multiplier ratio between investments and income will also be high. In other words, the smaller the additional saving called forth by additional income, the greater will be the multiplier.

The income-creating effect of investments diminishes progressively, it is said, because its income-generating power "leaks" away through savings, taxation, and foreign trade. With a low propensity to consume — which current economic theory says is characteristic of a highly-developed market economy — the income-creating effect of new investments is small, so that additional spending is required. It is expected that government spending will encourage entrepreneurs to maintain, or to increase, their own investment. Government spending will thus create additional income by way of consumption as well as private investments, and the budgetary deficit, which made the spending possible, results not only in a larger national income but also in a larger productive capacity. Although the income created by deficit-spending is offset by the increase of the national debt, it is assumed that new savings, result-

4 A. P. Lerner, *Everybody's Business*, New York, 1964, p. 112.

ing from the increased income, will in turn offset the national debt. It is held, in other words, that deficit-spending can be financed out of the savings it has itself created.

By suggesting that the sum total of subsequent increases in income is larger than the total amount of deficit-spending, the multiplier concept creates the illusion (by analogy with the velocity of money) that any given amount of additional income can multiply itself merely by traveling from one income group to another. Actually, of course, this is not so, just as a change in the velocity of money does not imply a change in its quantity or in the quantity of commodities in circulation. The same quantity of money merely serves more exchange transactions from the commodity-form to the money-form and *vice versa*.

The new government-induced investment does not fall from the sky but represents commodity-values in money form to be exchanged for other commodities. If a government spends a billion dollars, this sum has been either collected in taxes or borrowed on the capital market. In either case, this sum represents the equivalent of previously-produced commodity-values. On the unrealistic assumption that this billion dollars will be spent on consumption, these consumption goods must already exist or must be produced to make the transaction possible. Their owners, or producers, will exchange them for the one billion dollars. If they in turn spend this billion on consumption goods, they merely spend what in another form they already possessed and exchanged for the one billion dollars of the initial spenders. The same holds true for all the following exchange transactions. In each case, the commodities either already exist or must first be produced to make the transaction possible. There is no multiplication of income through the initial spending itself, though there may be the production of new income; and it is only insofar as the original spending leads to increased production that it can increase income.

All investments, whether of a private or a public character, will increase the national income as they increase national production. Capital, however, cannot accumulate except through profitability: no increase of production which is not also an increase of profits can increase capital. Since it does not depend on profitability, government-induced production can enlarge total social production; but it cannot enlarge the total capital. It is conceivable, however, that the mere increase or maintenance of a given level of production regardless of profitability may arrest a downward business trend, and may even be instrumental in reversing the trend. Although deficit-financing of non-profitable production increases only the economic activity of total capital, it does affect the profitability of those individual capitals which partake in government-induced production, and it allows for the accumulation of interest-bearing claims on the government. This may create a business climate more favorable to the resumption of private capital investments. And because any depression releases endeavors to recreate the conditions for a new prosperity, the combination of governmental and private efforts to reverse a downward trend may actually succeed. (In fact, deficit-spending was first conceived of as a temporary and limited anti-depression policy to alleviate social misery and halt an economic decline, itself conceived of as a temporary event.) As deficit-spending reduces unemployment and increases production, it may, under special conditions, induce an acceleration of private investments. If this should be the case, it would increase total income by more than that brought forth by deficit-spending, but this "multiplication" would be due directly to the additional profitable investments, not to the initial spending.

However, deficit-spending as a "regulator" of economic activity has found almost general acceptance and is widely practiced by conviction as well as by necessity. The remaining ambivalence toward deficit-spending stems from the fact that it involves an element of income redistribution because it channels funds into non-profitable spheres of production. Although the lack of investments for lack of profitability kept these funds idle in the first place, from a capitalistic point of view, they are nonetheless misused when used for non-profitable undertakings. For capital functions as such only insofar as it yields profit. Whatever the rates of profit may be, the more of the total social capital is engaged in non-profitable production, the smaller the total profit on the total capital. Although its profits would not be any greater were there no non-profitable government spending, they cannot be increased by way of such spending. From the larger total production — both profitable and non-profitable — a larger share falls now, as it were, in the sphere of consumption, and a correspondingly smaller share can be capitalized as additional profit-yielding capital.

The change in the amount of employment brought forth by government-induced production decreases the profitability of total capital relative to the magnitude of total social production. It is this decreasing profitability which shows up in the mounting national debt, and it is the latter which indicates the decline of private capital formation despite and because of the increased production. In bourgeois theory, the gross national product, or aggregate demand, is equal to the sum of consumption, investments, and government spending. Government deficit-spending, however, is not part of the actual aggregate demand, but a deliberate policy of producing beyond it. To be sure, individual businessmen are not concerned with the nature of the demand which they supply. To them, it makes no difference whether it stems from government or from private spending. Likewise, the financiers do not care whether loans are made to private entrepreneurs or to the government, so long as the loans are secure and yield the desired rate of interest. And to the individual it makes no difference whether he is employed by the government or by private enterprise, whether he produces commodities for the market or for "public consumption." In practice, no distinction is made between the public and the private sectors of the economy, and in both all transactions are money transactions, which veils their underlying social implications. From the individual's point of view, government-induced production may be no less lucrative and important than production for the market; and the accumulation of the national debt appears to him as an accumulation of private claims on the government equivalent to the accumulation of money and capital.

Deficit-spending means the spending of money derived from the sale of government bonds. Like consumption in general, "public consumption" does not add to the formation of capital. It does, however, increase the national debt. The costs of the debt, that is, the interest paid to the bondholders, must come out of the profits of the relatively diminishing private sector of the economy. The payment of interest transfers a portion of profits from productive to loan capital. But while in private capital production interest is always a part of realized profit, the interest paid to the holders of government bonds has no such profit counterpart, for this interest is paid on capital which yields no profit. The growing national debt and its interest burden cannot be related to total income as determined by both public and private production, but only to that part of the total which has not been injected into the economy by way of deficit-spending. That part which has been injected falls out of the economy as a profit-producing system. It yields income but, being unprofitable, yields no taxable income and, for that reason, cannot be considered a compensatory factor *vis-a-vis* the national debt.

What does the government actually do by bringing together labor and idle capital for the production of non-marketable goods? Taxes are a part of realized income through market transactions; if taken from capital they reduce its profits, regardless of whether or not these profits would have been consumed or reinvested into additional capital. If not, idle capital in its money form would exist as a private hoard. As such it cannot function capitalistically; but neither can it function capitalistically when taken by government to finance the nonprofitable production of public works and government waste. Instead of a capitalistically-useless money hoard there is then a capitalistically-useless production of goods and services. There is a difference, however: Whereas without taxation capitalists would be in possession of a money hoard, with taxation for purposes of public spending capital is actually "expropriated" to the extent of the otherwise possible hoard.

When used for government purposes, taxes taken from capital flow back to the capitalists in form of government contracts. The production resulting from these contracts is paid for by the capitalists through their taxes. Getting their money back through government orders, the capitalists provide the government with an equivalent quantity of products. It is this quantity of products which the government "expropriates" from capital. The size of this quantity determines the extent to which production has ceased being capital production, and the growth of production by way of taxation indicates the decline of the capitalist system as a profit-determined private enterprise system. Not only is this type of production non-profitable, it is made possible only through that part of total social production which is still sufficiently profitable to yield taxes large enough to extend government production by way of taxation. With the decline of profitability it becomes increasingly more difficult to expand production in this particular way.

But the government can borrow additional funds. These funds also flow back to the capitalists as payments for production contracted by government. The expense of government-induced production piles up, in part, as the national debt. The increase of the debt is held to be quite harmless as long as the national income increases faster than the debt. The growing national debt is then usually compared with the growing national income, to substantiate the claim that deficit-finding will be accompanied by a rising national income. This claim rests, however, on a curious way of accounting, for, to repeat, the growing national debt cannot be related to total national income, but only to that part of the total which has not been injected into the economy by the government. It is by counting an *expense* as an *income* that the illusion arises that the growing national debt is neutralized by a rising national income.

Unless the national debt is actually recovered through additional income in the private sector of the economy, that is, *additional income apart from that injected into the economy by government,* the "income" derived from the latter procedure remains, as far as capital is concerned, merely an expense of government. The utilization of privately-owned productive resources for non-profitable purposes is a partial "expropriation" of capital. The "expropriated" capital was no longer able to function on its own behalf, but that does not prevent the capitalists from demanding compensation for the government's use of *their* productive resources, even though the possibility of honoring the government debt depends on the future profitability of private capital. Unless this profitability actually materializes, the debt cannot be paid and today's additional income becomes tomorrow's loss.

The private sector of the economy must be taxed for current government needs *and* for the costs of the national debt. A larger part of its profits are taken by taxes and a correspondingly smaller part can be capitalized. Deficit-spending was resorted to in the first place because of an insufficient rate of capital growth. While taxation cannot increase this rate it can increase non-profitable production. The increase of taxation is made possible through the increasing productivity, which now benefits government-induced production rather than private capital accumulation. Instead of being capitalized, an increasing part of the social profit dissipates in additional government spending.

If not accompanied by significant expansions of private capital, the increase of productivity thus merely increases the capacity for non-profitable government-induced production, i.e., the government's ability to tax and borrow. How much can the government tax and borrow? Obviously not the whole of the national income. Yet the non-profit sectors of the economy have constantly risen in all capitalist nations. In the United States, for example, it rose from 12.5 per cent of the Gross National Product in 1929 to 27.3 per cent in 1963. If this trend continues, there must come a time when the non-profit sector outweighs the profitable sector and therewith endangers the latter's existence. There must then be a limit to the expansion of the non-profitable part of the economy. When this limit is reached, deficit-financing and government-induced production as policies to counteract the social consequences of a declining rate of accumulation must come to an end. The Keynesian solution will stand exposed as a pseudo-solution, capable of postponing but not of preventing the contradictory course of capital accumulation as predicted by Marx.

Government-induced production is thus limited by the limitations of private profit production itself. To change this situation through farther-reaching interventions in the economy would require the existence of governments willing and able to destroy the social dominance of private capital and assume control over the whole of the economy. It is for this reason that a continuous rapid growth of taxes and the national debt is viewed with some apprehension even by the advocates of compensatory fiscal policies. But so long as government spending merely affects unused productive resources and not the mass of labor and capital which can still be profitably employed, non-profit production is held to be preferable to an otherwise existing condition of economic depression. It is hopefully assumed that production via government deficit-financing will always remain a minor part of total social production, an aid rather than a hindrance to the further expansion of private capital. But to limit government-induced production in order not to destroy the market structure it is designed to defend means, of course, to limit the effectiveness of government interventions and to expose the capitalist development sooner or later once more to the vicissitudes of the business-cycle and, perhaps, to permanent crisis conditions.

As previously pointed out, Keynes did expect the return of pre-war conditions after the Second World War; he died before his proposals for full employment became government policies in the post-war world. Perhaps the manner in which his theory was put in practice would not have been to his own taste; still, the practice proved that even in "mature" capitalism employment can be increased through government initiative. There have been, however, short depressions (or recessions, as they are now called) since the end of the war, and a state of full employment has been the exception rather than the rule. This has caused much apprehension and frequent warnings that "all the structural changes and the new appearances of the movement of prices and production should not tempt us to draw hasty conclusions about the disappearance of the old [business] cycle."[5] In the Keynesian view, of course, the return to depressions finds its cause in the government's failure to apply the Keynesian remedies with sufficient resolution, and particularly in their neglecting to increase the propensity to consume by a planned redistribution of income in favor of the poorer classes. Suggestions are constantly made to strengthen the so-called "built-in-stabilizers," i.e., the monetary and fiscal reactions to emerging economic imbalances, which would increase the social demand and employment.

There are two wings of Keynesian economics, a conservative one and a radical one. Keynesian economists *out* of government office generally advocate increasing useful public works through more government spending and a general rise of living standards until full employment is reached — even if this should mean government interventions on a scale such as occurs only under war-time conditions. Keynesian economists *in* government office generally confess to the same goal, but hope to achieve it by less drastic means, i.e., through government policies which strengthen rather than weaken the private enterprise economy. The "radical" Keynesians seem to look upon government as an independent and neutral force, concerned only with the welfare of society and possessing the ability to take measures suited to this end. Actually, of course, the government has no intention of altering existing social relations and for that reason, will not institute the degree of "socialization" necessary to fulfill the "radical" Keynesian dream.

5   E. Lundberg, ed., *The Business Cycle in the Post-War World*, New York, 1955, p. XV.

The demand to raise the buying-power of the low-income classes disregards the fact that "mature" capitalism, even as a mixed economy, is still a profit-producing economic system. While it is true that this system's actual or potential productive capacity allows for a production of "abundance," with regard to its profit requirements it remains a "scarcity-economy." Because in capitalism the production of useful objects is merely a necessary medium for the production of profits and the augmentation of capital, the system's success or failure is measured not by the abundance or shortage of commodities, but by the rate of profit and the rate of accumulation.

Wages are "costs of production." Any increase in wages without a corresponding larger increase in the productivity of labor will reduce the profitability of capital. Wages do rise under capitalism, but only under conditions of rapid capital formation. Capital formation represents an excess of production over consumption. It may, and generally does, lead to increased consumption, but consumption itself cannot lead to capital formation. Each capital entity, large or small, must try to keep its production costs at a minimum in order to reach the profit maximum. Extra profits gained through monopolization and price manipulation increase competition between the less privileged capital entities and transfer profits from the weaker to the stronger enterprises. Although a partial escape from competition frees some enterprises from a steady and pressing concern with production costs, it magnifies this concern for other enterprises. In the long run, of course, the resulting decrease of profitability of the more competitive enterprises will also decrease the amount of profit that can be transferred to the less competitive capitals. As long as competition prevails it will center on the costs of production and will, thus, determine wages to the extent that they cannot be larger than is compatible with an enterprise's profitability. To the extent that greater profitability is reached through profit transfers via the marketing and price mechanism, higher wages in some enterprises are based on correspondingly lower wages in others. Just as the total social profit cannot be increased by the "inequality" of profit distribution, so total wages at any one time remain what they are no matter how they may be distributed among different laboring groups.

Government determination of wages presupposes government determination of profits and *vice versa;* the two are equally impossible (aside from taxation) within the market economy whether mixed or not. The demand for a higher propensity to consume by way of higher wages amounts to a request for ending the market economy. If taken seriously, it would require centralized control of the whole of the economy and a planned determination of its production, consumption, and expansion. Short of this, the propensity to consume will vary with the ability to accumulate capital. It is for this reason that government-manipulated wage increases are not among the various "built-in-stabilizers" of the mixed economy, and that it is always the lowest wage which sets the standard for government minimum wage legislation.

Any increase in the propensity to consume achieved by redistributing income in favor of the poorer classes should show up in income statistics. It is now generally admitted that in the pre-Keynesian economy, the distribution of income between the different classs did not change in spite of growing wages. It is, however, asserted that in the Keynesian economy there is a tendency toward a distribution of income favoring the poorer classes. This statistical tendency relates to what is called the *real produce,* which is that part of the gross national product which represents actually disposable income for consumption and savings purposes. Here, in some countries, the income falling to the capitalists as a whole has decreased relative to that of the workers as a whole. As there are now relatively fewer capitalists than before, due to the capital concentration process, and consequently more wage- and salary-earners, this is not surprising; particularly not under conditions approaching full employment. This statistical shift of disposable income from "capital" to "labor" as a whole does not tell much about the relationship between profit and wages; the less so, as the reduction of the capitalist's income share is due to some extent to their tax-evasion practices. Rather than part with dividends by way of tax payments, they reinvest them as undistributed profits, hoping to recoup present "losses" of directly disposable income at a more favorable future time. Recent American studies of income distribution have revealed that, although wages have increased, the distribution of national income among the different classes has not changed. There have been shifts within the high-income brackets, some of which undoubtedly reflect the expansion of the economy's public sector at the expense of the private sector. Despite these shifts, however, and with regard to total social production, both private and public, the gap between production and consumption is getting wider, not narrower. Because an increasing part of social production is of a nonprofitable nature, the decline of private capital production appears as an apparent redistribution of income without, however, increasing the propensity to consume, least of all by way of higher wages.

Social welfare measures such as unemployment insurance, old-age insurance, and health-insurance are also credited to the prevailing Keynesian spirit, even though most of them were instituted in the pre-Keynesian *laissez-faire* economy. These measures have nothing to do with any kind of income redistribution, even though in some countries special interests still combat them as anti-capitalist policies. They are "social" only insofar as they are legislated and, by that token, support the general trend toward increasing government control over social life. They do not increase the income of the workers; for the workers pay out far more in taxes and contributions to the various welfare-funds than what is expended for welfare purposes. In the United States, for example, "welfare spending has not changed the nature of income inequality, nor raised the standard of living of the lower-income classes above what it would have reached if they had not been subjected to Federal taxation."[6]

Because the profitability principle of private enterprise excludes the distribution of surplus products by way of the wage system, surplus-production increases in the form of waste-production. Government promotion of production by way of subsidization consists predominantly of "defense" expenditures, "military capital formation," and non-profitable endeavors such as nuclear and space technology, which have no conceivable application in other fields and cannot directly find commercial exploitation. This type of production diverts labor, materials and machinery into products that serve political-military functions. If these products are not utilized, they have no function at all. This production can serve neither the augmentation of profit-producing capital nor the general welfare, unlike other public works such as schools, parks, roads, etc. Because such a large part of government-induced production serves the alleged "defense" needs of the nation, the military enter into the picture as a third partner in the co-determination of public funds, acting not only in the military but also in the industrial sphere. The existence of a "military-industrial complex" is reflected

6 G. Kolko, *Wealth and Power in America*, New York, 1961, p. 39.

in the fact that the top echelons of industry and business are largely occupied by former military professionals. The interests of the
latter, just like those of government and private enterprise, are all
vested in the perpetuation of the prevailing corporate structure of
the economy and its continued profitability under conditions of
relative capital stagnation.

CHAPTER XV

MONEY AND CAPITAL

The Keynesians see the economy as a money economy and tend to forget that it is a *money-making* economy. In their view money appears as a mere instrument of manipulation for turning insufficient into sufficient social production. An excessive monetary growth by way of credit expansion and deficit-financing may lead to inflation, just as credit contraction and too little money tend to be deflationary. To avoid both excesses, there must be the "right" quantity of money; and it is the government's function to arrange for this "right quantity." Fiscal policies are in a way also monetary policies, as they merely allocate the "right quantity" of money in the direction most conducive to economic stability and growth. But in order to understand the dynamics of the mixed economy it is necessary to understand the relationship between money and capital.

Well into the nineteenth century different nations adhered to different metallic money standards — silver, gold, or both simultaneously. The precious metals were originally used not only as media of exchange but also as a convenient and relatively indestructible store of wealth. Whether gold or silver were produced within the money-using economies or appropriated abroad by colonizers and adventurers, the quest for gold in pre-capitalist times was mainly a quest for money. The individual's wealth, as well as the wealth of nations, was reckoned in terms of money, which meant quantities of gold and silver. Money was amassed for its own sake rather than for capitalization in other forms of material wealth. The capitalist system adapted this mercantilist money system to its own, different ends.

As capital, money is both money and more than money. Although capital is conceptually money, this category embraces not only gold but all other commodities as well, for any commodity can take the place of money by expressing its commodity-value as a money-value. The owners of capital are not trying to amass a particular commodity — gold in this case — but to accumulate the money-values of their capitals, which may take on any physical shape. Amassing money, even in the form of gold, would yield them nothing beyond the monetary hoard. Money yields additional value only when it is applied in a productive enterprise. The capitalistic accumulation of money presupposes the accumulation of capital, even though the accumulation of capital requires an initial accumulation of money.

Capital employs labor: if money is to function as capital it must first cease to be money and be turned into instrumentalities that put laborers to work. These instrumentalities, the means of production, are commodities with a value, or rather price, expressed in money terms. By themselves, these means of production are as unproductive as money is in its money form. They become productive only in the labor process. The labor not only reproduces the existing capital, and therewith its value in its money expression, but also produces a surplus which turns capitalist production into capital formation. This is again expressed in money terms by adding the capitalized surplus to the previously existing capital; but, as before, the addition of "money" implies the addition of means of production in a continuous capital expansion process.

Accumulated capital represents money values which have the form not of money but of commodities and capital. Capital is reproduced only gradually, for the means of production deteriorate, or become obsolescent, only over a number of years. The slow depreciation of capital is calculated in depreciation charges which, together with all other costs, are added to the prices of commodities to be realized in the market. Commodities offered on the market must be bought with money, but, since the commodities which are bought or sold on the market at any given time represent only a fraction of the total capital in existence, only a fraction of the total wealth of society need exist in monetary form.

Commodity exchange, or the circulation of commodities from one place to another, does not require a montary medium. It is actually carried on by human labor and the means of transportation utilized by labor. What money mediates and circulates are not commodities but property claims attached to commodities. However, it is only by way of such property claims that the actual production and distribution process is carried on. This need not involve a specific type of money, however; any medium able to designate the various claims and counter-claims in the exchange process will do as well as any other.

As money, gold enters neither production nor consumption; therefore, the labor and capital expended in its production yields no surplus. The gold producers themselves, of course, profit by gold production, just as other capitalists make profit in other branches of production; but from the point of view of society as a whole, monetary gold constitutes an expense of the circulation process. The less gold is needed as a medium of exchange, the less expensive is the exchange process. The corresponding saving in the production costs of gold can be applied to other, profitable, ends. Although money as gold was once the very incarnation of all wealth and power, in capitalism it is a cost of circulation. For this reason there was from the very beginning of capitalist development a strong tendency to change the medium of exchange from its material into an ideal existence, i.e., to replace commodity money with symbolic money.

The same development which led to the quite general adoption of the gold standard also witnessed the emergence of new and different categories of media of exchange, such as bank notes and checking money. There were then both physical and non-physical means of payment; the latter were brought into some relation to the former by means of a gold backing which served as a safeguard against the over-issue of token money. With the extension of credit institutions the monetary system became increasingly more complex. Bank credits became the principal medium of payment and standard money began to play a subsidiary part.

This development gave rise to the notion that the credit and debit system supercedes the money system. Although the concept of money, it has been said, is dependent on that of debt — for every sale of goods and services gives rise to a "debt" through the interval between purchase and sale — the concept of debt is not dependent on that of money, for a debt can be cancelled by another debt without recourse to money. Bank credit can thus exist without money. All debts, however, are reckoned in terms of money. And even if payments are made and received by check, and these checks cancel each other in the clearing system of the banks, these transactions involve other transactions in the production and exchange process in which currency serves as a medium of exchange. Moreover, business is not carried on in order that businessmen's claims on one another may be mutually cancelled, but in order to make profit. Receipts must be larger than expenditures; money must be made. Any quasi-monetary system of payment is merely an instrument to facilitate the making of money. To see in the credit and debit system of payments a form of money is to see money only as a medium of exchange. But though capitalist exchange is an exchange of commodities and of services treated as commodities, money is here more than a medium of exchange because commodity exchange itself is merely a means for the augmentation of capital.

The wealth of nations and the property of individuals can be expressed in terms of money and in terms of their physical possessions. But this wealth does not exist twice, once as real property and once as money. One may have either the one or the other. A business enterprise may be bought or sold for a certain amount of money. Money is here not a medium of exchange but is itself exchanged for property; it is the equivalent of real things — of property. To be exchangeable, money assets cannot differ from real assets. In this respect it is not correct to say that bank credit can exist without money, for the credit granted is granted for a collateral which represents money, even though this "money" has for the moment the form of real property.

In capitalism, money exists as capital, which appears in fixed or in "liquid" form. In its "liquid" form it may have the shape of commodity-money (gold), or the shape of token-money representing either gold or any other commodity that comprises material wealth. Since all real assets are potential money assets and all money assets are potential real assets, businessmen need not differentiate between quasi-money and real money. Both function equally well in settling exchange relations between business firms. But this is so only because real money as well as quasi-money are both covered by real capital assets. Where there are no real capital assets, credit money does not apply. Of course, there is always the risk that seeming real assets, which serve as collateral for credit money, may turn out not to be real; in which case the courts will finally have to settle debts based on "quasi-property."

Behind monetary transactions stand the capital values of business firms, not only in their monetary expression but also as material entities in their commodity form. The wage-earning (and salaried) classes do not generally have this kind of collateral. But they may have personal property on the security of which they can borrow money. These classes sell their labor-power as commodities for money. They get paid *after* their work performances in daily, weekly, or monthly intervals. The labor already performed is the commodity that is remunerated. Short of their savings, the total money income of the wage-earners equates with the total prices of the commodities they buy. There is, then, an exchange of commodities against commodities. The money mediating this exchange is here a mere accounting device, and as such need not have commodity form.

Usually, the value of money is measured by its *de facto* command over goods and services. For instance, the value of a pound, or of a dollar, is determined by what one can buy for one pound, or for one dollar. This leaves open the question why this is so. There must be something about a pound or a dollar which equates with something that adheres to the commodities which they can buy. From the standpoint of the objective theory of value, an answer is easily found. If gold is money and gold is a commodity, the costs of producing the gold contained in a dollar, or in a pound, are then considered equal to the production costs of the commodities which they are able to buy — modified, of course, by the changing demand and supply relations of the market.

Money thus has in theory a commodity-value equal to its production costs. Actually, this is not the case. The commodity-value of gold diverges from its money-value, although monetary authorities may set the same price for both. Furthermore, commodity-money comprises only a fraction of the total money supply; even under the rule of the gold standard, the actual convertibility of paper into gold affected only a small portion of the total money in circulation. To the extent that money has a non-commodity form, it cannot derive its value from its production costs. To be sure, non-commodity money may be evaluated in accordance with the labor costs of commodity money; but any such evaluation is a deliberate act. And since at present money in most nations is fiat money, it is clear that — at least nationally — money possesses purchasing power without having commodity-value.

Since the quest for money is now a quest for capital, modern monetary history reflects the history of capital formation. The more extensive use of commodity-money refers to an earlier stage of capitalistic development, characterized by a less-integrated production and marketing system. Capital was less concentrated and operated less routinely; the intervals between purchases and sales were more sporadic than under modern conditions. People prefered metallic money not only because they were used to it, but also because the accumulation of capital generally presupposed the hoarding of money. Money had to retain its value, a condition best assured by maintaining its commodity form. Besides, gold had been the money standard for too long to be easily displaced by mere symbolic money. The circulation of gold coins and the assurance that paper was convertible into gold supported a general confidence in the stability of the monetary system and the value of currencies.

The early preference for commodity-money found its international extension and most important rationale in the "automatism" of the gold standard as the "regulator" of the international exchange economy. The gold standard tied the value of the various national monetary units of account to their gold values and to one another by fixing the price of gold. A dollar represented a certain quantity of gold, as did the British pound and other gold-standard currencies. If one pound could be bought for four dollars, this meant that the gold content of one pound matched that of four dollars. Actually, of course, the exchange of currency was and is not that clean-cut, since prices for different currencies fluctuate with the changing supply and demand of different currencies in the foreign-exchange market. But these differences average out over time in the multitude of exchange transactions. The foreign-exchange market provides an international clearing mechanism. Since debits and credits between national claims may not balance, residual claims are settled by gold shipments in order to reach a complete, if temporary, payments balance.

Only part of newly-mined gold serves monetary purposes. Another part — probably less than half of total production — serves non-monetary needs in the arts and industry. In order to maintain the fixed price of gold, its supply must not exceed the demand; as long as the output of gold exceeds the industrial market demand, the excess must be bought for monetary purposes whether or not it is actually needed. In recent times, it has been found necessary to sell gold on the private market to maintain its fixed price. A steadily increasing demand for gold drove the price beyond its fixed limit, forcing England and the United States to meet the demand by selling some of their monetary gold on the London gold-exchange.

Like money itself, the gold standard was not meant to facilitate the international circulation of commodities in any physical sense; its purpose was to express and secure the property claims attached to the commodities and capital entering the world market. International monetary transactions had to be covered by commodity money for this was the only realistic form in which property claims could be settled.

The gold standard was an agreement between governments during *laissez-faire* capitalism; as such it was a conscious intervention in the market mechanism. Yet it was conceived as a self-regulatory system parallel to the self-regulatory market mechanism. Nationally, the gold standard implied that the central banks had to keep the value of their monetary unit at par with that of other gold-standard currencies by keeping a sufficient gold reserve. The maintenance of such a reserve set a definite limit to the creation of credit-money. The gold standard was then an instrument to circumscribe the expansion and contraction of credit and therewith the inflationary or deflationary tendencies which find expression in rising or falling prices. Under the rule of the gold standard, a disparity between supply and demand in the foreign-exchange market led to a flow of gold from one country to another: gold flowed to nations with a favorable balance of trade from nations with an unfavorable balance. It was assumed that the drain of gold from a particular country would reduce its economic activity and thus lead to deflation and lower prices, while the influx of gold into another country would stimulate economic activity and thus lead to inflation and higher prices. Because prices would be low in countries losing gold and high in countries gaining gold, trade would shift from the latter to the former. This shift in trade would again reverse the gold movements. It was through the effects of gold movements on the level of prices that the gold standard was adjudged an international equilibrium mechanism.

As an "equilibrium mechanism," however, the gold standard was as inefficient as the market itself. The assumed close connection between gold stocks and domestic prices did not exist: prices did not fall or rise because of gold movements from one country to another. At times, some nations experienced what seemed to be an unendingly favorable balance of trade and payments, while others were not able to overcome unfavorable balances regardless of their deflationary policies. At any rate, the First World War practically ended the gold standard by interrupting and dislocating the international capital and commodity market. Governments borrowed and issued money in complete disregard of their gold reserves. They paid for necessary imports with gold; so gold accumulated in nations able to sell. After the war, nations left the gold standard either by necessity or by design. By means of currency inflation, governments rid themselves of the enormous debts they had piled up during the war and kept consumption down in order to re-capitalize their industries. In some countries runaway inflation finally threatened to destroy all economic activity, at which point, of course, government-decreed money reforms brought it to an end, thus providing the circulating media with sufficient stability to function in the exchange and capitalization process once again.

It should be clear that it is not the mere availabiltiy of credit — due to the influx of gold — which induces new investments and creates conditions of prosperity, but the expected profitability of investments as indicated by the existing profitability of capital. And it is not the contraction of credit — due to an outflow of gold — which issues into capital stagnation, but a lack of profitability of the existing capital, which destroys incentives for new investments and therewith the demand for credits.

An increasing capitalization of production increases the productivity of labor and therewith the competitive ability of an enlarged capital. Where credit expansion leads to capital investments, it also leads to a cheapening of production relative to the production of countries with a lower rate of capital formation. By being able to sell at lower prices, the more-productive countries invade the

markets of the less-productive nations. It is therefore not true that
credit expansion must always lead to inflationary prices. With a
sufficient increase of productivity the supply can match and exceed
the demand and can thus not only prevent a rise in prices but even
lower them. Instead of losing gold because of adverse trade positions, rapidly expanding economies may increase their gold reserves and thus their money supply in accordance with their credit
policies. With a declining profitability of capital, both investments
and credit transactions decline. This does not necessarily bring
about an increase in sales through foreign commerce, for even the
low prices of nations with a contracting economy may still be
matched by the prices of nations enjoying a higher productivity in
expanding economies. There will then be no influx of money from
abroad to stimulate the economic activity of the relatively stagnating nations.

Moreover, with the establishment of the world market the conditions of prosperity, stagnation, and depression became world-wide
phenomena. While these conditions affected different nations to
different degrees, none remained unaffected. All capitalist nations
tended to expand credits in good times and contract them in bad.
In its credit expansion, each nation was limited by the size of its
gold reserve. In times of depression there was no pressure on the
gold reserve since demand for investment credits was low. At such
times, nations would simply wait for a turn of events and engage
in an intensified competition for markets and gold.

Despite the gold standard's disappointing results, only reluctant-
ly, and under the pressure of the Great Depression, was it finally
abolished. But since commodity-money was still necessary for settling international payments balances, an international gold exchange mechanism was substituted. Though gold still flows between
nations, these flows need not affect domestic money supplies. As
gold is now regarded simply as a special kind of money, as international money, gold movements need no longer determine national monetary policies. Inflation and deflation result from
governmental decisions to expand or contract the money and credit
supply. Precisely for this reason, some adherents of an unrestricted
market economy distrust the present arrangement and long for a
return to the "automatism" of the gold standard.

The fact that any decline in economic activity shows up as a money-contraction gave rise to the notion that such declines were caused by shortages of money and that these, in turn, were the result of limits set to credit expansion by the rules of the gold standard. Keynes, we recall, held that the gold standard was largely responsible for the crisis conditions which followed the First World War. He felt that the liberal argument against mercantilism as a system bound to a senseless accumulation of gold lost all its force and meaning because it was precisely the *laissez-faire* gold, competitive pursuit and competitive appetite for the precious metal."[1] For with strict adherence to the gold standard, there was no "orthodox means open to the authorities for counteracting unemployment at home except by their struggling for an export surplus and an import of the monetary metal at the expense of their neighbors," which tended to contract both domestic market and international trade. Keynes advocated freeing national money and credit policies from the requirements of the international gold standard.

It is quite obvious, however, that the existence of the gold standard did not prevent a rather rapid capital formation at the turn of the century; and it is equally obvious that when the gold standard was abolished, the rate of capital accumulation was reduced rather than hastened. Clearly, the expansion and contraction of capital production did not depend on the existence or non-existence of the gold standard.

An economy with a growing population, growing production and growing productivity will have a continuous increase in the quantity of money. This increase is modified by the application of non-monetary forms of exchange and by the decline of the level of prices due to the increasing productivity of labor. The development of the banking and credit system was a powerful means for speeding up the capital formation process. Not only were widely-dispersed money resources centralized in large money pools, but under the fractional reserve system these pools provided a wide base for a multiple credit expansion. And while credit allowed for an accelerated extension of industrial and commercial activities, the expansion of production thus fostered allowed for, and demanded, further extensions of the credit system. This reciprocal process im-

1 *The General Theory*, p. 349.

plied a steady displacement of commodity-money by credit-money.

However, if banks could create credit at will, the value of money would soon be lost. When the money supply is limited, so is the extension of credit. And with the supply of gold limited, the supply of money and credit was also limited. Cutting loose from gold freed the way for an independent national money policy designed to enhance economic activity through credit expansion, inflation, and deficit-financing.

While there is general agreement that the value of money is measured by its purchasing power, different notions prevail regarding the factors that alter this power. Most popular was the idea that changes in the volume of money would lead to alterations in the general price level. This was an application of the supply-and-demand theory of prices to monetary theory: quantities of money were contrasted with quantities of commodities. The quantity theory of money includes the principle of velocity, that is, that the same unit of money functions in more than one exchange transaction. Aside from the historical fact that an expanding economy also expands its money supply, the velocity of money varies with the increase or decrease of economic activity. If there is a downward trend in the circuit velocity of money this indicates real market disturbances rather than monetary difficulties, even though such a trend will intensify these disturbances on its own account.

In the quantity theory of money, money appears as an independent economic force determining the expansion and contraction of business activities, the rise and fall of prices, and the increase and decrease of income. Actually, the growth of production and incomes does not depend on the presence of any definite amount of money; more money or less may expand the scales of production and income. Moreover, prices are not high or low because more or less money circulates, but more or less money circulates because prices are either high or low. It is clear that if all prices should suddenly double, the existing money supply must also be doubled, for otherwise half of the circulating commodities could not be sold. And if all prices should suddenly fall by half, only half of the existing money supply would be required to clear the market. But doubling the money supply will not double, nor halving it reduce, the volume or value of commodities. The prices of commodities and services, though expressed in money terms, are not determined by but determine the quantity and velocity of money.

It is of course true that if money were commodity-money (e.g., gold) exclusively, its buying-power would vary like other commodity prices. A smaller or larger quantity of money would exchange with larger or smaller quantities of other commodities. A shortage of money would raise its value relative to other commodities, which would induce increased gold production — and this, in turn, would end the money shortage. If gold production could not be increased, this would merely mean that fewer quantities of gold would have to give expression to larger quantities of other commodities. However, the price of gold is fixed and money, which was based on gold solely to the extent of the fractional gold reserve, is at present entirely freed from its gold connection. Under these conditions, increasing the quantity of money beyond the extent of its "normal" growth within the rising market transactions would only mean to change the money expression of constant commodity-values. Assuming an "inflationary" situation in which all prices rise, all commodities would have higher numbers on their price-tags, but otherwise nothing would be altered. There would be no point in increasing the quantity of money.

However, if some prices should rise faster than others under inflationary conditions, a situation of advantages and disadvantages will arise. To be sure, some commodity prices always fall or rise relative to others because of the effects of increasing productivity, or because of changes in the competitive market situation. Such regular price changes do not refer to inflationary or deflationary conditions, which affect the general price level rather than particular commodity prices.

Although inflation affects the general price level, the price of some commodities changes more than others. Wages, for instance, rise less under inflation than do the prices of other commodities. As wages form part of the prices of commodities entering the market, a rise in wages due to inflation can be compensated for in this price. The prices of commodities are set after the labor costs incorporated in them have been settled or paid. A rise in the cost of labor, therefore, cannot prevent a still faster rise in the prices of commodities; so that, relative to the commodities it produces, the cost of labor power would have been reduced.

In this way, general inflation can raise particular prices at the expense of others. But the increase or decrease of money influences economic activity only by creating changes in the distribution of income. Because wages are more sluggish in their movements than commodity prices, inflation leads to higher profits and therewith to a more rapid turnover of goods and a higher rate of capital formation. Insofar as this keeps up the level of employment, inflation appears preferable even to the workers, for deflation may mean large-scale unemployment. Inflation does not suit all capitalists, nor does it suit those social layers who live on fixed incomes and thus suffer when prices increase. There are, then, social groups interested in inflation and others opposed to it, and these groups wage political struggles for either one or the other monetary policy.

Inflation is usually defined as a condition in which the money income rises faster than the real income, i.e., where there is too much money relative to the available goods. Under conditions of full employment, it is said, inflation occurs when expenditures for goods and services grow faster than potential output. On this assumption, inflation can be stopped either deliberately or automatically — deliberately, by the conscious contraction of the money supply on the part of the monetary authorities, and automatically, because according to bourgeois theory the increasing demand for money raises the rate of interest, which in turn decelerates the expansion process.

It is quite clear that prices will rise with a shortage of commodities and fall when there is a glut on the market, whatever the money supply may be. With given incomes, this merely means that people will be able to buy less at some times and more at other times. What some lose thereby others will gain. The social demand can be smaller than the social supply, but, except as a mere desire, it cannot be larger, for what is not there can be neither bought nor sold. An injection of money under conditions of a limited supply cannot increase the actual demand; it merely increases the prices of the available commodities. The supply can be increased only through additional production; and this depends not on the quantity of money but on the profitability of capital.

In fact, monetary authorities determine the quantity of money by their decisions, mediated through the banks, to make money available for loans and investments. The supply of money is a

matter of policy and not the unwilled result of uncontrolled economic events: economic difficulties may be resolved by deflationary
or inflationary means. Both these means conform to capitalistic
principles; if at a given time one is chosen instead of the other,
it is because it appears to be more effective and politically more
viable.

A period of extensive capital formation need not be inflationary
when sustained by a sufficient profitability based on an increasing
productivity. Likewise, a period of economic stagnation is not
necessarily deflationary. It usually is so, however, because the
preceding stage of expansion leaves a mass of capital and productive capacity too large for other than conditions of accelerated capital expansion. The excess results in idle capacity and idle workers;
prices collapse through intensified competition; and the whole system contracts. During a period of retrenchment the system slowly
restructures itself until conditions of profitable capital expansion
are restored. Because investments decline (or cease altogether)
during periods of depression, there are not only idle resources but
also idle money, i.e., money unable to find profitable employment.
Paradoxically, it is this idle money (and credit) which provides
the surface impression of a general money shortage. Such a situation does not call for additional money, but for the restoration of
profitability which will strengthen the inducement to invest.

Inflation results from monetary policies designed to improve the
profitability of capital internally and so enhance its competitive
capacity externally. Deflation, which can have the same effect, was
the method most used in the past to overcome crisis conditions.
It was not so much submission to the rules of the gold standard
which contracted the economy as it was the deflationary process
itself which upheld the rules of the gold standard. In other words,
it was the principle of *laissez-faire,* of non-intervention in the economy, and reliance on "automatic solutions" for business slumps,
which explain the earlier preference for non-monetary means to
combat a state of decreasing profitability. Not money, but capital
itself was devaluated and destroyed, in order to make room for
a more concentrated and more productive capital structure. Real
wages were cut without much concern for social consequences.

But depressions lost their "curative" power, or at any rate, became
intolerable. Under twentieth-century conditions the deflationary

process of "recovery" became increasingly more untenable because of the social convulsions it tended to release. Inflation became the preferred, if not unavoidable, way to react to depressions and to maintain levels of economic activity consistent with social stability. Inflation of varying intensity is now resorted to under conditions of full employment as well as of unemployment — under conditions of stagnation as well as of expansion. The depreciation of money has been consistent and universal, though the rate of depreciation has varied, often widely, for different nations. When prices rise faster than income destined for consumption (particularly wages), a greater part of total production can be turned into additional capital. While people without capital are victimized by the depreciation of money, the owners of capital preserve and augment theirs by the same process, provided, of course, they are able to realize their profits through market sales. But one good thing may lead to another: profit realization is itself enhanced by the inflationary process. Depreciating money is more rapidly spent than stable money.

The depreciation of a national currency makes capital not only more profitable but also more competitive internationally. However, as the power to devaluate is given to all independent nations, the devaluation of money in some countries leads to devaluation in others. In the end, it will again be the real capital structure, and not the money structure, which determines the relative competitive capacities of different nations.

Through government purchases with borrowed money the public debt is monetized and, with the exception of that part of the monetized debt which may be hoarded, increases the social demand. The process of debt-financing has been an inflationary process in both Europe and America. The purchasing power of the American dollar declined by more than a third in the first twelve post-war years, and to that extent deprived long-term lenders of part of their interest and part of their principal. It deprived all people with more or less fixed incomes of part of their income. This loss can, hardly be offset by wage increases, unless wage rates are based on, and actually move with, a cost-of-living index, which is rather the exception than the rule. Monetary inflation has been institutionalized and "has become subject to an institutionalized operation of co-determination by the government and all receivers of private income, among whom the financially potent private enterprises maintain a privileged position."[2] Inflation is then another form of subsidization of big business by government. It is merely one of the techniques by which income is transferred from the mass of the population into the hands of government-favored corporations.

Government intervention in the market economy is most pronounced in times of war. Inflation is used to reduce consumption by reducing the buying-power of money, so that a greater part of total production may be freed for the war effort. It is not much different in times of "peace," when a great amount of government-induced production is needed to compensate for a declining rate of private capital formation. The substitution of government-induced demand for an inadequate market demand has been an inflationary process. This obviously contradicts the notion that inflation results from the existence of too much money relative to the available commodity supply. In an economy requiring government-induced demand, the market demand could not possibly exceed the supply.

Inflation has different effects when it is used to enhance the expansion of capital and when it is used mainly to finance government-induced production. In the first case, it distributes income in a way conducive to capital formation; in the second, it sustains the expenses of government-induced production. It is generally assumed that government spending in a full employment situation will have inflationary effects because it increases the amount of money relative to the actual mass of produced commodities. This would not be so under conditions of unemployment and unused resources, it is said, because government spending would then enlarge the insufficient demand without pressing on the supply. Under such conditions, government spending need not be inflationary. But as there would be no need for compensatory government-spending in a full employment situation, we need not consider the first case. As to the second, the argument clearly rests on a misunderstanding of the character of the capitalist economy.

Although governments can create new money at will, they do so within the framework of the private enterprise economy. The central banks are agencies governments use to manufacture and control the money supply. They can alter the deposit-creating powers of

2 P. K. Crosser, *State Capitalism in the Economy of the United States*, p. 104.

the commercial banks by changing the discount rate (i.e., the rate of interest at which the central bank lends money to the commercial banks), by changing the legal reserve ratio for deposit money, and by buying and selling government bonds on the capital market. It is the banking system as a whole which creates additional means of payment through an increase in reserves as determined by the monetary actions of the central banks. Banks are thus both businesses and social institutions for the creation and allocation of money. They are in the fortunate position of profiting both as business enterprises and as the delegated instruments of monetary policies. They draw profits and interests not only from the money deposited with them, but also from the multiple amounts created by the fractional reserve system and the growth of reserves by the money-creating practices of the central banks.

Although it is the government which increases the money supply, it does not use this money directly to increase the market demand through government purchases. It finances its expenditures out of taxes and borrowings on the capital market. As far as the private contractors of government orders are concerned, the government-created demand is as good as any other. The government pays them money which must retain its value long enough for the private contractors to regain the value expended in the production of government orders and make the customary profits. If their returns were less than their expenditures because of a too rapid devaluation of money, they would find themselves in a state of disinvestment. Inflation must therefore be a controlled inflation; and it is controlled because it is based not on the government printing presses but on government borrowings restricted by legally set limits to the increase of the national debt.

Idle money and newly-created money are channeled through the banking system into industrial production to government account. But the large bulk of the products thus brought forth are neither capitalized new means of production nor additional marketable commodities; they appear as materialized expenses of government and as such reduce the total mass of private profit relative to the total mass of the existing capital. Prices are then raised to secure the customary profits, and the increase in prices necessitates additional money. Without this additional money the fall of the average rate of profit, due to the increase of non-profitable government-induced production, would lead to a further decline of private capital production; it would thus in some measure, and possibly decisively, undo the increase of economic activity through government-induced demand. It is then necessary to allow for a continuous increase in prices by a continuous increase in the money supply. It is not, as has been assumed, the pressure of an increased demand on a supply caused by government-induced production which leads to inflation. Rather, inflation is the means by which the non-profitable character of government-induced production by way of deficit-financing finds its partial compensation in higher prices.

"Normally," capital formation indicates a residual surplus of total production after the requirements of total consumption have been met. Accumulation consists of added capital-producing means of production. This occurs in decreasing measure when total production incorporates an increasingly larger share of products which cannot serve as capital-producing instruments of production. Total production, whatever its character, is "marketable," either in the actual commodity-market or through government purchases; but part of the money realized, which should take on the form of capital, does not do so. And this is because part of the existing non-consumption demand is a demand not for profit-producing capital, but for government purchases which do not include productive capital, or do so only incidentally. Although the total supply may match the total demand, the rate of capital formation declines.

Nonetheless, although accompanied by a low or stagnating rate of private capital formation, the increase in production itself may be formidable. Thus the economy may appear quite prosperous. The fact remains, however, that private capital formation finds itself in a seemingly insoluble crisis; or, rather, that the crisis of capital production which characterizes the twentieth century has not as yet been solved. When viewed from the perspective of profit production, the present differs from the past in that deflationary depression conditions have been supplanted by inflationary depression conditions. In a deflationary depression, production declines because part of the producible commodities cannot be sold profitably, thus preventing the realization of profits and their transformation into additional capital; whereas in an inflationary depression production continues, despite its lack of profitability, by way of credit expansion.

Controlled inflation is already the continuous, if slow, repudiation of all debts, including the national debt. It spreads the expense of non-profitable government-induced production over a long period of time and over the whole of society. Although government-induced production increases the scope of production, it cannot increase the profitability of private capital as a whole and thus restore for it a rate of growth that would make a compensatory government-created demand unnecessary. Capitalist profits can be increased only by increased productivity and an increasing quantity of capital capable of functioning as capital, and not by the mere availability of means of payments manufactured by government.

CHAPTER XVI

TECHNOLOGY AND
THE MIXED ECONOMY

Apart from its irrational aspects, the mixed economy can exist as long as an increasing productivity yields a sufficient social product. Production must be large enough to maintain the necessary profitability for the stagnating or relatively declining private capital, to secure existing living standards, and to allow for a growing quantity of non-profit production. Since the national debt can be refunded, it is actually only the interest on it which need be covered by either taxes or new borrowings. And since the rate of private investment decreases, more funds become available for government borrowings. In the long run, however, and with the continuous, faster growth of the "public" as against the "private" sector of the economy, profit-production must contract. To prevent this development, government-induced production must remain a limited part of total social production. If definite limits cannot be kept, the market system will eventually be superceded by a politically-controlled system of production as far removed from the mixed economy as the latter is from *laissez-faire* capitalism.

Once non-profit production becomes an institutionalized part of the economy, a vicious circle begins to operate. Government-induced production is begun because private capital accumulation is diminishing. Using this method diminishes private capital accumulation even more; so non-profit production is increased. The addition, in its turn, diminishes private capital expansion further; and so on. So long as the private sector dominates, there is no way of indulging in non-profit production except at the expense of private capital's profit production. The limits of private capital production are thus, finally, the limits of government-induced production. To change this situation through farthergoing state interventions requires the existence of governments able and willing to destroy the social dominance of private capital and to proceed from government control to government ownership.

How much can a government tax and borrow? Obviously not the whole of the national product. Perhaps fifty per cent? This would come close to war-time conditions: for instance, during World War II the American government purchased roughly half of the national product. Under these conditions, however, the rate of investment was 2.9 per cent of gross national product — a rate below that of the depression years, with the sole exception of 1932, when the rate was 1.5 per cent. Moreover, to indefinitely continue a war economy will destroy the capitalist system. However, until the end of 1965, actual waste-production in the United States, i.e., the military budget, comprised roughly 10 per cent of gross national product, while total government expenses accounted for about one-fourth of gross national product. There was, and at this writing still is, considerable leeway before the conditions of the peacetime economy approach those of the wartime economy.

Although private capital can exist and even flourish when government spending is high relative to national product, there is, of course, an absolute ceiling to government spending, past which point the taxation which finances it will reduce rather than increase social production. What this ceiling is, or when it will be reached, is not predictable. When the increase in government-induced production is enough to prevent private capital formation, its gain will be nullified by the loss of that production which private capital would have undertaken for expansion. A further increase in government-induced production would then be possible only at the expense of consumption in that term's true sense. This process may be understood by analogy with the war economy: the increasing amount of waste production which occurs during war is made possible by restricting consumption and cutting down new capital investments. Eventually, however, waste production is at the expense of consumption only; for the productive apparatus must be replaced and extended if waste production is to grow.

Although high taxes do not necessarily imply that private enterprise is being replaced by government production, some Keynesians recognize that "a high rate of taxation *is* closely related to socialism . . . If a government collects fifty per cent of the profits of

business, in taxes, and because of 'loss effect,' also carries fifty per
cent of the losses, it is just as if the government owned fifty per
cent of the business. . . The high tax rates can more properly be
said to *be* socialism than to *threaten* it."[1] It is for this reason that
"socialistically-oriented" Keynesians do not expect that the Keynesian "remedies" will be fully applied by capitalistic governments,
but look to the rise of socialist governments which combine "the
Keynesian economic policies with the traditional socialist measures
of public ownership and social reform."[2]

As the limits of private profit production are also the limits of
government-induced production, the latter will become less effective
as it increases in scale. A flourishing mixed economy can thus only
be considered a temporary state, or a transitory condition between
laissez-faire and state capitalism. Whereas Keynes himself did not
(in theory) shy away from the idea that the development of the
mixed economy may lead to a completely (unmixed) state-controlled economy, his bourgeois disciples look upon the mixed
economy as a permanent state of affairs. But their only answer to
arising difficulties within the mixed economy is a request for more
extensive state interventions, which must eventually rob the mixed
economy of its "permanence."

According to Marx, commodities must have both exchange- and
use-value. In capitalism the production of use-values ceases when
and wherever they cannot function as exchange-values. In the
mixed economy, however, material production (use-value production) continues even though no exchange-value attaches to it. The
increase of "use-values" in largely useless forms accompanies the
relative decrease of use-values capable of serving as exchange-values.
This is a modified reappearance of the discrepancy between ma-
terial- and value-production elucidated by Marx. Under *laissez-
faire* conditions, this discrepancy came to the fore in the crisis of
overproduction; it led to prolonged depressions, which restored the
capitalistically-necessary relationship between material- and value-
production. But in the mixed economy there is no restoration of
this "dynamic equilibrium" with its "proper" relationship between
profitability and accumulation; instead, a growing part of social

1   A. P. Lerner, *Everybody's Business*, p. 125.
2   J. Strachey, *Contemporary Capitalism*, p. 294.

production is carried on outside the profit system and to that extent indicates the system's decline.

The profitability of the existing and relatively stagnating capital can nonetheless be maintained through an accelerated increase in the productivity of labor, that is, through labor-displacing and capital-saving innovations. The more government-induced production grows, the more urgent is the need for greater productivity to maintain the profitability of capital. Yet the steady increase in production and productivity reproduces the need for further vast increases in productivity on an ever-narrowing base of private capital production. Even if capital-saving innovations check the growing discrepancy between that capital invested in means of production and that invested in labor-power, and in this manner curb the fall of the rate of profit, the consistent displacement of labor by labor-saving devices will enforce this tendential fall. Yet capitalism cannot do without the steady displacement of labor as the only effective means of coping with the intensified pressure on the rate of profit brought about by the increasing mass of non-profitable production. While the increase of productivity through labor-displacements is a way out for capitalism, it is a way which ends in a *cul-de-sac*.

Any particular state of capitalism is transitory, even though it may prevail for a considerable length of time. It is only by considering the general laws of capitalist development that its given historical stages reveal their transient nature. The question is, then, whether the general laws of capitalist development can be set aside by technological and political means, which attend to both the profit needs of private capital and the "general social welfare" by the simple expedient of non-profit production. For this is exactly what has happened. To see this process as a permanent and ever-widening social practice is to assume that capitalism can transform itself into another system in which — to speak in Marxian terms — it is no longer exchange-value but use-value which rules.

According to Marx, definite social relations, or production relations, correspond to definite social productive forces released by them and bound to their existence. The capital-labor relationship determines the unfolding of technological development as the accumulation of capital. Only within the frame of capital formation do science and technology expand the capacities of social production by increasing the productivity of labor. Capital is congealed surplus-labor in the form of surplus-value; it feeds and expands on living labor. Insofar as technological development is a function of capital formation, the capital accumulated is the materialization of unpaid labor-time. The reduction of labor-time implies the reduction of unpaid labor-time as well. To be sure, unpaid labor-time can be increased at the expense of paid labor time, even while total labor-time is decreased through the increase of productivity. As less labor-time is needed to produce the commodity equivalent of the workers' income, more of the total labor-time can take on the form of products appropriated by the capitalists. Yet the continuous reduction of labor-time through the displacement of laborers must eventually reduce the total unpaid labor-time, and where there is no labor, there can be no surplus-labor — and, consequently, no accumulation of capital.

Whatever the extent of automation and computerization, means of production neither operate nor reproduce themselves. Their owners, the capitalists, on the improbable assumption that they themselves engaged in production, would thereby cease to be capitalists, that is, buyers of labor-power for purposes of exploitation. Assuming what is more probable, that they succeed in continuously reducing the number of productive workers, they would also reduce the unpaid labor-time relative to the mass of the accumulated capital. It will then become increasingly more difficult to continue the accumulation process, which is only the accumulation of unpaid labor-time transformed into profit-yielding new means of production.

Capital-labor relations are value relations, which is to say that means of production are not that only but are also capital values, and that labor-power is not that only but is the source of value and surplus-value. To consummate the capitalist production process, surplus-value must be sufficient to ensure its enlarged reproduction. As value-relations are labor-time relations, it should be clear that a reduction of labor-time which would disturb the necessary relationship between surplus-value and capital is not compatible with capitalist production. However, while the reduction of social labor-time becomes a detriment to capital production, the reduction of labor-costs remains a necessary requirement for each single capitalist enterprise or corporation. Their profitability increases as their labor-costs diminish. It is for this reason that the displacement of labor by capital cannot be halted within the competitive capital formation process, even though it undermines the very structure of capitalist society.

All social progress is based on the ability to produce more with less labor. Capitalism is no exception. Technological development always displaces labor, which is only another way of saying that production increases with the increasing productivity of labor. A rapid rate of capital formation, however, can increase the absolute number of workers while decreasing this number relative to the growing capital. It is then only under conditions of relative capital stagnation that advancing technology diminishes the number of workers absolutely.

Although Marx experienced unemployment as a social fact, he held that full employment was as possible as unemployment. The level of employment depended on the rate of capital formation. Nonetheless, the displacement of human labor by the machine was what industrialization was all about. And this same process, according to Marx, turned the productivity of labor into the "productivity of capital." Although the means of production represent a definite sum of values and can be capitalistically productive only through the enlargement of this sum of values, it is the quantity and quality of the means of production in their physical form, rather than labor-time, which expresses the growing productive powers of social labor. But as long as exchange-value is the goal of production, labor-time quantities remain the source and measure of capitalist wealth. Although the "very development of the modern means of production indicates to what a large degree the general knowledge of society has become a direct productive power, which constitutes the life of society and determines its transformation,"[3] capitalism's particular contribution to this state of affairs consists of no more "than in its use of all the media of the arts and sciences to increase the surplus-labor, because its wealth, in value form, is nothing but the appropriation of surplus-labor time."[4]

Were it not for the capitalist relations of production, the growth of social wealth would be characterized by a continuous reduction of direct labor time, and the wealth of society would be "measured"

3 *Grundrisse*, p. 594.
4 *Ibid.*, p. 595.

not by labor time but by free time. According to Marx, "labor-time ceases to be the measure of wealth, and exchange-value ceases to be the measure of use-value, as soon as labor in its direct form ceases to be the source of wealth."[5] Although in an antagonistic form, the diminution of labor time as the source and measure of value already takes place under capitalistic conditions. But here it involves the reduction of surplus-value relative to the growing mass of capital. And here it is the productivity of labor, not the "productivity of capital," which accounts for the capitalistic profit. To be sure, profit presupposes the existence of capital. But profits can only be the difference between paid and unpaid labor. If they should in some mysterious fashion derive from the "productivity of capital," independently of the labor which first sets this capital in motion, they would not be profits in the capitalistic sense, for they would not be the result of labor exploitation. It would still be true that capital represents transformed past surplus-labor, but it would no longer be determined by living labor. Actually, of course, capital presupposes wage-labor just as wage-labor presupposes capital; they are the two necessary sides of capitalistic production relations. Where there is no capital involved in production, there is no capitalist society; and where capital is no longer dependent on wage-labor, capitalism has ceased to exist.

A vast increase in productivity makes it possible for private and government production to grow side by side. But the resulting prosperity is deceptive; for the credit mechanism which fosters increased production is based on future profits, which may or may not materialize. This pseudo-prosperity thus requires a continuous and accelerating increase in productivity, and the need only becomes greater as "prosperity" continues. Less-productive means of production must continually be replaced by more-productive ones, and a portion of realizable profits must be used as additional capital for this purpose.

In view of the present trend of automation, it is more generally discerned that the growing discrepancy between labor and capital tends toward a point of development at which further progressive capital expansion through labor exploitation would be impossible. This growing conviction implies an unconscious acceptance of Marx's theory of accumulation, if only because the idea is dressed

5 *Ibid.*, p. 593.

in non-Marxian terms. Instead of deducing the eventual collapse of capitalism from the growing "productivity of labor," which is only another expression for the accumulation of capital, the inverted "Marxists" deduce it from the growing "productivity of capital" and its tendency to displace labor. In either case, the system of capital production through labor exploitation comes to an end. Since the growing productivity of labor implies the growing productivity of capital, an end of capitalism by way of automation equates with the end of capitalism for lack of surplus-value.

Whatever the theory, however, the end of capitalism is not as yet in sight. Surplus-value is still produced in sufficient measure to secure the profitability of capital within the conditions of a declining rate of capital expansion; and automation, considered in relation to world-capitalism, is as yet no more than an exotic exception to a rather stagnant technology. In Marx's view, technological development is limited by the conditions of capital production; the full realization of its potentialities is impossible without the destruction of capitalist production relations. At a certain point in its development capital becomes a hindrance to a further unfolding of the social forces of production and changes from a progressive to a regressive system of production. The revolutionary working class is now alone able to overthrow the barrier to further development. By ending the capitalist system it clears the way for the social and technological advancement which can eventually abolish unwanted and disagreeable human labor. In Marx's view, capitalism's exploitative class relations made it an economically limited system and an obstacle to technological development.

On this last issue, too, Marx appears to have been wrong because of the so-called second industrial revolution, characterized by atomic power and automation. Strangely enough, however, this new triumph over Marx's gloomy prognostications is rarely celebrated as a solution to current social problems. Rather it is seen as the harbinger of new and perhaps insoluble difficulties. Suspicion that there is a possible incompatability between the new technology and the prevailing socio-economic relations runs through the growing literature on automation. While most of the difficulties of the capitalist system have seemingly been overcome, the problem of permanent and large-scale unemployment appears to be the last and most important of all capitalistic contradictions.

There is no dearth of data on automation. Its changing statistics appear everywhere, in the daily press as well as in scientific publications. These statistics simply indicate increasing productivity, production, and profitability through the reduction of the labor force. The impact of automation differs with different industries. It is particularly noticeable in textiles, coal mining, oil, steel, chemicals, railroads, and automobiles, but it affects all large-scale production in increasing measure as well as commercial and organizational activities and to some extent even agriculture. It does away with "white collar" and "blue collar" jobs; presently more of the latter than of the former, though this may change in time.

However, automation is still in its infancy and the existing number of unemployed may not be traceable to the labor displacements it causes. Clearly, workers lose their jobs due to automation; but their inability to find other employment may be the result of a declining rate of capital formation. After all, there were sixteen million unemployed in America during the Great Depression. Displacement of labor by machinery has been continuous and has not prevented a steady growth of the work force. It is feared, however, that automation is so different in degree from previous technological development as to amount to a difference in kind. The social problem it poses is thought to be unique and insoluble by analogy with past conditions.

Evaluating the impact of automation upon the American economy, Donald N. Michael,[6] for example, attempts a prognosis of its possible social consequences within the next two decades. His study is based on a number of assumptions, all of which imply that trends will remain largely what they are now and what they have been during the last ten years. Michael employs the term "cybernation" to account simultaneously for "automation" and "computers," which usually go together in the application of cybernetics to production processes. We will leave aside all the wondrous existing and potential capabilities of cybernation, and will merely indicate what Michael, among others, considers to be the advantages of cybernation. The advantages for both business firms and governments are plainly to "boost output and cut costs," leading to success in private and national competition. The other advantages Michael mentions, such as "reducing the magnitude of

6 D. N. Michael, *Cybernation: The Silent Conquest*, Santa Barbara, 1962.

management's human relations tasks; greater rationalization of managerial activities; freeing management from petty distractions; greater freedom in locating facilities," and so forth, are all aspects of, or different expressions for, the cheapening of production. Expressed in Michael's genteel fashion: "If the criteria are control, understanding, and profits, there are strong reasons why government and business should want to, and indeed would have to, expand cybernation as rapidly as they can."[7]

The advantages of cybernation will, however, be offset by the problem of unemployment, which will eventually affect all occupations — the unskilled more than the skilled, consequently Negro workers more than white workers. The present relocation from production to service industries will come to an end. "If people cost more than machines — either in money or because of the managerial effort involved — there will be strong incentive to replace them in one way or another in most service activities where they perform routine, predefined tasks."[8] As technology allows fewer people to do more work, many of the intermediary middle-class management jobs will also disappear.

There are, of course, answers to the projected dilemma, such as the retraining and upgrading of labor and the shortening of working hours for the same pay, or even price reductions leading to a larger consumer demand. But because all workers are affected by cybernation, Michael feels that such proposals will not solve the problem. His own suggestion is a large public works program, for "although the proportion of workers needed for any particular task will be reduced through the use of cybernation, the total number of tasks that need to be done could equal or exceed the absolute number of people available to do them."[9] He thinks, however, that such a policy would run counter to the capitalist spirit. It may, therefore, be self-defeating for free enterprise to encourage cybernation.

While the consequences of cybernation may endanger the free enterprise system, the very continuance of this system compels increased automation. Michael sees the dilemma: the outlook is unfavorable *with* cybernation, but it is just as bad *without* it.

7 *Ibid.*, p. 13.
8 *Ibid.*, p. 16.
9 *Ibid.*, p. 26.

Greater government control and national planning are, in his view, only partial solutions. Ideology and goals must change, and the required centralization of authority "would seem to imply a governing elite and a popular acceptance of such an elite." If newly evolving behavioral standards do not complement the cybernated future, feelings of frustration and pointlessness "may well evoke a war of desperation — ostensibly against some external enemy but, in fact, a war to make the world safe for human beings by destroying most of society's sophisticated technological base."[10] Obviously, however, it would more probably be a war in which the sophisticated technology would serve to destroy most of mankind.

However, both technological development and capital formation correspond to underlying social relationships and may be altered by changing these relationships. While automation enhances capital development it is also limited by the existing capital-labor relations. This is a familiar phenomenon: monopolization is an instrument of both capital expansion and capital contraction; the drive for profits reduces capital's profitability. Any prognosis about the cybernation process must, first of all, raise the question as to how far this process can be carried by the existing society. What is feasible technically may not be so economically; and what may be feasible economically may not be so socially.

Whereas Michael approaches automation from the point of view of technology, economists usually approach it from the economic point of view. S. Kuznets, for instance, thinks it necessary to distinguish between potential and actual technological change. Although the "concept of potential technological change is difficult to define precisely, let alone measure," he writes, "it is extremely useful, for it points to the fact that of the large flow of technological change offered, as it were, to society, only a part is embodied in the productive structure, mainly because of limitations of capital and of entrepreneurial ability."[11] Kuznets thinks, however, that the next three decades will witness an acceleration of the rate of technological change, mainly because of a quickening in the pace of scientific research. It seems certain, he says, "that the development of nonmilitary applications of nuclear physics, of electronics in automation and communications will have an immense impact

10 *Ibid.*, p. 46.
11 S. Kuznets, *Capital in the American Economy*, p. 442.

upon the production system."[12] All this will give momentum to the demand for capital funds and Kuznets thinks it not unlikely that the new technology — at any rate initially — will require an amount of capital that can be brought forth only at the expense of the national product. In other words, installation of the new technology may require a larger part of total production for new material capital equipment and leave a correspondingly smaller part for immediate utilization and consumpiton.

So it has always been in the past under conditions of capital formation. And even though the material requirements of capital formation may be more formidable for the second industrial revolution than they were for the first, they may be nevertheless attainable. The more so as the new technology may, eventually, demand a smaller amount of capital to yield a greater product than has been true for the "conventional" technology. But new capital investments must be financed. The question is then "whether the savings patterns in the private sector [of the economy] suggests saving proportions that will match the prospective demand for capital." The concern is with the private sector alone, for "the government sector is not likely to have net savings in the long term prospect. Indeed, it may be forced to draw upon the savings of the private sector."[13] Because of an actual decline of the private sector's savings propensity, Kuznets thinks that the previously experienced "pressure of the demand for goods upon the supply of savings will persist." He suggests, cautiously, that "during the 1948-1957 decade a combination of high-level demand for consumers goods and continued high level of government drafts for current consumption might have kept private savings and capital formation below the proportion required to increase productivity sufficiently to offset inflationary pressures."[14] Against this background, and in view of an expected growth of the non-productive population, rising government expenditures, and continued high levels of consumption, Kuznets fears that the supply of voluntary savings may not be adequate to the demand. For this reason "inflationary pressures may well continue, with the result that part of the savings needed for capital formation and government con-

12   *Ibid.*, p. 443.
13   *Ibid.*, p. 453.
14   *Ibid.*, p. 457.

sumption will be extracted through this particular mechanism."[15]

While a lack of investment capital may hamper cybernation, the same lack is also its *raison d'etre*. The expected rise of profitability is supposed to lead to increases in production and employment large enough to compensate for the labor displaced by technological improvements. This is the idea behind the argument that all technological advancement, sooner or later, creates new and additional work opportunities. It is usually illustrated with reference to definite enterprises and particular situations. For example, R. Calder points out that "in France the state-controlled Renault Company was able to undertake, after the war, the most intensive automation of any automobile factory in Europe," in consequence of which "three times as many workers are employed now as there were before the introduction of automation." Calder thinks that this is "a good example of the repercussive effects of modern technology."[16]

For the Renault Company this is no doubt true, at any rate for the time being. And it may well be true for many, or even all enterprises, in the expanding West European economy which has been experiencing the same process of growth that — for a variety of reasons — occurred in America earlier. While the rate of capital formation in the last ten years was higher in Western Europe than in America, there is no reason to assume that this will remain so. Obviously, the effects of automation will be different under conditions of rapid capital expansion than under conditions of capital stagnation. The present American situation may, therefore, be just as much "an example of the repercussive effects of modern technology" as Calder's experience with the Renault Company, or even with the whole of Western Europe.

From the viewpoint of a single capital, an increase of productivity by way of automation is no doubt a good thing, if it enables this capital to enlarge its markets by eliminating less-efficient competitors. The individual capital is not aware, and could not be aware, of the loss of profit through the loss of social surplus-labor; its only considerations are its production costs and its return on sales. No matter what the social consequences of automation, private capital will always try to increase its productivity to gain extra

15 *Ibid.,* p. 460.
16 R. Calder, *Europe's Needs and Resources,* p. 789.

profits, or just to maintain a given profitability. A declining rate of savings will not stop the cybernation process in corporations with sufficient reserves to finance their technological innovations. Because automation speeds up obsolescence, smaller businesses, unable to introduce automatic machinery quickly enough, will fall by the wayside. Automation thus accentuates the concentration process inherent in capital competition.

Capital concentration demands, and allows for, further extensions of automation. Short of an ever-increasing rate of capital expansion, unemploymnet is bound to grow. Such an accelerated rate of expansion is highly improbable; so that the increase of profitability which automation brings may well be nullified by the simultaneous increase in government expenditures needed to cope with cybernation's social consequences. To be sure, automation would also cheapen the products falling to the government and to that extent ease the burden of private capital. Yet this may be offset by an extension of government demands on the prviate sector of the economy — which, by itself, would hasten rather than hinder the automation process.

None of this will happen if the social conditions of the near future discourage both the growth of automation and that of the "public sector" of the economy — in other words, if society, by and large, "freezes" existing social conditions. But this requires a centralized control over the whole of the economy which the government does not possess. If it had this control, it would no longer preside over a free-enterprise economy. Aside from the internal difficulties of a stationary state, the nation's external relations preclude the maintenance of the economic *status quo*. For automation, it is said, must overcome foreign wage advantages by enhancing domestic productivity. And capitalist nations must compete not only in the economic sphere but also in the military, and weapons production already depends to a very large degree on automation technology.

However, many enterprises that would like to automate may not be able to do so without ceasing to exist. Subsidies may be extended to these businesses such as have been granted to sections of agriculture. This is not less likely than, or different in principle from, sustaining the unemployed out of current production. In this way, part of private enterprise (in its technologically backward form) may become a part of the "public sector" of the economy, as has long been true for sections of big business. Unless the latter's privileges, such as government contracts, tax exemptions, and extraordinary depreciation charges are cut back, the shrinking profitable sector of the economy will have to give up a still larger share of its production to the public sector. This course would reach its "logical" end in the destruction of the profitability of private enterprise by the demands of government.

The actual course of events, however, determined as it is by the interaction of diverse and contrary interests, is rarely, if ever, "logical." It may be both logically and economically possible to have a highly cybernated industry with, say, half of the working population unemployed; yet in practice this is quite improbable. Social movements would arise to change this situation. Similarly, the accentuation of capital concentration by way of automation would most likely bring political forces into play seeking to arrest this development. When theory conflicts with real necessities, fetishistic attitudes toward the production system and its technology lose their sway, and people will try to change the social structure rather than accomodate themselves to it indefinitely. In the end, the question of the degree of cybernation will be resolved by political actions.

Even on purely economic grounds, cybernation finds its limits where it begins to contradict the profitability of capital. Its full development would be a very long process at any rate, as it requires the displacement of most existing production equipment. To throw out the mass of capital based on the old technology is to throw out the congealed labor of generations. To create the capital of a radically new technology also requires the work of generations. Cybernation can only be applied in piecemeal fashion regardless of the nature of society. But in capitalism it is doubly hindered because it can be applied only insofar as it safeguards and promotes the growth of the existing capital.

Taking past developments into consideration and judging present conditions realistically, the future of cybernation seems not at all promising except, perhaps, for selected industries, particularly those engaged in the production of armaments. Indeed, it has been said that "these miraculous machines in which cybernetics could develop all its resources seem to be usable only as engines of death."[17]

17 P. de Latie, *Thinking by Machine*, Boston, 1957, p. 284.

One method of dealing with the increased productivity produced by cybernation would be to cut the number of hours of work and provide people with more leisure time. Almost uniformly, however, this method is questioned or totally rejected, not because it contradicts the capitalist mechanism, but because society has "failed to develop meaningful leisure." Boredom is considered a very serious and even dangerous problem because "it still remains true that the happy man is very often the one who has insufficient time to worry about whether he is happy or not."[18] All sorts of crimes and delinquencies are attributed to increased leisure, which, then, must be "organized" by competent authorities before it can be granted. This silly and insincere talk can be dismissed at once. The leisure class has always found the leisure of the lower classes obnoxious and dangerous to its own leisure. Looking at the wonders of the first industrial revolution, Delacroix mused about the "poor abused people, [who] will not find happiness in the disappearance of labor. Look at these idlers condemned to drag the burden of their days and not knowing what to do with their time, which the machines cut into still further."[19] Yet leisure is precisely what the majority of people need most and have the least of — leisure without wants, that is; for the leisure of the starving is not rest, but a relentless activity aimed at staying alive. Without greater leisure there can, be no betterment of the human condition.

This whole question cannot arise under prevailing conditions. Aided by special circumstances, one or another laboring group may succeed in cutting down its working time without diminishing its income. But this is an exception to the rule. For to cut down working hours generally and maintain the wages bill would defeat the capitalist's purpose in introducing technological change and make automation a senseless affair. The point of automation is precisely to reduce wage costs relative to overall costs of the "factors of production" and to recoup the higher capital costs by greater productivity. It can be argued, of course, that there is no longer a need for extensive capital formation and that mere replacement and modernization of the existing productive apparatus suffices to satisfy all social needs. Any increase in productivity could then immediately be translated into higher wages, shorter hours,

18 R. Theobald, *The Challenge of Abundance*, New York, 1962, p. 86.
19 *The Journal of Eugene Delacroix*, New York, 1961, p. 512.

or both. While this may be true, it is *not* possible within the capitalist system, and those who seriously propose this solution must be prepared to change the system.

The capitalist "solution" to the problem of automation is to be found not in higher wages and a shorter work week for the laboring population but in higher profitability and a larger capital. Each entrepreneur, or corporation, employs the minimum of labor relative to capital investment; each, of course, tries to increase this minimum by correspondingly larger investments. They are interested — economically speaking — not in a larger or smaller labor force but in that labor force which proves most profitable. They are not and cannot be concerned with the national labor force; the unemployed are the government's responsibiltiy, although it can sustain them only with funds extracted from the whole of society.

Because production in capitalist society is achieved by numerous independently operating and competing enterprises, each following the dictates of profitability, there is no way for the total labor force to share the available work. There will be overwork for some, unemployment for others. The employers will not cut working hours without cutting wages; and the more fortunate workers will insist on working enough hours to support their customary style of life. In place of shorter hours, there will be growing unemployment. Capitalism must attend to its victims well enough to secure their quiescence; but the system will bear this loss only if the increasing productivity of labor compensates for it. When increasing productivity itself gives rise to large-scale and permanent unemployment, it will no longer benefit capitalism: the profits it creates will be lost again by the cost of sustaining the non-productive population. Capital will have ceased to function as capital.

This is the general tendency of rapid technological development under conditions of capital production. Actually, because such a development cannot be fitted into the capitalist relations of production, it will remain a mere tendency. It will constantly be countermanded by the social reactions it releases. Nonetheless, the tendency assures the continuation of social crisis conditions. Capital production in the mixed economy thus faces a double dilemma: its future is challenged equally by the rapid growth of its public sector and by its labor-displacing technology. The more automation there is, the greater is the need to deal with its social consequences by an increase of public expenditures. The more the government spends, the more urgent becomes the need for more automation. In 1964 the American Congress set up a National Commission on Technology, Automation, and Economic Progress to deal with the increasing rate of technical change and its consequences. The Commission found the problem still "manageable," if technological change was accompanied "by vigorous fiscal policies" fostering economic growth and government employment for all those unable to find jobs."[20] Yet — such "vigorous fiscal policies" are just as detrimental to the private-enterprise system as are the social consequences of automation under conditions of relative capital stagnation.

20 The *New York Times,* January 24, 1966.

CHAPTER XVII

CAPITAL FORMATION
AND FOREIGN TRADE

The increasingly organized character of the mixed economy has induced some economists and sociologists to speak of it as a "post-capitalist" system. The possibility of an organized capitalist economy either pleased or worried many social theoreticians before — Rudolf Hilferding,[1] most notably, envisioned a completely organized capitalism based on a class-antagonistic system of distribution. However, a non-competitive capitalism, though perhaps conceivable on a national level, is quite inconceivable as a world-wide phenomenon and for that reason could be only partially realized on a national level. What national economic organization there is has arisen mainly in response to international competition; and the more such organization has entered into and transformed the market mechanism, the more chaotic and destructive the capitalist system has become. Capitalistic property relations preclude any effective form of social organization of production. Only where these property relations have been destroyed, as for instance in Russia, has it proved possible to have some measure of central economic control. But even here, the character of the planned economy is still determined by international competition and, to that extent, its organized nature helps perpetuate the general anarchy of capital production.

Although Keynes' theory evolved out of the consideration of a closed system, it had to relate itself to the real world of capital production. Keynes felt that by insisting on the self-regulatory nature of the market, *laissez-faire* doctrine condemned society to

---

1   R. Hilferding, *Das Finanzkapital*, Wien, 1910.

depressions and the decline of international trade which they brought. He hoped that an enlightened self-interest would induce national capitals to expand production by way of government interventions, and then to extend their newly-won more comprehensive point of view to international trade and finance. It is now quite generally held that governmental policies can control the behavior of the national economy. But this confidence does not extend to the international economy which, from time to time, is raked by trade and payments difficulties, such as the so-called dollar-gap after the Second World War and the more recent payments difficulties of England and the United States — not to speak of the rather permanent trade and payments problems of the capitalistically underdeveloped nations.

For Marx it was not trade but the process of capital accumulation which was the source of capitalistic crisis; the expansion and contraction of trade merely expressed the needs of the process of capital accumulation, as did expansion and contraction in other spheres of economic activity. He did not share the classical illusion that international free trade benefits all nations equally by bringing about an international division of labor in harmony with both natural conditions and the economic needs of men. Marx held that the international division of labor that developed through trade was largely determined by capital accumulation. Therefore, "just as everything became a monopoly, there are also some branches of industry which prevail over all others, and secure the nations which especially favor them the command of the markets of the world."[2] This monopolistic position is simultaneously an exploitative position. Marx was not surprised that the "free-traders cannot understand how one nation can grow rich at the expense of another, since these same gentlemen also refuse to understand how in the same country one class can enrich itself at the expense of another."[3] He declared himself in favor of free trade nonetheless, for in his day, "the protective system was conservative, while the free trade system worked destructively," and "carried the antagonism of proletariat and bourgeoisie to the uttermost point."[4]

Economic development "has been a process of growth from a

2 K. Marx, *Free Trade*, New York, 1921, p. 42.
3 *Ibid.*
4 *Ibid.*

center in which the countries outside the center have owed their development (and often their very existence) to the movement of factors, as well as of goods, from the center; and the center countries have in turn owed their development primarily to this movement."[5] Under these conditions it is true that international trade constitutes an "economic gain." However, the gain accrues largely and disproportionally to a few capitalist nations and transforms the world market into their dominion; so that the fortunes of the international market depend on the expansion of these few countries or, at times, of a particular nation.

In a world without tariffs, quotas and other restrictions, trade faces a discriminatory situation, for the strength of different nations varies according to level of productivity, degree of industrial development, and possession of natural resources. Over a period of time, "if there are divergent rates of growth of productivity, the trade will be progressively less favorable to the countries less rapidly advancing in productivity."[6] Thus "Free Trade" was the watchword of the more advanced capitalist nations, and the "free-traders" themselves were only concerned with making trade free so long as this meant an expanding economy and a growing world market. This specific freedom of trade, in turn, prepared the conditions for new waves of protectionism, which emerged as soon as capital formation began to decline.

Large-scale and diversified economies are less dependent on the extension of international trade than are more specialized small-scale economies. The dependence of the American economy upon the products of other nations is relatively limited: what other nations produce can, in most cases, also be produced in the United States; and what cannot be produced can often be dispensed with, or replaced by substitutes. Of course, the large-scale economies will use their "autarchic" possibilities only in an "emergency situation," since capital recognizes only profitability as a border to its expansion. But since these economies suffer least by a deterioration of international trade, they can set the conditions under which it is carried on. And though it is clear that the economic advantage of foreign trade does not consist in getting rid of exports but in

5 J. H. Williams, *Economic Stability in a Changing World*, New York, 1953, p. 24.
6 *Ibid.*, p. 38.

obtaining the maximum value of imports in exchange for them, countries in absolute need of imports are often forced to engage in trade practices quite contrary to their "economic interests."

Having one nation in a monopolistic position in the world economy does not necessarily impair international trade: indeed, in the nineteenth century, England's exceptional capital strength, accompanied by large capital exports, fostered trade. Yet structural changes in world capitalism may affect both capital accumulation and international trade negatively. It has often been said that America's relatively limited capital exports and the low percentage of exported goods to total production testify to her lack of "economic imperialism"; and that, consequently, American competition cannot be blamed for the economic difficulties besetting the world. From a consistently capitalistic point of view, however, it would be just this lack of "economic imperialism" — whatever its cause — which would account for the contraction of the world market. During the period from 1870 to 1913, for example, "Britain invested abroad about two-fifths of her savings, i.e., something like one-tenth of her income. By 1913 her foreign investments, equal to nearly four-ninths of her home investments represented one-third of all European investments and contributed one-tenth of her national income."[7] Expressed in terms of the scale of the now dominating American economy, "the equivalent would be an American foreign investment of about $600 billion yielding $30 billion a year income and growing somewhat like $15 billion a year."[8] Instead, United States private foreign investments after the Second World War were for a long time at a rate of less than $1 billion a year, representing less than one-third of one per cent of her national income, and only slowly rising to $3 billion in 1957 and to $4.5 billion in the years thereafter.

The world's recurrent trade and payments dilemma dates back to the First World War and acquired an apparently insoluble character in the wake of World War II. The consistently unfavorable trade and payments positions of the European nations were largely the result of the two wars, which led to the loss of most of their foreign holdings, their indebtedness for American supplies, and the shrinkage of their traditional markets. The relative scarcity of food-

7   W. L. Thorp, *Trade, Aid, or What?*, Amherst, 1954, p. 183.
8   *Ibid.*

stuffs and raw materials during and after the wars turned the terms
of trade against the European nations. The situation was further
aggravated by the deterioration of East-West trade which resulted
in part from political changes but in even greater part from the
industrialization of countries that formerly had been producers
almost exclusively of primary products. America's dominating position in the world economy, as not only the largest industrial but
also the largest agricultural producer, dislodged still further the
already precarious "international economic balance."

A payments balance may be lost through commodity exchange,
through capital movements, or through the requirements of war.
Deficit countries may balance their foreign transactions in various
ways. They may draw upon their foreign assets and reserves. They
may alter their exchange-rates, thereby affecting both imports and
exports. They may encourage exports to gain foreign exchange
and discourage activities that lead to a loss of foreign exchange.
They may also get help in form of foreign credits and aid. A trade
and payments balance — by itself — means only that, and does
not necessarily imply healthy and prosperous conditions. A persistent imbalance in foreign exchange transactions, however, points
towards the dissolution of the market system. After the Second
World War, America became a creditor-nation unable to collect
and Europe a conglomeration of debtor-nations unable to pay.
Between 1946 and 1952, the deficit of the "free" nations with respect to the United States rose to about $34 billion. Some $4 billion were covered by European gold and dollar reserves; over $30
billion by American aid.

Offset by loans and grants, America's "favorable balance" was
plainly fictitious, for, as a United States Senator expressed it, it "is
obviously an imbecility to attach the word 'favorable' to a situation
in which the outgo exceeds the income . . . It was unfavorable,
but unavoidable, in the years when we were a debtor nation and
had to ship out in servicing our debt more than we received. We
are now a creditor nation and continue that practice. Anything
which expands our imports and/or diminishes our exports tends
to mitigate our silly practice of shipping aboard stuff that can't
be paid for."[9] However, this "silly practice" reflected the indispensable interdependency of international capitalism. Requiring the

9 R. E. Flanders, *The American Century*, Cambridge, 1950, p. 49.

maintenance of private enterprise systems elsewhere, America's economic foreign policy could not follow the rules of good business.

Capitalism has always been at once a productive and a destructive social system, not only in every-day competition, but, in an accelerated and concentrated form, in times of crisis and war. The destruction of capital values both in peaceful competition and in competition by way of war was instrumental in bringing about new upswings in capital production. To serve as instruments of accumulation, however, the destructive aspects of capital production must retain a certain definite relationship to its productive powers. The destruction of capital values in a depression affects only a small amount of capital in its physical form. The material productive apparatus remains largely intact; it is merely concentrated into fewer hands. War, on the other hand, destroys capital in both its physical and its value form; and if too much is destroyed in its material form, the surviving capitals find themselves thrown back to an "earlier" stage of capital development in which their own advanced characteristics become an anachronism. Because their own profits are bound up with a definite mass of world production, too great a reduction of the latter is likely to reduce the surviving capitals' own profitability. The disproportionalities caused by the destruction and dislocations of war must be overcome before the general process of capital accumulation can again proceed.

The United States' favorable balance of trade in 1948 was $5.5 billion and her production in the same year exceeded that of 1937 by 70 per cent. The deficit of the Marshall Plan countries was $5.1 billion and their production was still below the pre-war level. Their share in American imports had dropped from 2 per cent of the American gross national product at the turn of the century to less than 0.5 per cent in 1948. Under such conditions, the trade and payments question could not be left to the vicissitudes of market events. The unbusinesslike procedure of shipping more out in aid than was received by way of trade was unavoidable.

International capital movements after the Second World War were dominated by the United States, and most of the American flow consisted of government funds. American aid enabled European governments to adopt much more expansionary programs of recovery than would otherwise have been possible. This aid was an extension of government-induced production to the international scene. Just as government-induced production in the domestic economy is intended to secure that amount of economic activity considered necessary for social stability, so government aid to foreign nations finds its rationale in the inescapable need to sustain the private-enterprise system abroad. In both cases, it is expected that current non-profitable expenditures will be recouped at a later time through a general upswing of economic activity.

In order to accelerate the general expansion of capital and to enlarge its markets, an economic integration of the nationally-dispersed European economies appeared indispensable and found strong American support. Economic integration can mean different things — the "automatism" of a free world market, as well as political unification with planned supra-national interventions in the economy. The latter type of "integration" was incorporated in the Nazi vision of a Europe under German control. During the war, English voices were raised for a United Europe under British tutelage. But the war reduced Great Britain to a secondary power, despite her far-flung but decaying Commonwealth connections. The future and character of continental Europe seemed now to be determined by the evolving power struggle between Russia and the United States. For the latter to win, or even to hold her own, a rapid European recovery was necessary. This induced the Marshall Plan and forced the United States to accept economic policies discriminatory to her own strictly economic interests.

Although the conception of "integration" of the European economies was at once economic and political, at its start it was a purely monetary matter in accordance with the Keynesian view of things which considers all economic activities mainly from the monetary angle. Several hundred changes in exchange-rates in concurrence with different degrees of inflation in various countries had led into an impenetrable jungle of inconvertibility. To restore at least partial convertibility was then regarded as the starting point for an increase of trade and a consequent rise in production. The first attempt in this direction was the European Payments Union, modeled after the International Clearing Union proposed by Keynes during World War II. It was to make possible a better transfer of European currencies, which was regarded as a precondition for the elimination of import restrictions, export subsidies, and other measures that hampered intra-European trade. It was also regarded

as a way-station on the road to universal convertibility in an altogether free-trading world.

European trade and payments problems were soon superseded,
however, by the overriding issues of Western defense and Germany's
incorporation into the Atlantic Pact. In the years since Potsdam
it had become clear that the extensive destruction and holding-
down of German industry played into the hands of the new Russian
adversary. In the spring of 1951 the Western allies revised the
Occupation Statute in exchange for guarantees that Germany
would honor her pre-war and post-war debts and for the assurance
that she would cooperate to the limits of her capacity in the Western defense effort.

The decision to revive Germany's economic power implied different things for France and England than for the United States.
For the latter, it was first of all a military decision, a preparation
for a possible new march on Moscow with the "experienced" German army as the spearhead of a European force covered by the
immense productive power of America. The revival of Germany,
both industrial and military, was acceptable to France only if it
was accompanied by guarantees that assured France a dominating
position in Europe. Yet France's actual weakness and inability to
oppose American policies induced French politicians to anticipate
the dangerous aspects of this development and to answer them in
advance with the Schuman Plan.

The purpose of the Schuman Plan, the conception of a European
Coal and Steel Community, was to create a single market for coal
and steel in all of Western Europe. Adherence of France and Germany made participation by the smaller nations practically man-
datory. Britain associated herself merely for the exchange of
information, without surrendering control over her own coal and
steel affairs. The new supra-national institution was hailed as the
beginning of a new era in intra-European relations, as the harbinger of better things to come. The drawing into the single
market of other products besides coal and steel, and the creating
of an European atomic energy program, were to culminate in a
Western European Federation, a United States of Europe.

In a more prosaic mood, however, the Coal and Steel Community appeared to be merely an extension of the European steel cartel
of pre-Hitler days. Coal and steel in France and Germany lie close

to the borders of these nations in the Saar, in Lorraine and the Ruhr. To combine the iron ore of Lorraine with the coal of the Ruhr has been the concern of both countries for a hundred years. The European steel cartel, which lasted until the Second World War, was a price-fixing arrangement whose existence indicated the relative capital stagnation at that time. And in 1950, when the Schuman Plan was born, there were signs of impending surpluses of coal and steel; so that the Plan was probably inspired in part by the desire to avoid another period of cut-throat competition. Yet, at the time of its ratification and during the period immediately preceding it, the situation had already changed in favor of a general expansion of coal and steel production. There was now a need for German and French collaboration not so much to secure the given market as to assure a larger production. Whatever the future would bring, the Coal and Steel Community satisfied all those engaged in its foundation. For America it increased the war-potential of the West; for Germany it offered a chance for a quicker recovery; and for France it provided the opportunity to partake in the control of the inevitable development of Germany's productive power and war-making ability.

In one sense the ratification of the Schuman Plan was also a result of the German recovery, which came to be widely regarded as a "miracle" and a manifestation of capitalism's undiminished power of expansion. This "miracle" was, of course, the result of the colossal destruction of capital, which both allowed for and necessitated an enormous amount of reconstruction. Recovery was aided by a radical currency reform, by American aid and investments, and by political conditions under which mere survival was incentive enough for the workers to endure the greatest degree of exploitation. Working-hours were longer in Germany than anywhere in Europe. While German wages were half of British wages, investments in Germany were 25 per cent of the national income as against Britain's 16 per cent. Per capita consumption of the West German population was only 60 per cent of that of Britain; in no country in Western Europe was a smaller percentage of the gross national product employed for personal needs than in Germany. This exceptional rate of exploitation tended, of course, towards the European average; but while in effect, it did restore Germany's economic position within the European economy.

What is, perhaps, of special interest in this connection is the close association between the German revival, the European recovery, and innovations such as the Payments Union and the Schuman Plan with the Western defense program under American leadership. In fact, the Coal and Steel Community and the European Defense Community were at first supposed to share the same Court and the same Assembly charged with the creation of a European Army, a supra-national force with a supreme commander under the terms of the North Atlantic Treaty. However, this concept of the Defense Community could not be realized, and the difficulties that arose with respect to the Defense Community found their reflection in changed attitudes toward the Coal and Steel Community. Although the latter became effective in the summer of 1952, no real progress towards a Common Market was made. To be sure, the single market was to be realized only in stages, with regard to both the varying conditions in the member nations and the variety of products brought forth by their industries. Italian steel and Belgian coal were kept out of the Common Market for five years and some coal and coke subsidies were continued. The recession of 1954 impeded the development still further and the High Authority soon had to admit that it was able neither to develop real competition in the steel industry nor to regulate the prices in accordance with the terms of the Community's constitution. The Market was a common market only in a formal sense. "If the Community were abolished tomorrow," it was said, "nothing would be changed and nobody would feel that a living thing had been killed."[10]

However, the Community's activities were speeded up soon after the Korean war. Its control was extended to all types of energy. A series of tariff reductions in 1959 were coupled with the proclaimed intention of reaching a single, six-nation, tariff-less market by 1965 or 1970. Although the first tariff reductions were not of great significance, they did help initiate a rash of economic changes of greater importance. A series of industrial agreements within the Community led to many capital mergers within and between the member nations. These encompassed joint selling and production, the pooling of resources, specialization and rationalization.

10 P. Ricard, Head of the French Steel Federation, in the *New York Times,* February 22, 1955.

As in previous periods of prosperity, the ensuing economic up-swing created a climate of optimistic readiness to forego some of the stifling measures of protectionism. But as the removal of trade barriers is bound to increase both competition and protection against competition, it fosters capital concentration. Less productive enterprises made room for more productive ones, thus strengthening the competitive ability of the European Community's industries. While this spelled "progress" for the six-nation economies, it also pointed to sharper international competition. But competition in a generally unfolding economy merely accelerates the upward swing. European production expanded and exports increased, cutting the United States trade surplus to its narrowest margin since the end of the Second World War. By 1959 the Common Market nations were prospering, with virtually full employment.

With the Common Market a reality, England joined six other nations[11] in a European Free Trade Association to counteract the possible competitive advantages of the six-nation trading bloc. Retaining full control over their national economic policies, including tariffs with countries outside the Free Trade Association, these seven nations pledged themselves to low tariffs within the Association, to fair competition, to the equalization of supply conditions, and to a full employment policy. The trading blocs created as many problems as they solved. While they increased trade across national boundaries, they tended to obstruct world-wide trade. And the new free-trade areas disrupted the trade patterns which had grown up from earlier patterns of production. While capital flowed more easily within the separate trading blocs, it flowed less easily from one bloc to another. The realization of the two trading blocs probably appeared as the first and only possible step toward unifying the world market; but it has also come to demonstrate the hopelessness of this task. Although these new institutions were regarded as preliminary steps in the direction of world-wide market integration, they are themselves constantly endangered by the particularistic and changing needs or opportunities of the participating nations, as is illustrated by recurrent crises within the Common Market. Celebrated by some as so many signs that narrow uneconomical nationalism is in the process of being overcome, these institutions are adjudged by others as futile because their sectional

11 Austria, Denmark, Norway, Portugal, Sweden, Switzerland.

character tends to block rather than further world-wide integration.

Whatever the expectations or apprehensions associated with the rise of the separate European market systems, one thing is clear: their existence points out that it is becoming increasingly impossible to maintain purely national economic policies, and that the "free" world market is not likely to return. This fact will not prevent futile attempts in either direction. Nations always tend to insulate their economies against the detrimental effects of international competition when this is necessary. Yet they cannot cease hoping for, and working toward, the restoration of an "automatically" or otherwise-internationally-integrated economy. Regional groupings constitute a kind of "compromise" between these extremes, so as to overcome the limitations of national economy in a world not susceptible to disinterested international controls. The European trade blocs initiated a general (though largely illusory) movement from Africa to Latin America for customs unions and intra-national market arrangements. But while the regional "solution" seems the only one available, it is a "solution" only on the assumption that it will move toward, and not away from, world-wide integration.

The "final" solution to the world's trade and payments problem is, then, conceived of as a merger of all the various trade areas and the "economic fusion of the free world's nations."[12] It is recognized, of course, that such a "fusion," involving the elimination of tariffs and other trade restrictions, would aggravate the problem of nations competing with the United States. But this is to be dealt with by a "relatively unimpeded movement of capital and labor," by agreement on the part of the "strong" nations to "extend great blocs of credit to weaker nations to tide them over their balance-of-payments difficulties," and by the creation of "an international fund to ease the pain of unemployment and of capital liquidation in segments of any economy hard-hit by the process of integration."[13]

However, the "relatively unimpeded" movement of capital works in two directions. A great flow of capital from a "stronger" to a "weaker" nation will, no doubt, improve the balance-of-payments position of the latter. The recent spur in American capital exports, for instance, is decreasing the balance-of-payments difficulties of

12   R. Vernon, *Trade Policy in Crisis,* Princeton, 1958, p. 21.
13   *Ibid.*

capital-importing nations for the time being; but at a later time it may have the opposite effect. For the outflow of profits and interests to the capital-exporting country may well exceed the amount of new investments her capital creates. Profits made in foreign countries must find their way back to the American base. If not, the exported capital ceases to be American capital and functions as foreign capital in competition with America and the rest of the world.

While it may be immaterial to a nation's economy whether its capital investment is of domestic or foreign origin (provided the rate of capital formation is not affected by the transfer of profits to the foreign investors), it is not immaterial to the domestic capitalists that their own traditional sphere of capital expansion is invaded by foreign capital. They could do likewise, of course, by sending their investment capital to foreign lands; so that there would be numerous European owners of American industries and numerous American owners of European industries, as well as both European and American owners of industries in other countries. Profits would flow (as they do) from Europe to America and *vice versa;* capitalist enterprises would have changed places of operation, but nothing else would change unless this very process proved to be more advantageous for one than for another capitalist group or nation.

Capital movements take place due to considerations of profitability and security. The most profitable economies attract most of the capital and thus become still more profitable. This diminishes the competitive ability of less productive nations, making them still less profitable areas. The *general* flow of capital is decreased as capital is concentrated in nations which are already highly capitalized. The movement of capital from less profitable and less secure to more profitable and more secure nations cannot have an "equilibrating" quality, as it is bound to increase the gap between the "strong" and the "weak" countries. To have a capital movement of an "equilibrating" nature implies the sacrifice of the profitability principle; that is, it implies not the *free* movement of capital, but a rational allocation of capital according to the actual requirements of world economy seen from the point of view of general human needs. This clearly transcends the possibilities of the private enterprise economy and even minimum requirements in this direction — enough to assure a necessary degree of social stability and international intercourse — depend upon government interventions which "socialize" the losses thereby engendered.

Although socio-economic problems appear as market and money problems, they find their real source in the growing incompatibility of the prevailing property relations and the national form of capitalism with the changing forces of production and the pressing need to integrate world production and distribution on principles other than that of profitability. What the world experiences is not so much a crisis of its monetary and trading system as a crisis of capital production. For the adherents of the system, of course, it is not the system itself but its temporary imbalances which have to be attended to; either by avoiding all interferences in the market mechanism, as in *laissez-faire* theory, or by governmental interventions in the mechanism, as in Keynesian doctrine. But whatever the theory and practice, trade and payments problems continue to agitate the capitalist world and will do so as long as production remains the production of capital.

For many years after the Second World War, as related above, the European nations had nothing to sell, but a lot to buy, and no money to but it with. Most of their foreign investments, as well as their gold and dollar holdings, had been sacrificed to the war. Due to a persistent favorable balance of trade, gold flowed to the United States until, in 1949, she had an excessive 70 per cent of the world's monetary gold. At this point, however, the situation began to change. America's aid program, foreign military commitments, and capital exports created this change. By 1965, America's gold reserve had been reduced to about $15 billion.

Foreign central banks as well as individuals hold dollars in their own countries and also in the United States in form of deposit accounts and securities which can be turned into dollars. There are far more dollars in the hands of foreigners than are covered by the gold in the United States. The owners of these dollars can at any time convert their dollars into gold, for the United States is committed to sell gold to foreign central banks at $35 an ounce. "Normally," the gold reserve need not be large enough to cover all dollar holdings of foreign banks, merchants, and investors, for "normally" the conversion of dollars into gold does not make much "sense." Gold, as such, yields no profit, whereas the invested dollar does; and if a "run on gold" develops it is because confidence in the stability of the dollar has been lost.

The United States left the gold standard in 1933. The Gold Reserve Act of 1934 gave the U. S. Treasury title to all the gold in the Federal Reserve banks. All circulating gold coins were recalled and their possession by individuals was declared illegal. The dollar was devaluated by raising the price of gold from $21 an ounce to $35 an ounce, a price which still prevails at this writing. By 1937 the United States, the United Kingdom and France agreed upon a gold exchange standard under which they settled international financial business on a gold basis, while conducting domestic money policies in accordance with their individual needs. The fixed gold price determines the value of the dollar and the values of other currencies are pegged to the value of the dollar.

Whereas in 1934 gold had been over-evaluated relative to the dollar, it is now under-evaluated, since prices have meanwhile risen in dollar terms. However, there is always the possibility that the price of gold will be raised, as it was in 1934, thus devaluating the dollar. The dollar and, to a lesser extent, sterling serve as world money. Both are reserve currencies; so that the stability of the world's monetary system depends on the actions the United States takes, either unilaterally or in concert with Great Britain. If the different national monetary authorities were certain that the dollar price of gold would increase, they would not hold dollars; and if they were certain that there would not be such an increase, they would most likely stick to their dollar and sterling reserves. But there is no certainty; and, consequently, central banks rush out of currency and into gold whenever the stability of the reserve currencies is in doubt. Their preference for gold reflects their desire to protect their reserves against the hazards of depreciation.

For some time now the American payments deficit has ranged between $2 billion and $4 billion yearly. The deficit is the difference between the inflow and outflow of money in all international transactions. In part it is caused by American capital exports. Usually, capital movements are considered a positive factor in that they lead investments where they are most productive, i.e., most profitable. Funds not employed in the United States have gone in great bulk to Europe, accentuating an already-existing expansionary trend. This brought an increasing number of European enterprises, as well as new foreign enterprises located in Europe, into American hands. In terms of money, it meant that American investors received real property for dollars which went to Europe. These dollars, it is true, are convertible into commodities or currencies, as well as into gold. For the individuals and firms involved in these transactions, all this is, without doubt, sound business. But from a "national point of view," the final result is that the European nations wind up with large dollar and gold reserves, while American investors wind up with productive, that is, profitable property — with capital.

The re-capitalizing European economies proved more profitable than the relatively stagnating American economy. For the same reason — profit being the determining element — no real incentive arose for European capital to offset America's penetration of the European economies with European capital exports to the United States. It is still expected, of course, that once the European reconstruction boom is over, capital movements will again change direction through the repurchase of assets now owned by Americans, the purchase of American securities, and European direct investments in American industry. And this could well happen; there is no reason why the current difference in economic activity between the West European nations and the American economy should be a permanent affair. Meanwhile, however, European governments are increasingly less inclined to welcome capital imports from the United States, even though — since they are capital-exporting nations themselves — they cannot directly oppose the international movement of capital.

There is no limit to the creation of dollars other than that which the American money authorities impose on themselves. The American capital export is an indirect extension of American government credit to the international scene, but it places profits made in other nations into the hands of American capitalists. It has led to a vast international accumulation of dollar debts. Foreign claims against the United States amounted to about $13 billion by 1965. They may soon add up to a sum exceeding the gold reserve. Even if the United States intends to pay its debts to other nations "down to the last bar of gold," it may not be able to do so. But unless convertible into gold it is the depreciating dollar, not the fixed gold equivalent, which stands behind the foreign claims on the United States.

It is basically the profitability of capital and the rate of capital formation which determine the state of the international payments system insofar as it relates to capital imports and exports. Money which cannot be capitalized in the stagnating United States is capitalistically applied in the expanding nations. Since the higher rate of growth in the latter is offset by a lower rate in the United States, the *general* growth rate is obviously too low for a generally profitable expansion of world capital. Since only a few nations generate an increasing demand for capital, the available capital flows to these nations and helps in the creation of an imbalance in the international payments system.

It is not very different with respect to international trade. If a country shows a persistent payments deficit, it obviously buys more from abroad than it sells to other nations. Its own production cannot compete with that of other nations. For example, England, once the leader in industrial development, utilized her dominant position to become the monopolistic intermediary of world trade and international investments. Her own industrial development was increasingly neglected in favor of her financial dominance in world economy — a dominance based on the great money reserves accumulated during her industrial ascendancy. But the world's financial structure, with England as its center, was undone during decades of depression and war, through the dissolution of the Empire and the financial ascendancy of other, more productive, nations. Once the banker of the world, Britain became a debtor nation, going from one payments crisis to another and overcoming each only temporarily by borrowings from abroad. There is no monetary means of escape from this precarious position, founded in fact on insufficient capital formation. The payments deficit is here actually a deficit of capital production.

A payments deficit can be ended only by ending the conditions that gave rise to it. If a deficit arises because of large capital exports, these exports can be halted by government decree, or by a variety of economic penalties which make them less attractive. Equally, if a government fears that capital imports lead to an undesirable state of inflation and to the gradual displacement of native by foreign capital, it can prohibit capital imports or subject them to discouraging sanctions. In both cases, the prevailing situation can be changed by government interventions. To the extent, however, that a government restricts the import of capital it will also limit its country's economic activity and, in consequence, limit the overall production of the world economy. In part at least, the recent West European expansion was due to the American payments deficit insofar as it resulted from the export of capital. Cutting the American deficit by restricting the export of capital means the reduction of economic activity in capital-importing nations. The possible end, or decisive reduction, of deficits due to capital movements may make money scarce even where it is still capable of finding profitable employment, and the achievement of an international payments balance may coincide with a general contraction of economic activity.

However, payments deficits are only partly caused by capital exports and, as far as the United States is concerned, not at all by trade. To some extent this holds true also for England, where the deficit is partly a result of her attempt to keep the Sterling Area and the remnants of her vanishing Empire under British control. The steady outflow of money for these purposes cannot be compensated for by an inflow of money such as results sooner or later from the export of capital. Britain and America cannot eliminate these "extra-economic" expenses without changing their foreign policies and renouncing their imperialistic ambitions and power positions. Short of fundamental social changes, these changes are not to be expected.

Gold is still the only fully acceptable means of international payments. The reserve currencies, sterling and the dollar, are acceptable only because of their assured convertibility into gold. If confidence in this convertibility should be lost, these currencies could not function as international means of payment. And this confidence weakens with the persistence of the payments deficits of the two nations whose monetary units substitute for gold. When both the purchasing power of their currencies and their gold reserves decline, confidence in the gold exchange mechanism is bound to diminish. It seems, then, that resolving the payments problems of the deficit nations could prove just as disastrous as allowing them to continue. For the former course threatens to destroy international "liquidity," i.e., the availability of money for an expanding capital and commodity market. To escape this dilemma, all kinds of monetary reforms have been proposed. The more dramatic of these proposals suggested a return to the old gold standard, the complete de-monetization of gold, and the de-nationalization of monetary reserves through their administration by international institutions such as the International Monetary Fund.

The least realistic of these proposals, suggested by Jacques Rueff, is the return to the old gold standard. This was, perhaps, advocated more as a rationalization of France's recent policy of changing her dollar holdings into gold than as a serious belief in the workability of a resurrected gold standard. Why the gold standard should now operate better than in the past was not made clear, save for the hopeful assertion that it would end the age of inflation to which all countries are now subjected. In all nations, however, inflation has become the major policy for coping with the problems of capitalist production under conditions of a declining rate of private capital formation.

The suggested resurrection of the gold standard prompted a counter-proposal: the de-monetization of gold was to solve the difficulties encountered with the gold exchange mechanism. If America unilaterally refused to buy and hold gold for monetary purposes, it was asserted, the world could be forced into accepting a dollar standard without a gold base. Once this happened, gold would become a mere commodity, subject to the law of supply and demand. Since the private demand for gold is limited, the released monetary gold would flood the market, which would drive its price below its production costs.* The reduction in the price of gold, it was argued, would make the dollar the more desirable item; and the dollar would become the ultimate international medium of exchange. This audacious plan overlooked one important fact:

---

* In the spring of 1968, this suggestion became "half a reality" through the establishment of a two-price system for gold. In order to arrest the rising price of gold without selling monetary gold on the gold market, the monetary authorities participating in the London gold pool decided to let the gold price in the private market be determined by supply and demand while central banks would continue to buy and sell gold to one another at the fixed United States price of $35 an ounce. This move was expected to bring the gold price down without a further depletion of the monetary gold stock. While higher prices in the private market would make central banks and private financial institutions less willing to hold dollars, gold prices below the official rate would devaluate the gold held in monetary reserves. It is hoped, however, that the commodity price of gold will not deviate too far in either direction from the monetary price. But with the growing demand for gold and the continuing depreciation of the dollar, the free market gold price of more than $35 an ounce will most probably be sustained and the disparity between official and free market price is bound to recreate the old difficulties that led to the two-price system for gold.

the real conditions of American capitalism make it impossible for that country to come close to full use of its productive resources without continuously devaluating its money. If gold should become unacceptable, a steadily depreciating dollar would be even more so.

A partial, though quite limited, de-nationalization of monetary reserves has already been achieved through the establishment of the International Monetary Fund, which, among other things, bears witness to the contradictory forces that work within the international private enterprise economy. On the one hand, the capitalists of each nation compete with capitalists of other nations by all available means, including monetary means. On the other hand, there is a general desire to limit this competition through international arrangements that will bring a modicum of regulation and stability into trade and money relations. The I.M.F. was to help its member nations alleviate their payments problems by supplementing their reserves. Its gold and currency holdings are available to member nations on the basis of an agreed-upon quota system. Countries in payments difficulties may draw upon the Fund's resources to avoid introducing restrictive measures at home while awaiting a reversal of the payments situation. Deficits are thought of as temporary occurrences. But if they should be prolonged, a country's credit with the Fund will exhaust itself, and its borrowings from this source will deepen its payments dilemma. However, the I.M.F. has worked reasonably well in its limited way. For this reason it has been suggested that the I.M.F. become the sole trustee of its member nations' money resources.

Proposals with regard to the establishment of such an international monetary authority differ in details, such as the spacing of the transformation period from the national to international monetary controls and the nature of the reserves, i.e., whether they should involve a total de-monetization of gold, or continue to use gold as monetary reserves in some fashion or another. But whatever the peculiarities of the various suggestions brought forth, the schemes are basically extensions of the national manipulated monetary system to the international scene. In order for them to succeed, the international monetary authority would have to be as free as national governments are now to create money at its own discretion, to supply it to the member nations in accordance with their particular and changing needs, and to determine economic activity over the whole area comprising its 106 member nations. In brief, it would have to function as a financial world government — an unrealizable capitalist utopia. To turn the I.M.F. into a gigantic central bank, holding the reserves of all nations, and empowered to create money, would make the further keeping of gold reserves superfluous. The gold base of money could be replaced by international law. The gold in the vaults of the world bank would belong to all and nobody; commodity-money would have come to an end. The elimination of gold as monetary reserve would mean the elimination of money "reserves" altogether. Only so long as money retains at least in part the form of commodity-money will it retain its character as the independent form of exchange-value, as capital.

The international money reform finally agreed upon in 1967 (subject to government ratifications) paid no attention to the multitude of preliminary proposals, including those modeled on Keynes' International Clearing Union, or world bank, seen as an instrument capable of providing for all the changing monetary needs of world commerce. But it did agree upon the deliberate creation of a new type of money with which to bolster the reserves of the member nations of the I.M.F., so as to help them overcome arising payments difficulties. The new "money" consists of so-called Special Drawing Rights, or SDR's, which are allotted to the nations in proportion to their previously established I.M.F. quotas. This new "money" is, of course, credit money; but it has been provided with a gold guarantee to give it the semblance of real money. The money resources of the I.M.F., i.e., gold, dollars and other currencies, provide a "monetary pool" from which member nations can draw short-time loans to bridge a negative payments situation. In contrast, the SDRs are not borrowings but "additions" to the world's money supply, even though they have no material counterpart such as gold or convertible currencies. The money pool of the I.M.F. has not previously been used as a base for issuing new money; in fact, it was part of the "money reserves" of all its members in form of their subscriptions to the Fund. This same money is now allowed to function as an independent "international money reserve" and as a backing for the SDRs. It is a further reduction of the real money base of credit money on an international scale, or the dilution of the monetary character of the "enlarged reserves" of the nations of the International Monetary Fund.

Presumably, the theory behind the reform is based on the fear that international trade might contract due to monetary troubles, which would then lead to a contraction of production. Increasing world trade, it is said, requires a growing money supply. While domestically governments can arrange an increase of the money supply in accordance with the growing volume of business, it has not been possible to manage the international money supply. The Special Drawing Rights are a first attempt in this direction. They are necessary, it is said, because the increase of the international money supply via the growth of reserves has been dependent on gold production and the gold market, which not only are highly erratic but also expand far more slowly than the volume and value of international transactions. Actually, however, the world's gold reserves have increased in accordance with the increase of international trade. If gold stocks fall behind the increasing requirements of international trade it is not so much because of an actual impossibility of increasing the production of gold, as because of a reluctance to immobilize capital by holding it in the form of gold. Be this as it may, the SDRs are supposed to take the place of gold as the ultimate resource for purchasing other currencies. "Gold reserves" are thus created without the production of gold, which can only mean that the total gold cover is being decreased to the same extent as the total money supply is increased.

Of course, after it is generally accepted to create monetary reserves out of thin air rather than by producing them, the SDRs will function as reserve supplements in the same way that paper money functions as commodity-money. Instead of gold, SDRs can then be transferred from one country to another in exchange for currencies to straighten out disparities in payments balances. But like the supply of gold, supply of SDRs is also limited, and nations with a persistent unfavorable payments balance are in danger of exhausting both their conventional reserves and their allotment of SDRs. Countries with a persistent favorable payments balance will accumulate the supplementary SDRs as well as the monetary gold. Both processes will merely take a longer time. There is always the idea that trade and payments disbalances are only temporary occurrences, to be ended sooner or later by the self-assertion of the equilibrium tendencies of the market. But as this seems now to happen rather later than sooner, time must be won. The access to greater monetary reserves is to give nations more time to reverse an unfavorable trade and payments position, and to enable them to do so more gradually, so as to avoid the shock of sudden retrenchments and the consequent contraction of international trade.

Just as deficit-financing on the national scale finds its rationale in its postponement effect — that is, in the idea that the mere delay of a crisis situation by government-induced production may lead into a new business upswing capable of bringing forth profits large enough to compensate for the non-profitable part of production — so the managed international money supply is thought to postpone a monetary crisis and by doing so perhaps avoid it altogether. But manipulation of the international money supply, just like deficit-financing, is necessarily limited by the market character of the capitalist economy. If it were *not* limited, payments would not need to balance and world trade would lose its private-property nature; debts would not be paid and profits not collected, and trade would have lost its capitalist character. As it is, however, the postponement of monetary crises makes sense only on the assumption, contrary to all evidence, that there is a tendency toward external equilibrium which will work itself out if given a chance to do so.

There is no need to go into the suggested administrative details of the projected monetary reform, the less so because it is not at all certain that it will become a reality. Even if it does, it may still undergo many alterations to fit the special needs or policies of particular nations. What is of interest is the wide-spread recognition, implied in the reform, that the nationally managed economy requires some degree of international manipulation in addition to and above the "regulatory" market forces. However, the contemplated attempt at managing the international money supply is a rather modest yearly increase of reserves by between 1.4 and 2.8 per cent of the existing reserves which, in 1967, amounted to about $71 billion. Over a projected five-year period this would increase monetary reserves by between 5 and 10 billion dollars. The use as well as the acceptance of SDR's is limited and proportional with respect to other reserves, and their acceptance is to be rewarded by a small rate of interest in an attempt to make them preferable to gold. The need for larger reserves rests on the assumption that international trade will expand in the near future as it has in the recent past, that is, at an average rate of between 7 and 10 per cent a year, and on the parallel assumption that this increase of trade will complicate rather than ease the payments problems.

Reserves must still be held in gold or in acceptable international money; and money is acceptable only so long as it is convertible into gold. Most European nations keep the great bulk of their reserves in gold. Some nations, Canada and Japan for instance, keep the smaller part of their reserves in gold. Elsewhere in the world nations have much smaller total reserves and out of these smaller reserves much lower proportions in gold. Until 1961, the United States kept its reserves entirely in gold. Presently, she holds some small amount in convertible foreign currencies. As a result of America's payments deficit, monetary gold stocks are now more evenly distributed, the American share amounting to about 37 per cent of the "free world's" monetary gold — approximately the same as it was thirty years ago.

The gold cover of the American dollar was legally set at 25 per cent of the total amount of Federal Reserve notes in circulation and the total deposits of member banks in the Federal Reserve System. "By the end of 1964, the total deposits came to 19 billion dollars and the notes in circulation to 35 billion. The combined total of 54 billion dollars called for a gold reserve of 13.5 billion. This left, at the time only about 1.5 billion dollars of free gold as a reserve against the official and unofficial foreign claims. Since the total required reserves tended to increase at the rate of approximately 750 million a year because of the normal rise in business activity and bank credit as well as Federal Reserve notes, this meant that the margin of free gold would have virtually disappeared some time in 1966."[14]

Previously under American law, the gold reserve put an upper limit to the reserve-creating and note-issuing powers of the Federal Reserve System. This reserve requirement has been removed and the entire gold reserve serves now only the international convertibility of dollars into gold. Still, there are only $15 billion of monetary gold. With the continuous conversion of foreign claims into gold, resulting from the continuing American payments deficit and the decreasing value of the dollar — not in relation to gold but in

14   P. Douglas, *America in the Market Place*, New York, 1966, p. 291.

its actual buying-power — the steady decrease of the gold holdings would imply the decline of the dollar as international money and as a reserve substitute for gold.

Though it is not immediately necessary, the United States must halt the drain of monetary gold as a long-run trend. With inflation no longer checked by reserve requirements, the dollar will be less and less acceptable for the settlement of international accounts, and dollar holdings will be more readily converted into gold. America, then, must have an adequate money supply to cope with the problem of non-profitable government-induced production — now accentuated by the war in Vietnam — and an adequate gold reserve to assure the dollar's international position. But these are contradictory needs; because the very process which increases the supply of dollars also reduces the gold reserve.

It is because of her declining gold reserve that the United States supported the projected international money reform more enthusiastically than other nations. European countries, with ampler reserves, did not see the urgency of the need for new and imaginary reserves at a time when America's sizeable balance of payments deficit provides the necessary "liquidity" for the given international trade. Under these conditions, the creation of new "reserves" might reduce efforts on the part of the United States and other deficit nations to overcome their payments difficulties which, in time, would diminish international trade even more effectively than a reduction of America's foreign expenditures and capital exports. But as the continued profitability of American capital demands external expansion, and consequently the expenditures of imperialism, there is no chance to overcome the American deficit except by an increase of income from abroad through capital imports and by an increase of America's favorable balance of trade.

However, all capitalist nations share these needs, for which reason Europe's recovery, however necessary, could only be of dubious benefit to the United States. Notwithstanding all declarations, and even actual policies, to the contrary, it cannot be America's objective to bring about a well-functioning world economy at the expense of her own superior position. America's dominance is the result not only of her own productive efforts but also of the occurrence of two world wars which left the European economies far behind the American. At least in part, the United States owes her exceptional growth to exceptional circumstances. Some of the blessings of these circumstances are disappearing as the recovery of the European economies narrows the gap between European and American production and productivity. Because European expansion is by sheer necessity geared to the world market, its continued profitability depends on a successful penetration of American and extra-American markets. European capital must compete with American capital and with the Eastern power bloc, whose existence sets further limits to the external expansion of both European and American capitalism. With increasing competition from Europe and the East, America's exceptional position during the first half of the twentieth century seems to be drawing to a close.

The war and post-war disruptions of the "traditional pattern" of trade were to be ended by a return to "normalcy" achieved through the stabilization of exchange-rates and the gradual dismantling of all discriminatory trade practices. Although the formation of the European trading blocs was accompanied by hopes that they would eventually merge and extend European free-trade into a free-trading world, neither expectation has been realized. The goal of an all-European market becomes more distant with every year of the trading blocs' existence. Newly evolving patterns of competition and control tend to harden, and the breaking-up of established regional arrangements may prove even more difficult than overcoming national protective practices. If one group should gain exceptional advantages by virtue of the regional arrangement, it will not sacrifice this advantage to the principle of free trade, even if restricted to the intra-European market. For instance, Great Britain's current readiness to enter the Common Market, in order to partake in the more rapid expansion of the West-European economy and to find refuge behind the common tariff wall, not only is sabotaged by the powers profiting both economically and politically by existing arrangements but may well disappear if and when the Common Market economies begin to stagnate.

Tariffs and trade in the post-war world were to be determined multilaterally, with due consideration to both the special but "temporary" needs of individual nations and the common goal of a tariff-free world. Under the General Agreement on Tariffs and Trade (GATT), there began in 1947 a process of multilateral tariff reductions which, 20 years later, (in the so-called Kennedy Round negotiations) brought tariffs among industrial nations to their lowest point. However, the agreements were hardly made public when new protectionist measures were introduced in the American Congress. Rigid import quotas were asked for more than a third of all dutiable imports, including items such as steel, oil, chemicals, lead, textiles, meat, and dairy-products — this despite the fact that America still exports more than she imports. If enacted, of course, such measures would lead to retaliations by all countries affected and the expected increase of trade by way of tariff reductions would not materialize. In any case, the liberalization of trade cannot alter existing economic difficulties, for these difficulties led to the trade restrictions in the first place.

The growth of international trade during the last decade, reaching in 1967 the equivalent of $200 billion, was of course due to the expansion of production. In the industrial nations the rate of increase in trade was even faster than that in production, indicating the growing international specialization of industrial production and the rise of multinational corporations. However, although profits are realized in circulation, they must first be made at the point of production. If profit-production declines, the realizable profits also decline. Government-induced production can maintain a necessary volume of production despite its partial loss of profitability. Although the end-product of government-induced production (with some exceptions) is not marketable, its intermediary processes enter into national and international market relations. The fact that trade increases with the increase of production, and lately even faster than production, alters in no way the decreasing profitability of capital. The profits to be realized on the market by way of trade are no larger than those brought forth by the profitable sector of the economy. The increase of trade under these conditions is thus a sign not of advancing capital production but merely of a larger production, and indicates an intensifying competition for the shrinking profits of a growing world production. While the rate of increase of international trade is determined by that of production, the mixed character of present-day capitalism excludes an effective control of market and payments relations. The mixture of free *and* controlled production, of free *and* controlled trade, excludes both an "automatic" and a "controlled" integration of world economy. It does not exclude economic manipulation, to be sure; but this manipulation, which can only attend particularistic interests, will not serve the actual needs of the world economy.

CHAPTER XVIII

ECONOMIC DEVELOPMENT

Keynes' theory dealt with "mature" capitalism and its apparent incapacity for further "automatic" development. This preoccupation with "mature" capitalism reflected a rather general disregard for the development of the world's industrially backward regions. In Keynes' view, to recall, it is the diminishing scarcity of capital, a consequnce of the diminishing propensity to consume, which explains insufficient demand and unemployment in the developed capitalist nations. In countries where capital is scarce and the propensity to consume consequently high, this problem does not exist, for a "poor country will be prone to consume by far a greater part of its output, so that a very modest measure of investment will suffice to provide full employment."[1] He also said that there has "been a chronic tendency throughout human history for the propensity to save to be stronger than the inducement to invest," and that "the weakness of the inducement to invest has been at all times the key to the economic problem."[2] Apparently, then, the propensity to save is not only a consequence of the diminishing propensity to consume but exists quite independently of the scarcity, or diminishing scarcity, of capital. However, all in all, Keynes gave slight attention to backward nations, for he "looked upon international *economic homogenization* as a path to universal prosperity and lasting world peace."[3]

A fully-developed capitalism implies commodity production and exchange on a world-wide scale — the world market. When Marx pictured the future of capitalism by citing the example of British

1 J.M. Keynes, *The General Theory*, p. 31.
2 *Ibid.*, p. 347.
3 K. K. Kurihara, *The Keynesian Theory of Economic Development*, New York, 1959, p. 22.

233

capitalism, it was not to imply that all other nations would copy England's development, but that the world market would be an extension of the basic social and economic relations dominant in the then most advanced capitalist nation. Competition and accumulation would characterize world economy as they characterized England. The English picture was that of *laissez-faire,* supported by colonial exploitation and a monopolistic position in international finance and commerce. Even though capitalistically-developing nations objected to the *laissez-faire* principle, they did so only in order to gain competitive strength to operate more successfully under its conditions. They also strove for monopolistic positions in one or another sphere of world production and trade and vied for the possession of colonies so as to gain and secure special privileges. All this implied international heterogeneity rather than "homogenization," as it involved the concentration of capital in more advanced nations and the exploitation of the poorer countries by these nations.

But as Keynes ignored the fact of exploitation at home, so he ignored the exploitation of underdeveloped by developed nations. And just as he believed that "unjustified" exploitation (excess yields) could be eliminated without altering existing social relationships, so he held that the interests of the capitalistically-dominating nations could be harmonized with those of the underdeveloped countries without changing anything basic in the social structures of either the underdeveloped or the developed nations. It was just a question of "making the saving propensities of the world's richer members compatible with the development needs of its poorer members."[4]

Seen from the standpoint of Western capitalism, Keynesian policy with regard to underdeveloped nations exhausts itself in aiding their economic development by way of grants, loans, and investments. Although often considered aid, private business investments have, of course, nothing to do with helping foreign nations; they are undertaken purely for purposes of exploitation. Loans, too, whether from private or public funds, do not constitute aid but are supposed to yield interest and are thus instrumentalities to partake in the exploitation of the production they finance. Capital is invested where it can obtain profits and interest, and it is merely

4 *Ibid.*

the height of these returns that determines whether capital will flow to developed or underdeveloped countries. There is then nothing specifically "Keynesian," or "new," about foreign capital investments or loans; what is new is the demand that they should be "compatible" with the development needs of the poorer nations, i.e., with their capitalistic development.

On the assumption that Western capitalism has solved its own problems via the Keynesian techniques that led to a state of general "affluence," and aside from the threat of nuclear war, the problem of underdevelopment is now considered to be of first importance. How did this problem arise? To all appearances, it did not exist in the nineteenth century. As in the time of Ricardo, some economists still think that "it is in the nature of less-developed countries that they are mainly producers of primary goods, i.e., agricultural or mining products. With a low level of human skill and capital, the type of production in which they will have a comparative advantage will usually be those dependent on natural resources. Not only the 'supply side' but also the demand side is geared this way, for the poorer nations' greatest need is food. To finance their imports underdeveloped countries will have to export primary commodities. The markets for such goods are often not such as to stimulate their development."[5] A solution to this dilemma in theory would be an increasing world demand for primary products, sufficient to raise their prices and to narrow the gap between imports and exports in underdeveloped nations. Another solution would be to increase food production at the expense of exports. An increased food production, geared to an increased production of manufactured goods, would enable these countries to reduce imports from developed nations. An increased world demand for primary products presupposes a much higher rate of capital formation in the developed nations than the prevailing one. Such a high rate of expansion in turn presupposes, among other things, larger export markets for the developed nations and, to that end, cheap importation of primary products. Capitalist nations which depend on overseas supplies of primary products cannot show any real enthusiasm for the industrial development of backward nations, for this would endanger their own favorable positions on the world market.

5   J. Tinbergen, *Shaping the World Economy*, p. 15.

By shrinking the world market, a slowing down of the rate of capital expansion in the developed countries hits the least industralized territories hardest. It diminishes the demand for primary products and reduces their prices without lessening importation needs. But even a rapid economic expansion of the developed nations rarely benefits the underdeveloped economies. The fast pace of investments in the capital-rich nations in the wake of the Second World War, for instance, soaked up most of the world's available capital, leaving little for the development of poorer regions. This Western "prosperity" led to large price raises for machinery and other finished goods, which worsened the terms of trade for the underdeveloped countries. Whether there is prosperity or depression, the poorer countries just cannot win in the competitive game. Their helpless dependency on changing market conditions comes to light in violent changes in their export markets and in export-prices for primary goods. It has been estimated that for the period from 1901 to 1950 export earnings from primary commodity producers fluctuated an average of 23 per cent a year.[6] The price fall for primary products after 1956 actually cancelled out all the aid poured into the underdeveloped countries by Western nations up to that time. Practically speaking, this "aid" was merely a partial compensation for their losses in international trade, which were so many gains to the importers in the developed nations. Data published by the Statistical Division of the United Nations[7] show that in 1964 the price level of primary commodities as related to that of manufactured goods was 22 per cent less than in 1950. The terms of trade have cost the undeveloped countries a value loss of $4 billion in comparison with their revenues 15 years ago.

Foreign loans and capital imports "aided" to some extent the capitalization and industrialization of underdeveloped countries and hastened their change from feudal to semi-capitalist conditions by increasing commodity production. These investments served largely to facilitate the extraction of primary products. Capital has been used to develop the plantation system and to increase efficiency in the mining and oil industries. This basic pattern has not changed. American investments in Africa, for instance, which by

6 United Nations, Department of Economic Affairs, *Instability in Export Markets of Underdeveloped Countries*, New York, 1952, II, p. 1.
7 November, 1965.

1964 had grown to a total of $1.6 billion, have "gone into extractive enterprises to take natural resources out of Africa; only a relatively small proportion has gone into local manufacturing and commercial enterprises."[8] Over-all capital exports to underdeveloped countries have been greatly reduced and for some of these nations have come to an end altogether. In brief, there is not enough capital investment to facilitate economic growth in underdeveloped nations, and, more often than not, more is taken out of them in the form of profits than is poured into them by new investments. "Profits derived from operations in underdeveloped countries have gone to a large extent to finance investments in highly developed parts of the world;"[9] so that, at least in part, the advance of one part of the world was made at the expense of another.

The main results of American penetration into underdeveloped countries were not different from those achieved by European colonial control. The countries in South America, for instance, are used as raw-material sources and as markets for finished products. America gained the benefits of imperial control by way of the "open door" policy based on productivity superiority, by means of capital exports, and, when convenient, by military intervention. However, the Latin American countries are not in the same category of underdevelopment as are those of Africa and Asia. Mexico and Brazil, for instance, experienced a rapid rate of native capital formation. In Mexico, this amounted to about 15 per cent of total national production in recent years. Nearly two-thirds of this capital investment belongs to private enterprise. American private investments here include not only the traditional raw material sources but also the newer industries such as chemicals, electricity, telephones, aviation, automobiles, banks, and insurance companies, which causes some political resentment because "the economic power of the large foreign enterprises constitutes a serious threat to the integrity of the nation and to the liberty of the country to plan its own economic development."[10] However, profits are high; the rate of earnings on foreign investments ranges from about 10 per cent to over 20 per cent, of which roughly half is reinvested and the other half repatriated.

8   The *New York Times*, January 31, 1966.
9   P. A. Baran, *The Political Economy of Growth*, New York, 1960, p. 184.
10 O. Lewis, "Mexico Since Cardenas," *Social Change in Latin America Today*, New York, 1961, p. 306.

By dividing the world's nations into three different groups in accordance with the world's income distribution in 1949 we get the following picture:[11]

	World income (per cent)	World population (per cent)	Income per capita
High-income countries	67	18	$915
Middel-income "	18	15	$310
Low-income "	15	67	$ 54

On the North American Continent, including Canada, there are "a mere 10 per cent of the world's population. But we have here about 75 per cent of the world's income. By contrast, the 75 per cent of the world's population whose income is below $125 per person a year receives altogether perhaps no more than 10 per cent of the world's income."[12] Whatever the limitations of these and similar comparisons, they reveal nonetheless that "on the international scene, a drama is now staged, which could end in a Marxian catastrophe on a vastly larger scale than Marx ever envisaged. There is a tremendous income gap between rich and poor nations, and the poorer nations represent the masses. The gap is widening. The poor nations become class-conscious. But it is possible that, once more, concessions by the privileged, as the underprivileged grow stronger, may create a new harmony."[13]

It is a question of concessions as the process itself cannot be reversed. And these concession imply the sacrifice of at least part of the privileges which the developed nations derived from the process. This means larger capital investments and more foreign aid to hasten industrial development in the poor nations. Private capital is preferred but government aid is also necessary, as there are many undertakings in which private capital rarely, if ever, invests. These undertakings belong to what is called the industrial infrastructure, i.e., roads, dams, canals, harbors, education, health, and often transportation and energy — the services of which are used by almost all other industries. It is now generally acknowledged that the infrastructure is best taken care of by public authorities, even though its development is also a condition of private

11 R. Nurske, *Problems of Capital Formation in Underdeveloped Countries,* London, 1953, p. 63.
12 P. F. Drucker, *Landmarks of Tomorrow,* New York, 1959, p. 164.
13 G. Myrdal, *Beyond the Welfare State,* New Haven, 1960, p. 222.

capital development. Because capitalists in both underdeveloped and developed nations are equally interestd in this infrastructure, its construction is not so much a form of aid to underdeveloped nations as one of aid to private capital in general. And where all other economic relations between the developed and underdeveloped countries remain what they had been prior to the development, the infrastructure will aid the former even more than the latter. This form of aid subsidizes private business at public expense in both the giving and the receiving countries.

Any other large-scale aid, such as consumption goods and foodstuffs for the immediate relief of suffering populations, would interfere with the existing market relations and the special interests vested in them. Whereas in the "mature" nations this merely means that the chronic overproduction will be resolved by waste-production rather than by the provision of higher living standards, in backward countries it often means actual starvation in the midst of various attempts to create the preconditions for capital development.

The overwhelming part of aid actually received by underdeveloped nations has consisted of military assistance. In this form aid is least detrimental to private interests. By relieving the governments of underdeveloped nations of part of their "defense" expenditures, funds are freed (theoretically but not necessarily actually) for purposes of development. Military assistance serves to shore-up governments sympathetic to Western policies: it is given to governments which represent social classes determined to maintain domestic property relations as well as international economic relationships unchanged. "Not without economic significance," it is said, "is the capability demonstrated by specialized units of the armed forces of Peru, Columbia and Venezuela to destroy or control Communist-led guerrilla groups attempting to mount large-scale liberation-front operations. Such efforts have failed to disrupt national confidence."[14] A minor part of foreign aid is of a non-military nature. Being a kind of auxiliary military assistance, it is determined by the political-military needs of the aid-giving nations, not by the development-needs of the aid-receiving countries. To provide aid of greater significance could lead to radical changes in the social and economic structure of the underdeveloped countries,

14 The *New York Times,* January 31, 1966.

which could affect the economic and political-military interests of the aid-dispensing powers. For the new social forces released by the developmental process may well upset and overthrow customary trade relations as well as political alliances; particularly because under present-day world conditions rapid social and economic development implies government control tending towards state-capitalism. Foreign aid is giving to contain, not to extend, the state-capitalist trend.

A real concern for "backward" nations would be strange indeed: not so long ago enormous energies were released, in two world wars, to turn industrially-developed nations into so many under-developed areas; and still greater energies are today stored-up to transform the whole world into so much underdeveloped territory and, perhaps, into territory incapable of any kind of development. The imperialist power struggles alone prevent any meaningful assistance to foreign development. The bombing of the Yalu power stations in the Korean war, for instance, "destroyed more capital equipment in a single night than the United States is investing in the whole underdeveloped areas in a whole year."[15] This "policy" is now repeated on a far larger scale in Vietnam, and will most probably be extended to the developed parts of China and the whole of Southeast Asia.

In 1959 government grants and loans by the industrial countries of the "free world" to the less-developed nations were roughly estimated at $4 billion, of which the United States supplied about two-thirds, and France and the United Kingdom most of the remainder. This was far less than 1 per cent of these nations' gross national product. In fact, in 1961, when a renewed effort to assist the poorer lands was proposed, the 1 per cent figure was proclaimed a desirable goal for aid expenditures. The total flow of government *and* private funds from Europe and North America to the underdeveloped countries averaged just under 7 billion dollars a year from 1956 through 1959. Of this annual average, government grants and loans accounted for $3.6 billion; various forms of private lending and investment for $2.7 billion; and contributions to international agencies for helping underdeveloped countries for $600 million. These compilations included eleven different forms of "aid," ranging from government grants to private purchases of World

15 The *New York Times*, September 5, 1952.

Bank notes, and including guaranteed export credits, plowed-back earnings of private companies in underdeveloped countries, reparation payments, and so forth — all of these categories being considered "foreign aid" because all of them represented a flow of money to underdeveloped countries.

The "aid" thus far provided for the backward countries has been too slight to affect living conditions and not of a kind to enhance economic development. Consequently, it has only widened the income gap between the rich and the poor nations, rather than narrowing it. In the Keynesian view it must then be enlarged and perhaps differently distributed or qualitatively altered. Just as additional government-induced production is the Keynesians' solution to the problem of capital stagnation in the advanced countries, so more foreign aid is their program for speeding-up development in underdeveloped countries. Having reached this conclusion, the Keynesians shelve the issue, for the implementation of their theories is not within their competence.

For the development of backward areas, however, the Keynesian generosity is as inapplicable as the miserly reality of foreign aid is meaningless. As pointed out before, government-induced waste-production in the developed nations is not considered superfluous by their governments or, for that matter, by their populations; it is seen as necessary for the internal and external security of the nation and of Western capitalism. Moreover, short of violating free-enterprise principles, there is no way to transfer funds from the sphere of waste-production to that of foreign aid, unless this foreign aid is a part of the defense mechanism of Western capitalism; in which case, it is itself another form of waste-production. In view of this situation, government funds for any and all purposes are always scarce. With an international armaments race in progress, there is little chance for an increase of foreign aid expenditures capable of making a difference in the economic growth of underdeveloped countries. But even a substantial reduction of waste-production via disarmament policies would not lead to a significant enlargement of foreign aid unless such aid served the profit requirements of the industrial nations.

It is held, of course, that foreign aid will prove a boon to the developed nations as the industrial growth of hitherto underdeveloped countries becomes the impetus for a general capitalist ad-

vance. Instead of making the rich countries poorer, the development of poorer countries can make all nations richer. The idea
finds support in Keynesian theory, according to which all capitalist
nations can reach a point of "maturity" where capital-demand falls
below savings propensities. It is then just a question as to how
the latter can be made compatible with the development needs of
the poorer nations. The answer is the simple request to *make* them
compatible by appropriate government measures. But it is precisely because the saving propensities of the richer nations are
incompatible with the development needs of the poorer nations
that neither private capital, nor governments representing private
capital, can accept the Keynesian suggestions.

Economic stagnation in the advanced capitalist nations is accompanied by stagnation in the underdeveloped countries because
in both further investments appear as unprofitable under the existing conditions of production. Obviously, stagnation is not a capitalist policy but is suffered by the capitalists, as by anyone else, for
reasons beyond their control and even beyond their knowledge. For
them the problem is not what to do with "savings" that cannot
profitably be invested, but rather how to increase the profitability
of capital so as to employ these "savings" capitalistically. But "savings" looking for investment opportunities will find them, if at
all, first in the developed and *not* in the underdeveloped countries.
Even if industrial development should get under way in the latter,
the fact that they are less-developed makes their productivity, and
thus their profitability, lower than that in the older capitalist nations. Thus, even their development will increase the disparity
between developed and underdeveloped nations.

Although it is frequently asserted that backward countries "have
the advantage of being able to adapt the latest equipment without
having to scrap existing equipment and without being handicapped
by the existence of obsolete buildings,"[16] this advantage does not
really exist. Rather, the slowly increasing industrialization of underdeveloped countries widens the productivity gap between "rich"
and "poor" countries for the very reason that the developed nations
enjoy all the advantages of modern technology. It is true, of course,
that some of the new technological innovations find application

16 P. Einzig, *The Economic Consequences of Automation*, New York, 1957,
p. 65.

in underdeveloped countries — in the extraction industries, for instance — but here they support foreign capital rather than native development.

The profitability of capital in underdeveloped countries is, of course, very high in the extraction industries. Operated with the most modern equipment and served by technicians from abroad, they are capable of competing with similar industries in the developed nations. In fact, such industries are often enormously profitable. This is not only because they are competitive, but also because there is no need for competition. The world price for crude oil, for example, is fixed so that its extraction from the relatively high cost oilfields in the United States will be profitable. This price has no relation to the cost of production in the low cost oilfields in the underdeveloped countries. "To sell for about 100 shillings a ton something which costs 13 shillings a ton to produce (in the Persian Gulf, for instance) is a remarkable achievement. Such a margin of profitability makes it far from ruinous to have to give back to the Arab States half (or more) of the profit."[17] It is for this reason, then, that the bulk of foreign private investments has been concentrated in the extraction industries. Private enterprise secures profitability for foreign investments by creating monopolies in particular industries and allowing them to charge prices independent of production costs. But even so, except for particular businesses, general backwardness implies low profitability and for that reason does not attract foreign capital.

Insofar as the underdeveloped nations could be developed through foreign private investments they are already "developed"; and insofar as they can be further developed by private capital they will be — quite apart from all government urgings. If they are still in a most frightful state of underdevelopment, this merely indicates that the capitalist mode of production — particularly in its free-enterprise form — is not able to develop an integrated world economy and a rational division of labor which could assure the existence and well-being of the world's population. For just as in any particular capitalist nation investments stop at the point where they cease to be profitable, regardless of actual social needs, so in the world at large, the existing investments indicate the borders

17 J. Strachey, *The End of Empire*, New York, 1960, p. 159.

set by their profitability. This situation testifies to capitalism's inability to extend its mode of production into a world system. All capitalism has been able to do is to create the world market; and it was this creation itself which divided the world into "poor" and "rich" nations.

The very notion of foreign investments implies that their owners reside somewhere other than where the investments are made. They may take all, or part, of the profits made abroad into the country of their residence. In this way, capitalists exploit the labor of other nations without accumulating much capital in these nations. It is true that in so doing they provide some people with work, people who otherwise might be idle or occupied in less-remunerative occupations; but they are not fostering economic development to the extent made possible by the exploitation of this labor. Native capitalists too, for reasons of either profitability or security, may and usually do send part, or all, of their profits abroad. All this is quite legitimate until it is outlawed, for it corresponds to the capitalist ideal of the "free" movement of capital in a "free" world market. The search for maximum profits and maximum security is precisely the mechanism supposed to distribute capital in the most "economical" way, which is supposedly also the way most beneficial for the world's population. What it actually does is to perpetuate and accentuate the income gap between the rich and the poor nations. More money leaves the backward nations than is invested in them by the developed countries. According to the United States Department of Commerce, for instance, investments by United States investors in Latin American countries, including both new capital and unreturned earnings, amounted in 1958 to $317 million, while earnings returned to the United States were $653 million. The respective figures for the following years were:

	INVESTED	REPATRIATED
1959	$347 MILLION	$600 MILLION
1960	$267 MILLION	$641 MILLION

Or to take a single country: "From 1943 to 1958 private foreign citizens invested nearly $250 million in Chile. Over the same 15-year period these foreigners took nearly $600 million in the form of repatriated profits. This outflow, mainly to the United States, represented a gift of $50 from every man, woman and child in

Chile. The country desperately needs to receive aid, not give it."[18] But this complaint rests on a misunderstanding, for capitalism has nothing to do with charity, except as another profitable business.

In spite of the fact that most of the profits made enrich the developed nations more than the underdeveloped, the latter clamor nonetheless for more foreign capital investments to buttress the existing property relations in their own countries. But capital is not eager to invest, not only because of the competing demand for capital in the developed countries, but also because investments in many underdeveloped countries — which are nations in permanent crisis conditions — are no longer secure. Interested mainly in natural resources such as oil and metals, foreign investors foster a one-sided development which perpetuates the poor countries' dependence on the rich nations and prevents their more general development. There are exceptions, of course, finding their cause in a geographical proximity between developed and underdeveloped nations. In Mexico and Cuba, for instance, American capital has tried to enter all strategic industries. American businesses owned 60 per cent of all Cuban industries from cosmetics to sugar cane. But this proximity did not prevent the rise of revolutionary social movements and governments. They restricted and even expropriated foreign capital in the name of a free national development, and set themselves against the specific profit needs of the great industrial and financial empires. Because such movements have been widespread and threaten to raise their heads again, private capital has no great desire to invest in underdeveloped areas, where it faces not only economic but also political risks.

Because only a limited amount of capital is available for government-to-government aid transactions, and because all government aid is designed to strengthen and secure as much as possible of the "free world," this aid has the twofold function of maintaining the existing property relations in the aid-receiving countries and of assuring wider fields of operation for the capitalists of the aid-dispensing nations. With few exceptions, based on purely political considerations, aid is not provided for the development of state-owned industries, except those that fall into the category "infrastructure." To encourage capital exports to the underdeveloped nations, governments often underwrite and guarantee such invest-

18 J. Becket and K. D. Griffin, *The New Republic*, December 29, 1962.

ments against currency disorders, exchange controls, confiscatory taxation, and expropriation. But even the elimination of risk at the expense of the public purse does not greatly stimulate foreign investments; what needs to be assured are larger profits than those available at home.

Capitalism's inability and unwillingness to extend the industrialization process to the underdeveloped areas of the world has led to national-revolutionary movements which emphasize the role of the state in the general process of economic development. This conviction is here not the result of a long process of increasing government control as experienced in the advanced capitalist nations. Rather it is the starting-point for nationally-determined capital development directed against both native backwardness and foreign control, and often is accompanied by a partial, or total, expropriation of foreign and native capital. The ordinary business of profit-making becomes thus a matter of national concern and power politics. Because some Western firms lose out to "nationalization" in Iran or Guatemala, for instance, they get their governments to restore and secure their privileges. And because the businesses of these enterprises — as of all enterprises — are in some ways already an integral part of government policy, their governments will intervene on their own accord. Foreign business involves the interests and the prestige of governments. It is furthered and protected by political means. The attempts of nations to escape the detrimental economic consequences of being raw-material producing territories for the great capitalist powers, their insistence upon price and profit policies more favorable to themselves, are treated as "conspiracies" not only against special business interests but against Western civilization itself.

While political, military, and strategic considerations stem from economic interests and from necessities inherent in capital accumulation, and while this is often quite obvious — as, for instance, in the great interest displayed in Southeast Asia as a rich raw material-producing area and in the oil-producing Middle East — the national form of competition obscures the close relationship between political and economic interests. The latter, to be sure, have always included more than just the immediate or expected profitability of specific corporations. But never before has capital accumulation been so closely associated with either imperialism or nationalism. This is still another indication of the general decline of the market-economy and its slow transformation into a government-directed economy which operates, first of all, in terms of territories actually controlled, of raw material sources and manpower actually secured, and of lines of communication actually monopolized, instead of in terms of supply and demand in a world regarded as an open market place. And thus, though national and imperialist interests are still economic interests, seldom or not at all are they expressed in business terms.

Even in the past industrial development required a great effort on the part of the state. In Japan, for example, fear of colonization and foreign exploitation led to the deliberate introduction of capitalism by government. Already in its first stages the Japanese development showed elements of "Keynesianism" which were later to become characteristic of modern capitalism. By limiting the import of foreign capital, Japan retained a large degree of economic independence, and though this required an extraordinary degree of exploitation it achieved its goal — a Japanese capitalism capable of competing with other capitalist nations. Backed by politically favored financial houses, modern industry was introduced both with respect to economic-competitive and military needs. "These industries most highly developed in the technical sense and fashioned after the most up-to-date Western model, were the pride of the state bureaucracy which jealously guarded them even after large parts were acquired by private capital."[19] But Japan was the exception. Her rapid change into an industrial power took place around the turn of the century, at a high point of international capital expansion, and under the favorable political conditions occasioned by America's challenge to European colonialism in the Far East. What the European powers had reached by intervention, America was out to reach by trade, and the "open door" policy was to operate against both the colonizers and the less-developed nations.

The crises and wars of the twentieth century destroyed most of the European colonialism. But the political independence gained by former colonies was no longer a sufficient condition for their economic development. They were already too impoverished from

19 E. H. Norman, *Japan's Emergence as a Modern State*, New York, 1946, p. 135.

the stagnation of previous decades. Their situation has been described as a "vicious circle": "a low capital stock implies a low level of production, and so of income. But a low income does not permit large savings, and hence the capital stock cannot easily be increased."[20] The level of income cannot be raised without industrialization and industrialization cannot be developed without higher incomes. But higher incomes cannot be gained by way of trade in nonindustrial products. It must be gained internally through a still more ruthless exploitation to yield surpluses large enough to set labor free to construct an industrial base, without thereby diminishing the exports required to pay for imports necessary to the industrialization process.

Aside from colonial control and trade discrimination, a country or area may stay underdeveloped because of a deficiency of natural resources such as arable land and mineral deposits. Surpluses may be unattainable; and thus industrial development will be impossible, except such as is introduced from without, which affects only particular resources — oil and gas in the Sahara for instance. However, underdevelopment exists in countries or territories whether or not they have adequate natural resources. It even exists within capitalist nations as, for example, in Italy, whose highly industrialized North and very backward, agricultural South repeats on a national scale the international division of poor and rich territories. While there are some parts of the world that cannot in any meaningful way be industrially developed, this has nothing to do with the problem of underdevelopment in nations potentially capable of economic growth.

In economic parlance a country is considered to be progressive if it consumes less than its net production, so as to permit a net addition to the existing stock of capital. It has been estimated that in recent years underdevloped economies' net investments have been between 3 per cent and 5 per cent of national product, in contrast to developed nations, where the rates have been between 10 per cent and 15 per cent. But the increase of production in underdeveloped countries has been largely offset by an equivalent population increase. It is said that these nations consume as much as they produce; this, of course, is true only when one disregards the uncapitalized savings of the rich as well as those surpluses which

20   J. Tinbergen, *Shaping the World Economy*, p. 14.

disappear by way of trade to reappear as capital in the developed nations.

Because the underdeveloped countries are high-cost producers there is a great amount of unemployment in both agriculture and industry. According to Keynes, unemployment in "mature" capitalism finds its cause in a deficiency of effective demand because of oversavings due to a relative abundance of capital. This does not apply to underdeveloped nations. There are surpluses, of course, but they are not productively applied. The rich of the underdeveloped countries tend to amass fortunes in the form of hoards rather than in the form of productive capital. Income disparities between the rich and the poor in the underdeveloped countries are even larger than in the developed nations or, at any rate, appear to be larger because of the extremely low living standards of the great bulk of their populations. Being quite satisfied with the existing state of affairs, the rich ruling classes find no reason to alter the conditions which grant them their privileges.

In bourgeois economic theory, including the Keynesian version. income inequalities are justified as a source of capital formation. Only the wealthy can save on a significant scale; and the more they "save" the more rapid the development will be. Only under conditions where too much has already been "saved," i.e., in "mature" capitalism, may an increased demand require greater income equality. As these conditions are the opposite of those prevailing in underdeveloped countries, Keynesian theory can only suggest what all other bourgeois economic theory also proposes and what, in fact, is the capitalistic practice — namely, the increase of "savings" through increased exploitation and their application in industrial development.

To reiterate, Keynes thought that throughout history the inducement to invest has always been weaker than the propensity to save. He wrote that "the desire of the individual to augment his personal wealth by abstaining from consumption has usually been stronger than the inducement to the entrepreneur to augment the national wealth by employing labor on the construction of durable assets."[21] However, though the poor cannot help but abstain from consumption they augment nothing but their misery. And though the rich consume in a quite fantastic fashion they get richer nonetheless.

21 *The General Theory*, p. 348.

Keynes speaks only about the rich in both developed and under-developed countries, under capitalist and under pre-capitalist conditions. In "mature" capitalism the inducement to invest is weak because "maturity" destroys profitability; whereas in "immature" capitalism people can get rich, and stay rich, just because there is no capitalist development. "Non-consumption," writes a disciple of Keynes, "does not necessarily carry with it the implication that it thereby releases just the kind of human and material resources which can be used to produce capital goods and with nonchalant ease at that."[22] The rich of the poor nations must not only "abstain from consumption" but must "abstain" in order to invest in the "construction of durable assets." In short, the Keynesian program for industrial development is capitalism. And this comprises about the whole of Keynes' contribution to the "theory of economic growth."

The meagerness of Keynes' contribution to the "theory of growth" did not prevent the fact that the actual, or anticipated, industrial development of backward economies is now largely recognized as either a "Keynesian" or a "socialist" development, depending on the extent of state-participation in the capital formation process. Although state interventions under pre-capitalist conditions have an altogether different function from those advocated by Keynes to solve the problems of the advanced capitalist nations, it is possible to apply the Keynesian "techniques" for speeding up the process of capital formation in underdeveloped countries. State control of economic development preceded Keynes' theory not only in the limited "Keynesian" sense of state-*control*, as experienced in Japan, but also in the wider and more consistent non-Keynesian sense of state-*ownership* of the means of production, first realized in Russia.

National revolutions took on a variety of forms and characteristics within their basically capitalist nature, in accordance with the individual histories of the countries where they occurred and the world situation they faced. Russia's proximity to the Western world, the amount of foreign capital that had been invested in highly-advanced industries (however small in relation to the size and the needs of the nation), the weakness of her bourgeoisie within the ruling social groups, and her peasant population which

---

22 K. K. Kurihara, *The Keynesian Theory of Economic Development*, p. 57.

strove to escape the persistent semi-feudal conditions — all this gave her revolution the character of a "revolution from below," an uprising of workers and poor peasants and their middle-class allies against all *experienced forms* of exploitation, whether of landlords or of native or foreign capital. Based on Marxian ideology, the goal was socialism and its realization through the agency of a revolutionary state. In India the revolutionary ferment was of a different nature. Within the colonial conditions, there slowly emerged an identity of interests between the native and foreign bourgeoisie. Fostered by the circumstances of two world wars, there was a merger of foreign and native capital and a rapid expansion of the latter. Yet the greater primitiveness of her industrial and agricultural production and the consequent lack of social awareness in the lower classes gave her revolutionary aspirations the character of a national movement for political independence, awaiting deliverance through the decline of British imperialism. Whereas Russia is considered a state-socialist, or state-capitalist, system in the non-Keynesian sense of state-ownership of the means of production, India, considering herself a socialist welfare-state, represents, at least ideologically, a "Keynesian system" which limits itself to state control of the economy. For in "socialist India," as of 1958, "it was estimated that 90 per cent of the country's enterprises, including agriculture which is entirely in the hands of individual owners, were in private hands, and furnished 92 per cent of the country's total income, with only 8 per cent of total income coming from government-owned enterprises."[23]

With Russia's development into an industrial power and with the rise of the Eastern bloc after the Second World War, the world's national economies in both developed and underdeveloped countries divided into systems of state-ownership and systems of limited state-control. The division is not absolute; the various nations adhering to one or the other principle of social organization display various degrees of either state-ownership or state-control. There are no two countries exactly alike in this respect either among the so-called communist nations or among the nations belonging to the "free world," or among those which are considered "uncommitted" to either one of the existing power blocs. But in all nations governments intervene to some extent into the economic

23 V. M. Deans, *New Patterns of Democracy in India,* Cambridge, 1959, p. 106.

mechanism. In the "communist" nations investments are presumably directly determined by government decisions. In the controlled, or mixed, economies, developed and underdeveloped, investments are the result of market forces which the governments
seek to influence by monetary and fiscal means, and which they
supplement by directly-determined investments in public enterprises and government-induced production. The fiscal and monetary policies which have come to be associated with the name of
Keynes are applicable in all existing economic systems regardless of
their specific character or their particular stage of development.

Whereas in the "mature" nations Keynesian policies serve to
stabilize the economy, underdeveloped countries can use them to
organize and coordinate economic growth. Fiscal and monetary
policies may distribute income in such a way as to increase the
accumulation fund. The government may itself undertake the task
of savings and investments, enacting what Keynes conceived as a
somewhat comprehensive socialization of investments through the
collection of communal savings. If Keynes himself saw this only as
a possibility of the future, he was nonetheless convinced, or so he
said, of its desirability, not only because of the declining propensity
to consume but also because he believed in the state's superior
capacity to calculate the profitability, or marginal efficiency, of
capital in the long-run and to give due consideration to the "general social advantage."

All the Keynesian suggestions as to how to overcome capitalist stagnation and decline in the developed nations refer to government
activities which bring a measure of "planning" into the market
mechanism. But if partial "planning" is possible, so is total planning; there is nothing in the Keynesian system which would exclude
its application in a state-capitalist, or state-socialist system. Advocates of the state-capitalist system object to Keynesianism not because it suggests manipulating income distribution to create the
desired relationship between investment and consumption, but
because Keynes wished to make only limited use of such manipulative techniques.

Although Keynesian manipulative techniques are applicable in
all capitalist systems regardless of their stage of development,
Keynes' "general theory of employment" loses its "generality" by
a consideration of unemployment in underdeveloped countries. In

these countries, unemployment is the result not of an abundance but of a lack of capital. This unemployment, disguised as over-population relative to the existing means of production and to their productivity, is itself a hindrance to capital formation, not only because of the cheapness of labor competing with capital, but also because planned development must here necessarily be of an employment-generating instead of a capital-increasing nature. The planning authority must start out with a kind of social planning not conducive to rapid capital formation, or destroy a large part of the population. Under such conditions the Keynesian techniques will not suffice to yield the surpluses necessary to initiate capital development.

A country may be so impoverished that neither fiscal nor monetary policies can successfully channel funds from consumption to investments. It may then be found necessary to organize production and consumption by purely political means and to force populations into behavior patterns that will yield surpluses not otherwise attainable. The collectivization of Russian agriculture, as well as the whole of the Stalinist terror system, was such an undertaking. It finds a modified repetition in present-day China because there is no other way to capital formation. "Given a backward and over-populated agrarian society as a starting point," it has been said, "any emotionless practioneer of economics might have prescribed most of what is being done in China today even if he had never heard the word Communism."[24]

But not all underdeveloped countries are in such an impoverished state, and even if they were, some of them would still not be able to solve their developmental problems in the authoritarian ways of state-capitalism. In some cases, a developed capitalist nation may prevent an underdeveloped nation from following the state-capitalist model; or the underdeveloped nation may be too dependent on capitalist countries to consider such a move. State-capitalist systems must to some extent free themselves from traditional world market relations. They must be able to exist under predominantly autarchic conditions, and they must be capable of withstanding imperialist pressure. They must therefore be large countries with large populations, well endowed with natural resources. Since the end of the Second World War, however, state-capitalist

24. T. Mende, *China and Her Shadow*, New York, 1962, p. 16.

nations have been combined into an Eastern power bloc which, in its economic relations, represents a kind of "second world market." This allows even weak or small nations to break out of their previous dependence on the private world market and to organize their economic life on state-capitalist principles.

The synchronization of various national economies appears to be less difficult than economic "integration" by way of private trade on a monopolistic world market. And just as the Western powers distribute some "aid" to underdeveloped countries within their spheres of interest, so the stronger countries of the Eastern bloc come to the "aid" of their underdeveloped allies or potential allies. Economic "aid" by the Soviet bloc to underdeveloped nations had reached the equivalent of $3 billion by 1960. Most of this "aid" was in the form of loans and credits, some of it ($750 million) comprising military equipment. This "aid" has been regarded in the Western world as "aid competition"; and so it is. Like the "aid" of the Western nations, it is given to further the political and economic interests of the dominating powers within the Eastern bloc. The direct or indirect control of underdeveloped countries adds important sources of raw materials to the power base of the state-capitalist systems and subtracts these raw materials from the "free world's" resources.

Although Soviet "aid" serves the same purposes as "aid" extended by the Western nations, it is often provided under conditions more favorable to the underdeveloped countries. Russia's rate of interest on foreign loans, for instance, is 2½ per cent as against a Western interst-rate of between 4½ and 5½ per cent. Russian investments in the oil-industry of India demand 10 per cent of the returns as against the 50 per cent asked for by British and American companies. And, most important, industrial establishments erected through Soviet aid measures become the property of the receiving countries, whereas Western private investments in underdeveloped nations continue to be owned and operated by foreign companies. There is much barter dealing and government-to-government trading, which is favorable to underdeveloped countries since it by-passes international payments problems. There are also no restrictions or preferences with regard to types of industrial development; complete factory installations of all descriptions are offered and delivered. Extensive use is made of experts working in the underdeveloped countries. For all these reasons, trade too is expanding between the Soviet bloc and the underdeveloped nations, though not on a scale that will make a real difference in the conditions of the backward nations for some time to come.

The Soviet bloc's policy of expanding trade with underdeveloped countries began on an extremely small base of foreign trade. "For the underdeveloped countries as a group, Soviet bloc trade can be expected to make a positive though distinctly marginal contribution. But even a manifold increase of trade would not alter the fact that the economic future of these countries will continue to be interwoven with the trade of the free world."[25] Trade with the "free world," however, is trade for private profit and as such is determined by the conditions prevailing in the developed, not the underdeveloped, countries. If this trade has hitherto not much profited the backward nations, it can hardly be expected to do so in the future — a future already restricted by the existence and the growth of competitive state-capitalist systems.

The alignment of nations in Eastern and Western power blocs is not based on the existence of the "two world markets." Rather is the opposite true: the "two world markets" have some reality only because international competition (and cooperation) now has a political-military character. The Western powers desire the maintenance of capitalistic property relations, and favor government controls only to that extent which appears necessary to secure these relations and to allow them to develop in countries on the verge of capitalization. All foreign policy is designed to strengthen private enterprise wherever possible and to sabotage state-capitalist aspirations wherever they arise. Economic relations with state-capitalist systems are held to a minimum, or are done away with altogether, by the Western nations, though some are more consistent in this policy than are others. Trade with China, North Korea and Cuba, for instance, has become a crime under the American "Trade with the Enemy Act." For the state-capitalist nations, the international market is thus largely restricted to other state-capitalist nations and to nations not as yet committed to either of the dominating and competing power centers.

Most of the underdeveloped countries suffered, and are still suffering, under the double yoke of native and foreign exploitation.

25 J. S. Berliner, *Soviet Economic Aid*, New York, 1958, p. 94.

The social struggles in these nations are still fought against both
native ruling classes and foreign capital. Both struggles involve
questions of property expropriation for the rearrangement of national production and distribution in greater conformity with
national interests, even if these "national interests" become once
more the basis of new special interests vested in the political control of the state. "Middle-class groups," it is often pointed out,
"are the Promethean elements in the underdeveloped societies today — the only conscious, active and capable agents of social
change. The communists have long recognized the crucial role of
the middle classes and have been making major efforts to reach
and influence them. In contrast, the West has done far too little
to reap the benefits of its own advantages over the communists."[26]
With regard to social change the West has no such advantages.
The change required in these nations can only be disadvantageous
to the Western capitalist nations. It is precisely because of social
change, or the desire for change, that the underdeveloped nations
find themselves in open or latent rebellion not only against their
own ruling classes but also against the latters' supporters in the
advanced countries. These rebellions can have no other objective
than the change of existing conditions and therewith of the property relations at the base of these conditions. It is because the
"middle classes" find no prospect for advancement in underdeveloped countries, and these countries find no prospects for development in the monopolistically controlled capitalist world, that any
serious attempt at development will base itself on state-capitalist
ideology and a state-capitalist program, even where for the time
being it must actually be satisfied with state-control in the Keynesian sense.

The development of capital-poor countries presupposes social
movements against the social forces favoring the *status quo*. It is
thus first of all a political problem. Because the nation is the largest historically-evolved unit for coherent social organization, and
because conditions in all countries vary, development appears as a
national program. In some ways it must be coordinated with similar programs of other nations; but this larger unit of organization
will be composed of a number of national units and will have no

26 The National Planning Association, *The Political Economy of American
Foreign Policy*, New York, 1955, p. 161.

permanence until the institution of the nation-state is altogether abolished. The development of capitalism and the rise of the nation-state were one and the same process. It was the function of the state to assure and secure the growth of the national capitalist economy, as it is its function now — but in far greater measure — to stabilize the capitalist system so as to assure its continued existence. Development under present world conditions is far more difficult than the stabilization of advanced capitalist systems and requires even more government controls. As these controls affect various social groupings differently, they are established by way of political struggles, which are not confined to the national scene but involve other nations by affecting their political and economic interests.

To do justice to the problems of underdeveloped countries, it would be necessary to deal with each nation separately, for each is unique not only in its physical and social structure but also in its connections with other nations and with the world at large. Measured in terms of national income per head, Southeast Asia appears to be the world's poorest area; but it is also one of the areas most contested by the imperialist powers representing the two competing social systems. China and India follow closely, the one attempting the state-capitalist path of development, the other that of state-aided private capital development. The nations of tropical Africa, though even less developed, fall into an entirely different category. No attempts as yet are made here, either by foreign capital, or by the Africans themselves, to diversify production. Largely self-sufficient in food production and in relative isolation from one another, the various African states restrict their production and trade to primary goods intended for the Western, predominantly European, markets. The capital in evidence is foreign capital invested in extraction industries. Nonetheless, some African governments, Ghana and Senegal for instance, call themselves "socialist" or "welfare-states" because they have transformed existing private marketing organizations into monopolistic government agencies. The various nations of the Middle East display different degrees of state-control, from government participation in private enterprise and some form of government regulation for almost all economic activities, as in Egypt, to an almost complete absense of government intervention in business, as in Lebanon. Israel, being entirely dependent on foreign support, assumes the character of a mixed economy merely because assistance from abroad is distributed by the government and channelled into government and semi-government undertakings. As this assistance has been ten and twenty times as large as private capital investments, it is the government, not private capital, which determines economic activity. Some of the poorest countries in terms of per capita income are found in Latin America: Bolivia, Paraguay, and Ecuador are examples. Latin America also contains some of the most rapidly developing nations, such as Mexico and Brazil. Yet all these nations find themselves in permanent crisis conditions; some because no development takes place, others because there is development, and also because of the international repercussions of one or the other of these situations.

As regards Latin America any intensive development requires opposition to both the existing semi-feudal internal relations and to the exchange relations between the South American and the developed foreign nations. Only about 10 per cent of Latin American trade is internal, 90 per cent consisting of trade with the United States and Western Europe, which is trade in primary products such as coffee, bananas, cocoa, wool, meat, oil, sugar, copper, etc. This situation suits the industrial nations, the hereditary ruling classes in Latin America, and the foreign investors in primary industries. The native *haciendas* and *latifundia* operate under a peon system of obligatory labor. Although native labor is thus extremely cheap, foreign investors in large commercial plantations have found it more profitable to replace labor by machinery, a policy soon adopted by native plantation owners. There arose a rural proletariat, landless and unemployed, which has been held down by military dictatorships subservient to the native and foreign ruling classes. Foreign, particularly American, exploitation has allied itself, if not always ideologically at any rate factually, with the semi-feudal interests controlling the Latin American nations.

With the exception of Cuba, the combined powers of the American and Latin American ruling classes have until now proved capable of maintaining the basic social relationships in the Latin American nations despite a series of social upheavals. The Mexican Revolution was halted midway and turned into an instrument of private capital formation. However, new social movements confront the Mexican government with fresh demands for the completion of the interrupted nationalization process. The social restiveness in the Latin American nations forces their governments, at times, to assume greater controls over the national economy. Mexico has been joined by Bolivia and Brazil in the division of some large estates and the nationalization of natural resources and selected industries. The chronic instability of most of the Latin American countries, and the increasing misery at the base of this instability, induced the United States to offer more "aid" within the framework of a new Latin American "Alliance for Progress." But this "progress" is still envisioned in terms of the market economy and private capital accumulation.

Unavoidable government interventions in the economic activities of these nations modify their capital development to such an extent that these "developing" nations may be considered "developing mixed economies." Whereas in the developed nations the "mixed economy" feeds on the capacity of private enterprise to produce more than it can capitalize, in the less-developed nations the "mixed economy" must create the conditions of capital development. Agricultural output must rise but less must be consumed in order to gain investment capital. To bring consumption down in spite of the increased economic activity there must be monetary inflation. And thus the more and the harder people work the less they are rewarded. It is this preference of inflation to other methods of capital formation which gives these "mixed economies" their "Keynesian" connotation. But being already near starvation levels, this method will not suffice to bring forth the capital necessary to turn the underdeveloped into competitive industrial economies. Rather, it will increase social unrest and bring forth social movements for more efficient and less horrible ways of overcoming their present economic impasse.

Partly by choice and partly by necessity, private enterprise and government control operate simultaneously in each capitalist country and also as competing social systems in the world at large. Side by side there exist, then, the most ruthless general competition, the subordination of private to national competition (or *vice versa*), and the subordination of national competition to supra-national requirements intended to serve national ends and therewith the ends of private capital formation. This situation makes consistency and persistence in any and every form of competition and cooperation impossible; and the various and changing attempts at organization and collaboration which result from it only increase the anarchic character of capital production. Nationalism as imperialism, and nationalism in opposition to imperialism, lead to an always greater international economic disintegration. And this at a time when world conditions and physical production processes make the satisfaction of the most immediate needs of the world's population dependent on the closest economic integration.

Instead of working for such integration, industrial countries increase their agricultural production to reach a high degree of self-sufficiency in expectation of war, or merely to satisfy their own agricultural producers as a measure of "welfare economics." They protect both their agricultural and their industrial markets from all possible competitors with a great variety of tariffs and import restrictions. While increasing their agricultural surpluses, they hinder the primary producers to diversify their production, thus forcing them to contract their agricultural production which is already insufficient to feed their populations. The great mass of the world's population stays hungry, while surpluses are piled up in nations unable to sell them and unwilling to give them away. These people are supposed to starve themselves still further so as to raise the capital which will make their work more productive, while industrial labor in the developed nations is idle, or producing waste, instead of producing for world-wide use. These irrational economic contradictions manifest themselves in political tension and the diversion of an always greater part of world production into arms production. The nation-state, in its government-controlled or government-owned avatar, proves to be no less irrational a social form than private capital production on a supposedly free world market. The difficulties of capital accumulation in both the developed and underdeveloped nations defy not only market but also national solutions.

CHAPTER XIX

THE IMPERIALIST IMPERATIVE

Marx's model of capital accumulation represents a closed homogenous system in which the rising organic composition of capital results in a fall of the rate of profit and therewith in the decline of capital expansion whenever the conditions of production do not allow for a sufficient rise in the rate of exploitation. But capitalism is not a closed system: it is able to slacken the rising organic composition of capital through its outward extension and to better its rentability through importation of profits from abroad. It is the value-expansion of the existing centralized capital, however, which determines the size as well as the character of the world market, and which limits the capitalization of underdeveloped nations to serve the specific profit needs of the dominating capitals. Given this world market, it is no longer posssible for the underdeveloped part of the world to further its own capitalization independently of the profit requirements of the highly-developed capitalist nations.

The world as a whole is obviously short of capital and surplus-value. The overproduction of capital relative to its profitability in one part of the world confronts undercapitalization in another part. Considering capitalism as a world system it is indeed a miserable system of social production. For capitalism as a whole, of course, the organic composition of capital is not high enough to reduce the rate of profit below its accumulation needs. But due to the centralization and monopolization of capital, the inherent contradictions of capital production erect barriers to its expansion long before the abstract borders of Marx's theory of capitalist development find some kind of approximation in reality.

Capitalism has ceased to be a socially progressive system of production and has become —notwithstanding all superficial appearances to the contrary — a regressive and destructive one. It has led to the division of the world into a few highly-industrialized countries and a large number of nations unable to lift themselves out of a state of increasing misery. Yet the destinies of all nations are inextricably intertwined; it is the world situation which finally determines the future of any and every nation. Prospects for even the most "prosperous" nations must be considered in the light of existing world conditions; seen from this perspective, they are indeed bleak. No longer able to extract out of their own working population quantities of surplus-value which assure an accelerated profitable private capital expansion, the dominating capitalist powers find that the sources of additional profits in the underdeveloped parts of the world are also drying up. To keep on exploiting the backward areas will slowly destroy their exploitability. But not to exploit them means to reduce even further the already insufficient profitability of capital. The great capitalist nations will thus try to increase rather than relax their exploitation in the hope that their own expansion will be the vehicle for, or yield as a by-product, the development of the capital-poor nations. Western policy still rests on a deep faith in the profit-creating powers of competitive capital accumulation — a faith sustained by the recently-experienced period of government-induced "prosperity." It is still competition on the widest scale — the world market — to which expansion is oriented, even though on the world-scale, and in each nation separately, the market-economy seems irretrievably lost.

The big corporations in the industrial nations, which dominate the capitalist economies, can no longer function within the national framework; they have become and must remain multinational corporations. "Any company of importance that wants to survive has to be international and multinational," it is said, "for companies with world-wide operations may find it easier than purely national companies to reduce costs by moving raw-materials, production and distribution facilities, and manpower in conformance with optimization objectives."[1] Big corporations such as Unilever and IBM, for example, have interests in nearly every country in the world; IBM, specifically, operates in one hundred nations and maintains

1   G. A. Steiner, *Multinational Corporate Planning*, New York, 1966, p. 316.

fifteen manufacturing plants in thirteen countries. "Nearly 3,000 American firms have foreign subsidiaries and their sales are double what the United States exports. These American-based corporations that operate on a multinational basis conduct manufacturing enterprises abroad, extract and process natural resources, provide services, and market the resulting goods and services on an international scale."[2] The growth of multinational corporations is an international phenomenon but because of America's dominant position in world economy it is most pronounced in the United States. The latter's interests in multinational corporations is revealed in the value of her direct investments abroad. "These increased from $11.7 billion in 1950 to $31.1 billion in 1962. In the manufacturing category alone, the increase was from $3.8 billion to $13.2 billion." Since World War II, "every President, every Congress, and numerous public and lay leaders of national and international thought have emphasized the importance to national interest of the role of private companies operating on a multinational base. From 1950 through 1962, $29 billion was received in earnings, interest payments, management fees, and royalties from direct investments abroad. This compares with the $16 billion capital outflow from the United States for direct investments abroad in the same time."[3]

Whether or not the world structure of capitalism is such as to preclude profitable capital expansion on a world-wide scale, every capitalist enterprise, and every capitalist nation, tries to expand its own capital — at the expense of other enterprises and of other nations if necessary. The elimination of competition and the international centralization of capital, while perhaps not benefiting the capitalist world as a whole, will still benefit the advancing capitals and the stronger nations. The Canadian economy, for instance, has long been regarded as an extension of the American economy. "By 1963, foreign residents, mostly Americans, controlled 60 per cent of Canadian manufacturing, 74 per cent of her petroleum and natural gas industry and 57 per cent of mining and smelting. . . Control in the food-canning industry rose to 90 per cent. . . Some business observers attribute the continuing take-over trend to the growing internationalization of business. For Canada, however, internationalization means mostly Americanization, and this is

2 H. H. Fowler, *National Interests and Multinational Business,* in Multinational Planning, p. 123.
3 *Ibid.,* p. 124.

often regretted."[4] Opposition to actual and potential foreign domination of various industries becomes increasingly more vocal in the European nations. Both of the European trading blocs tend toward a continental allocation of capital resources and the curtailment of American investments in European industry; but the existence of these blocs spurs greater investments on the part of American corporations in order to get inside their tariff walls. Still, the developed capitalist nations comprise only the smaller part of the world. Their future depends not so much on an intensified competition within their own ranks as on gaining a broader base of capital expansion.

The big corporation must produce for, and profitably sell within, an expanding international market. If its profits and production on the world market do not expand, the corporation will face stagnation within its national market; and this will increase the need to maintain social stability through government-induced production. In other words, private capital production must be accentuated abroad to arrest its internal decline. A larger part of the world must be capitalized to accomodate the expansion needs of the big corporations. (This is the reason why development, or growth, once reserved for Marxian theory, has now become the predominant issue of bourgeois economy.) But it must be a development conducive to private enterprise and its accumulation requirements, that is, a development which subordinates the developing nations to the rules of the capitalist world market.

The "mixed" character of the capitalist market economies obliterates an earlier distinction between government and capital. Government is no longer merely the political arm of the capitalist class. Its economic interests are so intertwined with those of the capitalist class that government-policy and corporation-policy are one and the same. The need for external expansion of capital in order to halt its internal contraction takes on the form of an aggressive imperialism and of imperialistic competition. But this imperialism differs from the imperialism and colonialism of *laissez-faire* capitalism because capital competes for more than just raw-material sources, privileged markets, and capital exports; it also fights for its very life as a private-property system against new forms of capital pro-

4 The *New York Times,* February 11, 1966.

duction which are no longer subject to economic value relations and the competitive market mechanism.

For Keynes, imperialism and war certainly affected the economy but were not an integral part of capitalism. For Marx, structural changes in capitalism, national as well as international, imply competition, crises, imperialism and war. The Second World War was quite obviously connected with the long depression period preceding it, and the current world-wide trend of supplementing economic force with political-military means attests to the imperialist nature of modern capital competition. Although the miseries of war may not be regarded as the exclusive property of capitalism, their origins and their results are necessarily connected with the competitive character of international capital expansion.

Imperialism may be described in political terms even though it finds its material basis in the requirements of capital accumulation. The current imperialist activities find their direct cause in the shifts of power relations brought about by World War II. At first sight, these shifts could lead only to a new war or to the acceptance of a world divided into two different systems of capital production, with separate spheres of interest dominated by the two strongest military powers, Russia and the United States. The second possibility seemed, however, "unacceptable" to the Western powers, even though it has in some manner constituted Western post-war policies. It was less obnoxious to Russia, confident as she was of her ability to attain security, and possibly supremacy, without the intervention of a third world war. Aside from such "preferences," however, and despite various adventures of the "cold war" and even the Korean war, neither the East nor the West showed any real inclination to provoke a major war. Though often on the "brink" of war, both sides have thus far always retreated in time, leaving things more or less as they were.

The West European nations, occupied with their recovery and with futile attempts to defend their foreign possessions, were not in a position to act upon the "long-run" needs of Western capitalism. The United States, emerging from the war as the strongest power, had to consolidate the Western world as a precondition for resuming effective international power politics. As it turned out, there was no really urgent need to deal with further Russian expansion or to deprive Russia of those spoils of war which the West

— though with some unrealistic reservations — had agreed to allow her. Russia, too, weakened by the destruction and exertion of war, needed time to recover and consolidate her gains. The general inability to act upon the new problems posed by the post-war world expressed itself in the cold-war *status quo*.

Everything else was based on hope — either that "historical development" would come to the aid of the East, or that "human nature" would reassert itself and restore the conditions of Western capitalism in the world at large. Both the East and the West have looked forward to a cumulative growth of the internal contradictions besetting each power bloc. The fact that Russia's satellites are "captive people" and for that reason are a steady source of trouble to their new masters, and the possibility of arising differences of interest between Russia and China bolstered Western expectations of a possible disintegration of the Eastern power bloc. As soon as the expansion of the Eastern bloc was checked, whatever economic and political development went on in the world would by sheer necessity gravitate to the stronger power center. Whatever the merits of such expectations, they turned America's foreign policy into a continuous postponement of decisive political actions while awaiting a more favorable future.

Stalinist Russia's policy, too, was permeated by the recurrent hope that peace would prevail despite, and because of, the cold war. Stalin saw the capitalist world in nineteenth-century terms: to him, capitalist development was a crisis-ridden competitive process, setting nation against nation, and transforming economic rivalries into imperialistic wars. He felt, however, that for some time to come, the West was not ready to wage a new war against Russia. Western Europe was quite defenseless and the effects of the Chinese Revolution upon the whole of Asia put America at a strategic disadvantage despite her military might and superior productive power. This conviction was made apparent in the challenge of the Berlin blockade, in Russia's ruthless policy toward her satellites, in the covert support given to national liberation movements, and finally in the major test that the Korean war provided.

By this time, however, the situation had already changed due to the partial recovery of Western Europe, the ebbing of the post-war revolutionary wave in Asia, and, last but not least, the altered character of Western capitalism itself. The immediate post-war situation could well suggest the recurrence of those very conditions that emerged out of World War I — a semi-permanent crisis for some countries and a general sharpening of international competition. The Potsdam agreements promised to realize what the Versailles Treaty of 1919 had failed to do, and the destruction of German capitalism was bound to weaken the whole of Western Europe and produce new economic and political frictions within Western capitalism. Yet something different happened. Although national interests still dominated the policies of all capitalist countries, it was soon realized that only international power politics could safeguard those national interests, and that this required economic as well as political collaboration. This implied that economic policy remained the responsibility of governments, the permanent transformation of capitalism into government-manipulated capitalism, and the emergence of some degree of international cooperation affecting the whole of Western capitalism.

The Korean compromise clearly indicated that though the West was still not willing or ready to launch another world war, it was determined not to lose further ground to the Eastern bloc. In Geneva, in 1954, the Korean compromise was repeated in the Southeast Asia compromise. The Southeast Asia "liberation move-"Geneva spirit" remained purely spiritual, however, even though ment" came to a temporary halt. Whatever else comprised the the Russians pressed for a "general solution" of East-West differences in the direction of clearly demarcated and respected spheres of interest and free-for-all economic competition in the as yet uncommitted parts of the world. Russia's readiness for compromise betrayed the post-Stalinist regime's fear of war and its real concern over the restiveness of satellite nations as well as over conditions in Russia proper. Prevention of war, the new Russian leaders realized, required more than the principle of Churchill's dictum, "peace by mutual terror." It demanded not only that Russia and the United States come to terms, but that they mutually control the activities of other nations which might lead them inadvertently into general war.

The apparent trend towards the peaceful solution of imperialistic antagonisms in the wake of the Geneva Conference came to nothing. The world is simply beset by too many problems and particularistic interests, and neither Russia nor the United States has the degree of control over other nations which could secure peace under all circumstances. Because change and development go on relentlessly and affect the fortunes of the great powers, their own possible desire for peace remains a temporary inclination. The erosion of Western colonialism led to many national-revolutionary movements which could not be controlled by either the West or the East. China, at any rate, could not be subjugated to Russian rule — relations between China and Russia gave the lie to Western propaganda which depicted China as a "colony" of Russia.

The ceaseless erosion of Western influence in underdeveloped areas must be arrested. Yet, short of military suppression, this can be done only by assisting a development detrimental to the economies of the Western world. In the American view, the end of Western colonial domination created a "power-vacuum" in certain regions of the world, which the East will fill if the West does not. What is meant by "vacuum" here refers to the fact that hitherto-controlled regions have been freed: the former colonies' possession of "national self-determination" leaves them open to internal and external "communist aggression;" so the West must step in and guarantee their "independence." In other words, "national self-determination" cannot include a free choice of social systems and allies, although it may include preferences with respect to "protecting" Western powers. America's pose as an "anti-colonial" power in this special sense was not a deliberate policy to weaken her Western allies — though in fact it did so — but was adopted in the belief that it would strengthen the "free world" as a whole. To benefit the "free world," the colonial powers were supposed to sacrifice special political-administrative interests, and national-revolutionary movements were to be induced to stay within the confines of Western capitalism. That any policy in the interest of the "whole" of Western capitalism benefits America especially was, after all, not the fault of the United States but is merely a consequence of international capital development.

America's all-embracing view, which judges the needs of the world by the needs of American capitalism, includes, of course, numerous narrower special interests. American competition tends, or at any rate attempts, to drive out weaker capital entities wherever possible; thus there is a degree of truth in the assertion that by opposing the colonialism of other nations, America merely fosters her own. American foreign policy is not, however, exclusively determined by such narrow special interests; there is also the factor of her justified fear that continuous shrinking of the "free world" will come to affect the American economy itself and hasten the destruction of its private-enterprise nature. It does not make much difference, then, whether the foreign holdings that have to be protected, and the foreign markets that have to be kept open, are of great or small importance; the point is to prevent, and if possible to "roll back," any social movement or nation, which intends, or might intend, to restrict or abolish private-enterprise capitalism.

Until recently, national-revolutionary movements have tended to gravitate to Russia to find protection and support. Now it is China, which, by its very existence, threatens to eliminate Western capitalism's shaky foothold in Asia by calling forth new national-revolutionary movements that might preempt the present and future exploitation of Asian nations by Western capital. It is more China's "bolshevism" than her "nationalism" which agitates America so greatly, even though it is the combination of the two which proves deadly to private enterprise.

Quite independent of the meaning of these terms, the world-wide defense of "freedom" and "democracy" expresses America's chauvinism at home and her imperialism abroad. Bound to and taking pleasure in the realm of their own existence, America's ruling class cannot tolerate an expanding social system different from its own. It is no consolation that business may be carried on with state-capitalist no less than private-enterprise systems, for in the absence of private capital abroad, they see the harbinger of their own possible obsolescence at home. The ruling class' hatred of state-capitalist systems, which, rightly from their point of view, they equate with "communism," is genuine: the purely ideological expression of this hate does not alter the fact that it stems from the very material advantages that fall to the privileged within the private-enterprise system. It is not an empty, superstitious hate, but rather a capitalist class-reaction to all social change that could be detrimental to private capital.

Competition and national antagonisms lead to wars between capitalist nations. In a sense, war between state-capitalist and private-enterprise systems is also a form of international capital competition. But with this difference, that it involves not only economic interests of nationally-organized capital groups but also the defense, or destruction, of different social structures. A "civil-war" element enters the imperialist rivalries, even if this type of "civil-war" is carried on not within but between nations. "Anti-communism" means opposition to any and all movements and aspirations that threaten either the existence or the future of private capital.

To keep the world open to capitalist exploitation has been America's general policy since 1945. It springs directly from the expansion requirements of private capital and, short of the aboli-tion of the market system, cannot be changed. Particular interests may be lost, as for instance the investments and business of Cuba, and similar interests may be preserved, as by the occupation of the Dominican Republic and the overthrow of governments in Guate-mala and Iran. But the general policy must be directed toward extending America's role in world economy. Thus it must seek to prevent the rise of state-capitalist systems in regions mapped out for capitalist exploitation.

The imperialist imperative of capital expansion is often denied; European colonialism is ended and, it is said, imperialism no longer pays. Indeed, the time seems past when a few regiments could control hundreds of millions of people, and the returns from col-onial rule are dwindling while the costs of empire are rising. The "white man's burden" has become an actual burden instead of a blessing. Although individuals and corporations still enrich them-selves enormously, from an overall point of view colonialism pays less and less; so that, in part, the principle of profitability itself suggests a new approach to imperial rule. Imperialism by indirec-tion appears more promising than nineteenth-century colonialism. In view of the national-revolutionary movements, indirect control may be superior to direct control in the same way that the wage-system proved superior to slave-labor. Just as monopoly over the means of production is largely sufficient, by itself, to control the working class, so monopolistic control over the destiny of world economy may be enough to determine the behavior of nations subjected to it. In either case, of course, political-military force stands ready to ensure the workings of the indirect methods of control; and while the latter do work they create the illusion of general consent.

Although thus far Western capitalism has done very little to promote industrialization in the underdeveloped parts of the world, it is not opposed to such a development wherever it might prove profitable. It does not prefer the exploitation of its own laboring population to that of other nations; quite the contrary. There exists, then, an apparent contradiction between the need to keep the world open for free enterprise and the refusal of free enterprise to avail itself of its opportunities. But this contradiction merely reflects the contradiction of capital production itself. It is not different from the contradiction that bursts into the open with any capitalist crisis — namely, that production comes to a halt in spite of the fact that the needs of the vast mass of the population are far from being satisfied. Production is slowed down not because there is too much of it but because it has become unprofitable. Still, it will not enter the minds of the capitalists that their inability to increase production is reason enough to abdicate in favor of a different social system capable of coordinating social production to actual social needs. Nor will it enter their minds that because they have not industrialized the world and are, apparently, incapable of doing so, they should leave the world to others who presumably can do so by employing principles of social production different from those of private capital. Just as they defend their control in each particular country irrespective of their own performance, so will they defend it in the world at large.

As there is no chance of breaking the capital monopoly of the long-established capitalist powers by way of market competition, the industrialization of underdeveloped nations must proceed in opposition to the capitalist world market relations, on a nationally-organized, not a free-enterprise, basis. This possibility, however, is open only to larger countries, such as Russia and China, where some degree of "self-sufficiency" is possible. In most underdeveloped countries "national independence" does not alter their dependence on the developed capitalist nations, unless opportunities arise for aligning their economies with those of the large-scale state-capitalist systems. Having already been "integrated" into the capitalist world market, and being incapable of a self-sustaining existence, they remain, as so-called "third world" countries, objects of foreign exploitation and imperialist competition.

The national-revolutionary exertions of such countries are dis-

sipated in internal power struggles instead of being utilized in an
actual reorganization of their socio-economic structures. They gain
a measure of political control without losing their economic dependence upon the imperialist powers. "Even the militantly socialist
leaderships," it has been noted, "are very careful not to jeopardize
their economic survival by nationalizing foreign enterprise, lest
they kill the goose that lays the golden eggs . . . The usual course
for the socialist governments has been the kind of tactic adopted
in Ghana, where the rate of company tax was stiffened, wage-increases of 20 per cent were insisted on, plus an increased investment locally of 60 per cent of net profits after tax. Since this left
the mining companies still with dividend rates of 45 per cent, the
prospect did not terrify them. The companies now scrupulously
steer clear of any suggestion of direct interference in the national
economy, and are rapidly 'indigenizing' their staffs. But the 'colonial' character of the economy remains."[5]

However, the continued indirect economic domination of the
less-developed nations by Western capital offers no solution for the
actual needs of the vast mass of their populations, nor will it solve
the basic problem of profit production for Western capital. All
that it may do is to sustain somewhat longer the disintegrating
capitalist world economy. This will require the brutal suppression
of all resentment caused by growing and unrelieved social misery,
It is quite safe to predict that at least in the underdeveloped part
of the world the prevailing misery will lead to ever new rebellions
against the dominating foreign powers and their native collabor-
ators whether they belong to the traditional ruling classes or to
new ruling classes tossed up by the anti-colonial movements.

The colonialism of old is over, it is true. But it has been replaced by a system of neo-colonialism, in which nations that are
nominally independent continue to be exploited by foreign capital.
Within this setting, the contest between the state-capitalist and
private-enterprise systems for an increasing share of world production and trade necessarily concerns itself with the future of the as
yet "uncommitted" nations of the "third world." If these nations
should transform themselves into state-capitalist systems, they would
prevent a further penetration of private capital into their economies and get a measure of control over their trade relations which

5 P. Worsley, *The Third World*, London, 1964, p. 241.

would restrict or even exclude their exploitation by the capitalist nations. This would hamper the expansion of private capital and enlarge the "socialist world," leading to a more rapid general transformation of capitalism from its private-property to its state-organized form. Imperialism is thus not only an instrument of exploitation and aggrandizement; for the West, it is the only instrument with which to safeguard the future of private capital.

Like the old colonialism, neo-colonialism is practiced not in the interests of the imperialist nation as a nation but in the interests of its ruling class, and to the special benefit of that powerful segment of that class which operates internationally and co-determines foreign policy. "What is the real value of their Indian dominion to the British nation and people," Marx once asked; for "directly, that is in the shape of tribute, of surplus of Indian receipts over Indian expenditures, nothing whatever reaches the British Treasury. . . Such being the case, it is evident that the advantage of Great Britain from her Indian Empire must be limited to the profits and benefits which accrue to individual British subjects . . . Against all this a very large offset is to be made. The military and naval expenses paid out of the pockets of the people of England on Indian account have been constantly increasing with the extent of the Indian dominion . . . Add to this the career of endless conquest and perpetual aggression in which the English are involved by the possession of India, and it may well be doubted whether, on the whole, this dominion does not threaten to cost quite as much as it can ever be expected to come to."[6] The fact that the costs of empire became far greater than the returns was one reason that direct subjugation was replaced by neo-colonialism.

Although the returns from colonialism accrue to individuals while its costs are carried by all taxpayers, the difference between costs and returns finds a limit in the limitations of subsidization by way of taxation. Until these limits are reached, the fact that the income from colonial exploitation may be less than the national expense involved, far from deterring colonial activities, will rather spur them on in the expectation of a final reversal of the imbalance. It is not just to safeguard the returns of special interests, for instance, that the American government accepts the so much larger

6 K. Marx, "British Incomes in India," in *On Colonialism*, Moscow, pp. 157-161.

costs of its wide-spread foreign interventions. It pays the latter in the hope of increasing the former. This might be, and most probably is, a hopeless task, so that the whole imperialistic effort may accomplish nothing more than safeguarding the returns of special interests, if even that. But the probability of such negative results does not free the capitalist nations from the compulsive need to operate on an international scale.

Even an isolationist, non-imperialistic America would be forced to subsidize its dominant capital groups by way of government purchases, if only to avoid the depression conditions of capital stagnation. These subsidies have to come out of total production; the "returns" of subsidized capital imply the social "costs" of waste-production. This is precisely the dilemma which capitalism tries to overcome by external expansion. Imperialism projects the national dilemma to the international scene. But there is a difference. If waste-production in the form of expenditures for imperialistic purposes should result in the creation of conditions for an accelerated private capital expansion, the future "returns" may well exceed the present "costs." In that case, the production of waste would have turned out to be the instrument for the production of capital, the necessary expense of an increased exploitation, as has been true for all previous imperialistic activity. Whereas waste-production on a national scale merely increases the difficulties of capital expansion of which it is itself an expression, waste-production by way of war might bring about structural changes of world economy and shifts of political power relations conducive to a new period of capital expansion for the victorious capitalist powers.

Such cynical notions rest on the illusion that capitalism in general, and American capitalism in particular, has no historical boundaries. But even if they recognize the trend towards the progressive dissolution of the market system, capitalists can only act as if the trend was non-existent, or could be halted and reversed. Being in fact determined by the trend, their activities become increasingly imperialistic, in order to contain and, if possible, to destroy socioeconomic systems different from their own. The more mixed their own economies become, the more urgent becomes the need to arrest the spread of "nationalization" and "socialization" within the world economy, not only to gain more control over it but also to limit government-induced production in their own countries. It is for this reason that the mixed economy remains geared to war and mobilization for war; indeed, the mixed economy is nothing other than the capitalist economy as a semi-permanent war-economy. What during the depression appeared at first as a possible solution to the economic problems of the market system, now displays itself as an added cause of capitalist imperialism.

However, the consequences of war are bound up with the forces of production. These forces now make possible the destruction of most of the world and its population, which seems to preclude the utilization of war for purposes of capital accumulation. Shortly after World War II, it was still possible to look upon war as a "new industry" capable of solving capitalist problems, including that of pecuniary profits. "The destruction of the European economy," it was said, "has solved the problem of effective demand for the American economy. During the depression we got nowhere. The great lack was the absence of effective demand. Lately, these demands have been created out of sheer necessity, and . . . we are in a dawn of the greatest industrial era this country ever had."[7] This kind of optimism cannot prevail in view of the destructiveness of modern warfare which may well include the use of atomic weapons.

However, it is not possible to proceed rationally in an irrational world. The recognition that war can no longer solve the problems that harass the capitalist world does not change a behavior pattern which may, at any time, issue into war. No capitalist desired the losses of depression, yet the relentless competition for capital nonetheless led into crisis and depression; in other words, "normal" behavior caused the "abnormality" of the crisis. It is no different with regard to war. The relentless drive to gain or to retain political and economic dominance is the outcome and sum total of all the asocial behavior that characterizes social life under capitalism. The recognition that war may be suicide, which is by no means unanimous, does not affect the drift towards a new world war. Those who make political decisions are no less trapped in this *cul-de-sac* than are the emasculated and indifferent masses. Simply by making the "right" decisions, as determined by the specific

7 Proceedings of a Conference sponsored by the Economic and Business Foundation. New Wilmington, Pennsylvania, December 20, 1948, p. 18.

needs of their nations and the security of their social structures, they may destroy themselves and a large part of the world. Foreign policy in the post-war world has been essentially nothing but preparation for war, and only the perspective of war made possible that measure of collaboration which the Western alliances manifested. Aside from this, there has been no "policy" at all, just that impenetrable amalgam of contradictory actions and reactions by which uncounted special interests try to assert or defend themselves. America's post-war policy consists of the Truman Doctrine, the Marshall Plan, the North Atlantic Treaty Organization, the Korean War, the Caracas declaration, the Southeast Asia collective defense treaty, the mutual treaty with Taiwan, the Bagdad Pact and the Eisenhower Doctrine — a foreign policy made consistent by the actuality or expectancy of war.

The defense of Western capitalism is generally expressed in political-ideological terms. "Communist aggression" is fought not to make money — at any rate not immediately — but to defend "freedom" even where it does not exist — "freedom" being presumably understood in terms of democratic institutions such as prevail in the United States and Western Europe. The outcome of World War II assured a rapidly developing American interest in the nations of Southeast Asia. The collapse of Nationalist China only gave it greater urgency. "Because of its ideology," it was said by an American policy-maker, "Communist China is a model, so to say, of domestic totalitarianism, in complete contrast to the sort of development that we believe would foster the true welfare of these countries." Although "we seek no preferred economic position in this area . . . our policy seeks to deal with the central aggressive Communist power and its satellites by preventing their expansion as the first and essential step towards whatever relationship may later evolve."[8] China must be contained; that is, the nations of Asia and Southeast Asia must be prevented from leaving the Western fold.

Given the weak position of the rising native bourgeoisie, it is clear that the political structures of emerging nominally-democratic nations are as authoritarian as they are in the nominally-communist nations. Both "communism" and "democracy" are here purely

8 W. P. Bundy, "The United States and Asia," in *China and the Peace of Asia*, Ed. by A. Buchan, London, 1965, pp. 17-21.

ideological terms, indicating no more than two different developmental tendencies — the one toward state-capitalism and away from
Western domination, the other towards a market economy to be
kept in the neo-colonial structure of Western capitalism. To make
the second course prevail requires at times the physical presence of
American military power and the return to old-style colonialism.
The war in Southeast Asia, according to Secretary of State Dean
Rusk, not only is a moral imperative but also is necessitated by
national interests. "Within the next decade or two," he has said,
"there will be a billion Chinese on the mainland, armed with
nuclear weapons, with no certainty about what their attitude toward the rest of Asia will be. Now from a strategic point of view,
it is not very attractive to think of the world cut in two by Asian
Communism, reaching out through Southeast Asia and Indonesia,
which we know has been their objective; and that these hundreds
of millions of people in the free nations of Asia should be under
the deadly and constant pressure of the authorities in Peking, so
that their future is circumscribed by fear. Now these are vitally
important matters to us, who are a Pacific and an Atlantic power.
After all, World War II hit us from the Pacific, and Asia is where
two-thirds of the world's people live. So we have a tremendous
stake in the ability of the free nations of Asia to live in peace; and
to turn the interests of people in mainland China to the pragmatic
requirements of their own people, and away from the doctrinaire
and ideological adventurism."[9] However, America is not only a
Pacific but also a capitalist power and it is as such that she desires a
"peaceful" capitalist Asia — because America cannot do what she
suggests the Chinese should do, namely concentrate upon "the
pragmatic requirements of her own people."

9 The *New York Times*, October 13, 1967.

CHAPTER XX

STATE-CAPITALISM AND
THE MIXED ECONOMY

While Marx's theory of accumulation covers the mixed economy, it seems to lose its validity for the completely-controlled capitalist economy, i.e., state-capitalism or state-socialism as represented by the so-called communist societies of the Eastern power bloc, where government decisions and economic planning determine production, distribution and development. These societies are not the product of a slow transformation from a "mixed" to a state-directed economy but are the direct outcome of war and revolution. In practice, they have continued and extended the state-directed wartime economy; theoretically, they regard their activity as the realization of Marxian socialism. This is somewhat plausible because they adhere to an "orthodox" interpretation of Marxism which sees in private property relations the main, or only, condition of exploitation. Actually, the conditions which Marx expected to result in the "expropriation of capital" did not even exist in the industrially underdeveloped nations engaged in social revolution. Their leaders were convinced, however, that total state control over all of the economy would bring about a more rapid capital development than would be possible under competitive market relations, and that this more rapid development under the auspices of socialist governments would enable a slow transition to socialism.

The development of capital production in the name of "socialism" or "communism" is a paradox too farfetched to have entered Marx's mind. Yet from the vantage point of the present it is not strange at all. Although constructed with an eye on England which, at that time, represented capitalism in its most advanced and purest form, Marx's model of capital production represented neither the national nor the world economy but was an imaginary system of basic capital-labor relationships. The actual development of capitalism brought with it a variety of more-or-less developed capitalist nations, colonization, and imperialism. Yet the world economy was inextricably interconnected with, and dependent upon, capital expansion in the dominating capitalist nations. In underdeveloped countries revolutionary theory had to relate itself not only to still-existing pre-capitalist conditions but also to the overriding capital-labor relations that dominated world economy. As there was no way to develop new independent national economies except in opposition to the monopolistic powers and their fetishistic capital expansion, the ruling capitalist ideology could not serve national-revolutionary needs in backward countries, the less so as their own pre-capitalist ruling classes secured their existence in close collaboration with the imperialist powers. Even though it could serve no more than national capital development, the revolutionary ideology had to be an anti-capitalist ideology. And as the carriers of this ideology operated in the twentieth and not in the eighteenth century, their concept of progress by way of capital production was no longer associated with private enterprise and general competition but with the highly concentrated mixed or state-controlled economy of modern capitalism. Able only to reach those social conditions that Marxian socialism intended to eliminate, they could see themselves as "Marxists" by assuming an engagement in two revolutions at once — the "bourgeois" revolution which created the capital-labor relations of modern industry, and the "socialist" revolution, which prevented the determination and utilization of this development by private capital.

Though carried out in the name of Marx, the state-capitalist, or state-socialist, revolutions would be better described as "Keynesian revolutions." What is usually designated as the "Keynesian revolution" is Keynes' recognition and acceptance of the fact of intensive state interventions in the economy. It is only because of Keynes' preoccupation with "mature" capitalism that the application of his theory has a reformatory rather than a revolutionary connotation. But as a measure of reform, stopping at the "mixed economy," it is self-defeating, for it slows up but does not prevent the destruction of the private enterprise system. Arising at the same time as the mixed economy, the state-capitalist system may be regarded as Keynesianism in its most consistent and most developed form. It is not a mixed economy in the limited Keynesian sense of safeguarding private capital by way of government controls. But it is a mixed economy in the projected wider sense of a "comprehensive socialization of investments," geared to the promise of alleviating the prevailing "inequitable distribution of wealth and income" by leaving it to the "common will, embodied in the policy of the State," to determine "how far it is safe to stimulate the average propensity to consume" in a full-employment, crisis-free economy. Moreover, state-capitalism remains a "mixed economy" by being part of a world economy still largely determined by private profit production, and by virtue of the fact that it is marked by all the antagonisms that characterize private capital production except that of private profit appropriation.

Whereas the mixed economy in the narrow Keynesian sense is limited by the nature of private profit production, in its wider sense — as a complete state-capitalist system — it is limited by international capital competition. In theory, state-capitalism should allow for a nationally-planned determination of both the volume and the direction of production. The kind of "planning" actually undertaken is, however, determined by the needs of capital production within a setting of international capital and power competition. The possible advantages of complete government control can be only partly enjoyed and the fate of the state-capitalist economy remains bound to the fate of capitalism in general. Its economic expansion is not of the type which characterized the rise of capitalism but of the type characteristic of its decline. "Overproduction" in the form of waste-production in a relentless power competition now accompanies the early stages of capital formation and even that of "primitive accumulation." As in the capitalism of old, the accumulation of capital, not the real needs of the producers, determines the direction of production.

As capital formation is a concern of government in the mixed as well as in the state-capitalist system, what, in the Keynesian view, divides "capitalism" from "socialism" is merely the degree of government control. But as capitalism, according to Keynes, has the "tendency to socialize itself," socialism is now defined as a fully "socialized capitalism." In this sense state-capitalism represents "socialism" and is generally recognized as such by spokesmen of the "Marxist" and "anti-Marxist" camps. The dissolution of the private property system through capital concentration in corporations, some of which "are units which can be thought of only in somewhat the way we have heretofore thought of nations,"[1] changed the capitalist economy into "something which differs from the Russian or socialist system mainly in its philosophical content."[2] Contrariwise, it can also be argued that if the word *capitalism* is still used for the economies of the Western world, it "ought not be used to describe only the private ownership of capital; it ought to describe any community which believes in steadily increasing its wealth-creating capacity by a constant investment of resources in productive capital. So defined, there is nothing controversial about capitalism, since the leading examples in today's world of progress-by-capital are the United States and the Soviet Union."[3]

Already during the Great Depression, President Roosevelt realized "that what we are doing in the United States are some of the things that are being done in Russia and even some of the things that are being done under Hitler in Germany. But we are doing them in an orderly way."[4] Because of the affinity of the mixed to the state-capitalist economy, their actual enmity is now largely related to "philosophical" differences that are supposed to determine their political institutions but not their socio-economic structure. To be sure, "orthodox Marxism" maintains that the mixed economy is still the capitalism of old, just as "orthodox" bourgeois theory insists that the mixed economy is a camouflaged form of socialism. Generally, however, both the state-capitalist and mixed economies are recognized as economic systems adhering to the principle of progress by way of capital accumulation.

During the Great Depression, Keynes deviated from this principle and envisioned an early change of emphasis from investment to consumption in a society of capital abundance which would render superfluous the socialism conceived by its founders and adherents. It was precisely this deviation which distinguished his theory from the "orthodoxy" of his contemporaries. After the war, however, bourgeois theory insisted again on an accelerated rate of capital formation. "The extraordinary progress in Russia, with its

1 A. A. Berle, Jr., *Economic Power and the Free Society*, New York, 1957, p. 15.
2 *Ibid.*, p. 13.
3 *The Economist*, London, October 16, 1954.
4 *The Secret Diary of Harold L. Ickes. The First* 1000 *Days*, 1933-36, New York, 1953, p. 104.

distinct capitalistic tendency, has contributed to this general change of attitude and has greatly impressed the rest of the world. Never before has a people imposed upon themselves such severe restrictions in order to accumulate savings to be converted into real capital. It is now clearly realized that this immense display of [Russian] power is based on an abundant supply of capital created by an abnormal reduction in current consumption. Everywhere, people are demanding an economic policy which will lead to a progress similar to that in Russia."[5] While in the capitalistically less-developed nations this masochistic "demand" comes to the fore in various attempts to emulate the Russian example, in the highly-developed capitalist nations it takes the form of frantic attempts to reach Russia's higher rate of capital formation.

It also brought the question of "growth" to the forefront in a rather shamefaced return to political economy, which characterizes current bourgeois economic theory and practice in its new concern with the "macroscopic" aspects of the economy and its dynamics. However, contrary to Marxian theory, bourgeois theory holds that capitalism has proved to be reformable and is now securely on its way to solving all remaining social problems. There is, then, no need to see in the class struggle the motive force of social development, or even to approach still-existing social evils from a class position. These evils may be dealt with as general human, not specifically social, problems. (This point of view may, by the way, help explain the recent vogue of the socialist humanism of the young Marx, who considered the alienation of labor in capitalism a result of the "alienation of man from his true nature." This un-Marxian Marx well fits the welfare-state and can even be used in the ideological war against the ideological Marxism of the state-capitalist adversary.)

At present, moreover, there exists a tendency to view the developments of both the Soviet and Western systems as converging, pointing to the eventual establishment of a socio-economic structure as much removed from free enterprise principles as from those of the regimented economy. "The Soviet system does not remain the same," it is said, "and neither does the Western system. Both are moving and the movements are, generally, converging ones."[6]

5 G. Cassel, "The Role of Capital in the National Economy," *Skannaviska Banken*, Quarterly Review, January, 1945.

It is no longer true, the argument goes on, that "the systems are diametrically opposite," they have "already many features in common; elements from each can be combined, leading to new mixed systems."[7] But while both systems undoubtedly agree on the importance of capital formation, they disagree on the far more important question as to what particular social layers are to be its beneficiaries.

As regards this question, nationalized capital is the opposite of private capital, even though — as regards the producers — both forms of capital production thrive on exploitation. This common point encourages the empty hope for their eventual convergence; but they remain divided on all other issues. The nationalized economy is no longer a market economy, even though it may retain, or reintroduce, some quasi-market relations subordinated to over-all government control. Good or bad, it can actually plan its production and distribution, although the nature of the planning itself is co-determined by internal necessities, the world market, and the changing requirements of imperialist competition.

The strictness of the opposition between private and government ownership of means of production, between market-determined and consciously-regulated capitalist economy, seems to be contradicted by the existence of the "mixed economy" and its projection onto the international scene as a possible harmonious co-existence of different social systems. Yet an indefinite peaceful co-existence of state-capitalist and market-oriented economies is no less illusory than the indefinite existence of the "mixed economy" as a market-economy. In fact, it is precisely the advancing state-control in the private-enterprise economies which accentuates the conflict between the two different capitalistic systems. The wars between identical capitalist systems have made it clear that capital competition turns into imperialistic competition and that wars would occur even if there were not a single state-capitalist nation. The Second World War demonstrated the feasibility of temporary alliances between state-capitalist and "liberalistic" systems of capital production; but it demonstrated at the same time their fundamental irreconcilability, based not merely on newly-arising imperialistic interests but also on the difference between their social

6 J. Tinbergen, *Shaping the World Economy*, New York, 1962, p. 34.
7 *Ibid.*, p. 39.

structures. Far from bringing "traditional" capitalism closer to
state-controlled economies, the advent of the mixed economy inten-
sifies the enmity between the two, if only to curtail the expansion
of state-control in the market economies.

Capitalism will not turn itself into state-capitalism; and it would
be just as difficult to make a state-capitalist revolution as it is to
make a socialist revolution. Since a conscious organization of
social production presupposes the expropriation of private capital,
the transformation of the mixed economy into state-capitalism can
only be a revolutionary, not an evolutionary, process. In thought,
of course, it could be otherwise. In a "democracy," it is not entirely inconceivable that a government may come to power committed to the slow or rapid nationalization of industry. But such
a government would be a revolutionary, anti-capitalist government,
insofar as capitalism is identified with private ownership of the
means of production. In order to realize its program, it would be
forced to displace the market system by a planned system. As far
as the capitalists are concerned, this would be their death-warrant,
and it is not easily conceivable that they would accept it without
protest. Most likely, the complete nationalization of industry would
lead to civil war. It is fear of the social consequences of extensive
nationalization which prevents those ideologically committed to it
from actually attempting its realization.

Although there is no precedent, it is not inconceivable that a
state-capitalist system could be instituted with capitalist consent.
The mixed economy would then have been a step in this direction.
Keynesian reforms and political movements associated with them
may bring about a "social climate" in which the nationalization of
essential industries may appear inescapable, or even a good thing,
to a majority of capitalists. Arrangements may be made to safeguard property rights in terms of income while delegating control
of production to national agencies. Various "socialization" schemes,
based on capital-compensation, are aimed toward this end — to be
achieved within the legal structure of political democracy. Nationalization of industry, however, no matter how capital owners may
be compensated, amounts to their abdication as a ruling class;
unless, of course, they regain this position as members of government. Compensations are based on the value of the capital turned
over to the State. But accumulation now becomes the accumula-

tion of national capital and decisions over the employment of surplus-value become the decisions of government. Compensation comes out of surplus-value but cannot be productively accumulated to private account. The income it represents is secured by nothing but the good will of government, and the latter may at any time repudiate this claim to unearned income and complete the expropriation of private capital. Whether by consent or by revolution, the nationalization of capital ends the class rule of private capital.

The disciples of state-capitalism can if they wish have an easy time recognizing the inconsistencies and aimlessness of the neo-liberalism of the "mixed economies." They can point to the fact that capitalism is continuously changing in the direction of state-capitalism. For a long time, however, they were not willing to conceive of peaceful abdication by power groups in the interest of the general developmental trend. The Bolsheviks, for instance, never had the illusion of a frictionless side-by-side development of capitalism and "socialism," nourished by the war alliances between democratic and totalitarian nations and by the growing "similarity" between the Keynesian welfare-state and the state-capitalist system. They were convinced that the transformation of a partly-controlled social system of capital production into authoritarian state-capitalism involved social struggles, and if they envisioned a future world-unity, they saw it in the image of their own social system and thus defended the latter as much for the sake of "world-revolution" as for its own sake. Convinced of their progressive calling, theirs is an optimistic attitude and their policy is "dynamic" in contrast to the neo-liberal attempt to arrest the development at whatever particular point it happens to find itself.

Of course, like any social group, the Bolsheviks too can blow hot or cold. "Co-existence" allows for a variety of interpretations and so does the content and strategy of "Marxism." The latter has often been played down. This was the policy during the Second World War, for instance, to allow the Grand Alliance to discover a previously non-existent harmony between Russia and the anti-Nazi Western world — and this policy also suited Russia's internal needs, as she required at that time a return to traditional ideologies to support the war of "national liberation." On the other hand, with the end of the war and the extension of Russia's power the oppositional character of Bolshevik ideology and practice was stressed

once more and Russian "communism" was revived with the help
of Western "anti-communism." But at the time of Stalin's demise
Russia took the initiative in attempting to moderate the world
situation. In view of the precarious international situation and the
still more precarious conditions in Russia, Stalin's death was an
event capable of leading to great disturbances internally and
abroad. His successors sought a reduction of tensions in both areas
— in the first, by scrapping the internal course planned by Stalin;[8]
in the second, by an apparent willingness to open the "socialist"
market to capitalist trade.[9]

Concord between Russia and the Western world is, of course, the
hope of people horrified by the prospect of a new and more devas-
tating war, and of those who envision a future reconciliation between East and West on economic grounds. They recognize that
any rapport demands decisive changes in both the East and the
West and they try to help them along by developing the appropriate ideology. They tend to believe that the industrialization of

8   According to his last writings on the *Economic Problems of Socialism in
    the U.S.S.R.* (New York, 1952), Stalin thought that intra-capitalist rivalries
    would grant Russia time and opportunity to speed up her productive capa-
    city by way of a further strengthening of state control. In his eyes, Russian
    socialism was still weak because the government controlled collective-farm
    property only incompletely. "In order to raise collective-farm property to
    the level of public property," he wrote, "the surplus collective farm output
    must be excluded from the system of commodity-circulation and included
    in the system of products-exchange between the state-industry and the
    collective farms." (p. 70) This was an expression of dissatisfaction with the
    existing rate of farm labor exploitation. And, as it is clear that in a still
    largely agricultural nation an increased rate of industrial expansion depends
    on increased profitability of agricultural production, Stalin's statement
    formulated a policy detrimental to the interests of farm labor. A preoccu-
    pation with the agricultural problem also characterizes post-Stalinist re-
    gimes. But the latter do not seem to dare to base their policies on the
    assumption of a prolonged period of peace. If war is imminent it would be
    unwise, in their views, to alienate the farm population; if war is not immi-
    nent, more palatable, if slower, methods may be used to increase agricul-
    tural production. Most of all, it is necessary to assure a prolonged peace.
9   In Stalin's view, the breakdown of the world market led to the rise of "two
    world-markets, confronting one another," as socialism and capitalism do.
    He predicted that the nations of the "socialist camp" would soon "not only
    be in no need to import from capitalist countries, but will themselves feel
    the necessity of finding outside markets for their surplus products," which
    would increase the capitalists' difficulties and lead to new wars between
    the capitalist nations. (*Economic Problems of Socialism in the U.S.S.R.*,
    p. 26). What is implied here is a program of "autarchy" for the Eastern
    power bloc, and beyond that, a perpetuation of the "cold war" in the
    sphere of international trade. Against this policy, Stalin's successors pro-
    claimed a great interest in the strengthening of international economic
    relations in order to ease international tensions.

totalitarian nations and their increasing ability to trade will transform them into more democratic systems more akin to modern welfare capitalism. A partial abandonment of "Marxism" is urged upon the Russians in the interest of their own survival and final success. "Marxism for our time," it is said, exhausts itself in a full employment program, though not necessarily in the Keynesian fashion. But as private capital relations are declining anyway, there is no need to stress the inevitable. The general trend in the direction of a regulated economy will on its own accord serve Bolshevism better than a senseless harping on by-gone issues of expropriation and capitalist collapse. And if the Russians are not able to change their ideology, they should at least grant others what they deny themselves. Marxist propaganda in the old capitalist countries, it is pointed out, "would not necessarily lose in impressive strength were it clearly stated to non-Russians, non-Chinese, etc., that the further evolution of their national ways of life cannot simply be derived from the experiences made by civilizations with a completely different background."[10] In this view, Bolshevik propaganda would be more successful "if the claims for maximum realization of the original Marxist pattern were dropped," because with the receding of the egalitarian approach in the Marxist camp, the desire "for wholesale nationalization, as distinct from that of the commanding heights of economics, has lost its *raison d'etre*."[11]

By looking at the hands of Bolshevism rather than its mouth, Western capital may then find little reason to oppose the totalitarians, because their social system seems not too different from the future of its own. This is not a one-sided matter, of course, for while the Western world tends to adopt many of the innovations of state-capitalism, the Bolshevik East seems to adapt itself to the ways of the West. "Thus some ideas which sprang from early Communist preferences but proved difficult to apply have been given up. It is no longer held that workers can manage productive units by themselves, that all incomes should be more or less equal, or that money is superfluous. Incomes are geared to productivity and money concepts are increasingly used in planning. Interest, though not recognized as a possible source of private income, has gradually been accepted as representing a real cost element. The

10 R. Schlesinger, *Marx: His Time and Ours*, New York, 1950, p. 293.
11 *Ibid.*, p. 369.

value of an international exchange of products has been increasingly understood and some autarkic preferences weakened. Some decentralization in economic decision-making has been introduced and consumption has been given more attention in the new party program. Mathematical methods in economic planning, at first considered 'bourgeois', are now increasingly applied."[12]

However, just as it is highly improbable that in the absence of social revolution, the market economy will slowly transform itself into a planned economy, so it is equally improbable that a once-nationalized economy will return to capitalist market relations. The restoration of the market would mean the restoration, *de facto* if not *de jure*, of private capital. In the Western capitalist nations there exists the false concept of a "people's capitalism," by which is meant a system wherein a wide dispersal of stock-ownership results in a division between the ownership and the control of capital. The alleged divorce between ownership and control supposedly turns the non-owning managers of industry into acting capitalists. If the functions of the capitalists can be exercised by management without ownership, the rewards of ownership may also become the rewards of management. Although hardly likely, it is not inconceivable that the managers of Russian industry, in collaboration with the government and with the consent of large layers of the population, might proceed to restore a competitive market economy based on profit production, in the sense that each enterprise would operate as any private enterprise does in the West. As before, government would siphon off the equivalent of its own requirements from both paid and unpaid labor by way of taxes. But this would constitute a private-capitalist counter-revolution under the guise of a "managerial revolution," and would at once reintroduce into the Russian economy all the contradictions which are immanent in competitive private capital production.[13]

What a private-enterprise economy can engage in, short of social revolution, is a form of pseudo-planning, and what the

12   J. Tinbergen, *Shaping the World Economy*, p. 34.
13   The Yugoslav "market socialism," for instance, in which a combination of Workers' Councils and professional management runs industrial and commercial enterprises in accordance with the profitability principle and in competition with other enterprises, and where agriculture is mainly carried on by private peasants, suffers all the contradictions characteristic of capitalistic market relations, such as disproportional development, business failures, unemployment, and the ups and downs of the business cycle.

nationalized economy can restore, short of social counter-revolution, is some sort of pseudo-market. Either case, that of spurious planning or that of spurious market competition, indicates the existence of difficulties within the market system or within the planned economy. In combatting these difficulties, however, the use of instrumentalities which — despite their possible temporary usefulness — are foreign to the respective systems and their special needs will have to be arrested in time if the system's basic characteristics are to be secured. There is no congruency between the planned and the market systems, even though some economic-technical arrangements, in distinction to socio-economic relations, may be common to both.

All the state-capitalist systems resemble the capitalist market economy in their maintenance of capital-labor relations and their use of capitalistic business methods. Instead of being owned by capitalists, the means of production are now controlled by governments. The latter set a certain value (in money terms) on productive resources and expect a greater value (in money terms) following the intermediary of production. Money wages are paid to the workers, whose function it is to create a value greater than that represented by their wages. This surplus is allocated in accordance with the decisions of governments. It feeds the non-working population, secures national defense, takes care of public requirements, and is re-invested in additional capital. All economic transactions either are exchange-transactions or appear as such. Labor-power is sold to management of some enterprises and wages buy commodities from management of other enterprises. There is quasi-trade between the management of some enterprises and the management of other enterprises, like that which is carried on between the various divisions of large corporations in all capitalist nations and which reaches its complete form in the fully centralized state economy. Formally, there is not much difference between private-enterprise and state-controlled economies, except for the latter's centralized control over the surplus-product.

All actually-existing state-controlled systems were, or are, to be found in capital-poor nations. The first requirement of such nations is the formation of capital, a presupposition for their national independence and a precondition for the intended socialization of production and distribution. Bound more or less (depending on the country and its particular situation) to the capitalist "international division of labor," they must relate their economies to world market conditions and partake in international commercial competition. This limits or excludes any desire they may have not to make the money-economy and its expansion the motive force of their activities.

The "socialization" of the means of production is here still only the *nationalization of capital as capital*. Though private ownership no longer exists, the means of production still have the character of capital because they are controlled by government instead of being at the disposal of the whole of society. Although private capital accumulation is now excluded, the exploitation of men by men continues by way of an unequal system of distribution in both the conditions of production and the conditions of consumption. This inequality perpetuates competition as a struggle for the more lucrative positions and better-paid jobs, and carries the social antagonisms of capitalism into the state-capitalist system.

State-capitalism is still a "surplus-value" producing system, but it is no longer a system which finds its "regulation" through market competition and crisis. The surplus-product no longer requires market competition in order to be realized as profit; it derives its specific material character, and its distribution, from conscious decisions on the part of the state's planning agencies. That these decisions are co-determined by international economic and political competition and by the requirements of accumulation does not alter the fact that the lack of an internal capital market demands a centrally-determined direct system of decision-making with regard to the allocation of the total social labor and the distribution of the total social product.

Under these conditions, the use of quasi-market relations is a convenience, so to speak, not a necessity, even though it may have been forced upon the state-capitalist systems by circumstances they were unwilling to resist. In the U.S.S.R., for example, the quasi-market relations provide enterprises with a quasi-autonomy, consumers with a quasi-freedom of choice of consumption, and workers with a quasi-choice of occupation. But all these quasi-market relations are subordinated to over-all direction by government.

Within definite limits, this restricted "free play" of market forces can be extended or contracted without seriously affecting the planning system as such. It is presently being extended, in the belief that this will make for greater "efficiency" without diminishing the effectiveness of the planning system. This involves some decentralization of the decision-making process and more self-determination for individual enterprises — in support of the overall direction of the economy as a whole. The goal is not to change the character of the economy but merely to provide it with greater profitability through a more extensive use of capitalistic techniques of incentives.

Individual enterprises are given more leeway in determining their production processes, so as to fulfill and excell their planned production quotas; a greater regard for consumers' preferences is expected to aid production plans and to eliminate waste; interest charges on borrowed capital are supposed to lead to greater rationality in investment decisions; wage differences within the plant are left to some extent to the discretion of management; portions of the profits made through higher productivity and improved organization may be retained by management and reflected in wage increases. These and other "innovations" are intended to accentuate what has always existed, namely, the use of capitalistic incentives in state-capitalist economy. They do not affect the control of investments by government, nor its control of total social production and its division in accordance with a general plan. Wherever the outcome of these "innovations" does not suit the general plan, a government veto can change the situation either by decree or through a change in pricing policies. The limited "free market" can at any time be suspended by the real power relations which stand behind the pseudo-market relations.

It should be obvious in any case that at a time when not even the private enterprise systems are able to exist except through extensive government intervention, no state-capitalist system will find itself on the road of return to private-enterprise. In fact, the only advantage of the latter over the former type of system consists in its complete control over economic affairs, which compensates for its economic ineffectiveness *vis-a-vis* the highly-developed private-capitalist systems. The state-capitalist system does not suffer that particular contradiction between profitable and non-profitable production which plagues private-property capitalism, and which offers it as an alternative to stagnation only its slow destruction. With this destruction already behind itself, the state-capitalist system may produce profitably and non-profitably, without facing stagnation.

CHAPTER XXI

MARXISM AND SOCIALISM

Although often proclaimed as an established fact, the conjunction of free enterprise and government planning does not really produce a "mixed" economy. The combination of automatic market relations and conscious determination of production cannot be more than a side-by-side affair. In the course of development, one must come to dominate the other; this means the maintenance of either a competitive or a planned economy. But to avoid the transformation of the mixed economy into state-capitalism, as we have seen, it is not enough to curtail its domestic development, for it is no longer possible to consider the national in isolation from the world economy. The general trend toward state-capitalism must be halted because the continuous expansion of the one system implies the contraction of the other. And in fact the cold war which agitates the world relates not to an evolving struggle between capitalism and socialism, but to a divergence of interests between partly and completely state-organized systems of capital production. Capitalism is no longer what it used to be; and "socialism" is not the anticipated classless society of Marxian theory. The current political and economic competition is rather between the mixed economy and state-capitalism, and merely finds expression in the traditional ideologies that once separated capitalism from socialism.

The identification of state-capitalism with socialism was preceded by the indentification of socialism with state-capitalism. Revolutionary Marxism was the product of a period of development in which capital accumulation indeed meant increasing misery for the laboring population. Around the turn of the century, however, it became clear that in its decisive aspect the Marxian prognosis deviated from the real development; i.e., capitalism did not imply the continuous impoverishment of the industrial working class, and the workers themselves, far from becoming more class-conscious, were increasingly more satisfied with the improvement of their conditions within the capitalist system. This process reached its climactic expression in the First World War in which nationalist ideology triumphed over class interest. Some socialists even regarded the war-time "nationalization" of capital and labor as the beginning of the end of class conflict — as the dialectic synthesis, containing and negating both labor and capital in a higher social entity.

To others, however, this was merely the betrayal of Marxism by a corrupt labor bureaucracy. With the slogan "Back to Marx" the labor movement was split into radical and reformist wings. This division had been foreshadowed in earlier discussions centering around proposals to describe the social-democratic practice honestly in bourgeois-democratic terms instead of in an outdated Marxian phraseology. Social-democratic "revisionism" had its basis in the relatively prosperous conditions that preceded World War I. Since this very prosperity was in the Marxian view only the harbinger of a new crisis, more consistent socialists pointed to the imperialist tensions at the turn of the century rather than to the growing class harmony which, at any rate, affected only a few advanced nations. The debate between "reform" and "revolution," revisionism and orthodoxy, retained an academic character until war and revolution provided it with practical meaning. Marxian "orthodoxy" became identified with Lenin's Bolshevism; and the adjustments that the right-wing movement made in theory and practice turned it into an anti-Marxian movement, though its Marxian past was not denied. From then on any discussion about Marxian problems was a discussion about the theory and practice of Bolshevism and its relation to the Marxian creed. The success of the Russian Revolution made possible an almost complete identification of a specific Russian version of "Marxism" with Marxism in general. The more the Russians stressed their Marxian "orthodoxy," the more urgent it seemed to Western socialists first to oppose this "orthodoxy" and then to widen their distance from Marxism itself.

Lenin's "orthodoxy" had its source in the adaptation of Western socialism to Russian conditions. It has often been pointed out that the Russian situation at the beginning of the twentieth century

was in many respects similar to the revolutionary state of Western
Europe in the middle of the nineteenth century. Like Lenin at a
later time, Marx had faced a belated bourgeois-democratic revolution unable, or unwilling, to realize its own demands because of,
first, the existing revolutionary potentialities of the working class,
and second, the immediate need to fight the competitive advantages of earlier-developed capitalist nations with national protectionism. This fight required close collaboration of the democratic
bourgeoisie with their still largely reactionary governments. Marx's
positive attitude towards bourgeois revolutions was based on the
hope that the proletarian element in these revolutions might push
them beyond the restricted goals of the bourgeoisie. The undeveloped character of Western capitalism in 1848 gave Marx's political theory a certain ambiguity with respect to the bourgeois and
the proletarian revolutions. He could not help being greatly interested in the former, if only because it was a precondition of the
latter. This ambiguity paved the way for the class-collaborationist
and social-reformist Marxism of the *Second International* and, finally, for the theories of Bolshevism. In Lenin's view, the Russian
bourgeoisie was even less able to carry through its own bourgeois-
democratic revolution than the Western European bourgeoisie had
been; and thus the working class was destined to bring about both
the "bourgeois" and the "proletarian" revolutions in a series of
social changes that would constitute a "revolution in permanence."

The twentieth-century Western labor movement, however, faced
the choice between two different goals: it could seek a purely proletarian revolution or it could follow the program of Marxian
revisionism, and work for a slow transformation from capitalism
to socialism by way of reforms. While the Marxism of 1848 no
longer had meaning for the West, for Lenin it was a call to parti-
cipate actively in the Russian Revolution and to engage in world-
wide movements against backward as well as advanced capitalist
nations. The new situation seemed to repeat the revolutionary
situation of 1848 on a more grandiose scale, affecting not merely
the European scene but the world at large. Instead of the earlier
temporary alliances of proletarian internationalism with bourgeois-
democratic movements, there now existed a world-wide amalgam
of revolutionary forces of a social and nationalist character. These

forces might be led beyond their restricted goals to pursue social-istic ends.

With regard to the Russian Revolution, however, Lenin's confi-dence in the validity of Marx's theory of revolution found only partial justification. True, the Russian democratic revolution yielded quickly to the Bolshevik dictatorship; but the "revolution in permanence" turned out to mean only the slow process of the consolidation and centralization of power in the hands of Lenin's party. The Bolsheviks were dedicated to maintaining their power position against dangers from within and without, rather than to carrying out a world revolution determined to end all forms of backwardness and oppression. The focus of this dedication de-termined the character of the changes in the economic and political structure of Russian society.

The critique of Bolshevism rests on the "bourgeois," or capitalist, aspects of the Russian Revolution. For the social reformists, the Bolshevik dictatorship was an outrage: it was unnecessary, because democratic liberalism alone could bring progressive social changes, and, more than that, it was dangerous, because the type of social control it created threatened the even course of progress in the West. Lenin's dogmatism envisioned and enacted a program that went far beyond the need for democratic reforms; and, by doing so, it destroyed the very basis for a successful evolution from bour-geois to socialist society.

A more interesting but less popular criticism of Bolshevism came from the left. The anti-Bolshevik, left-wing labor movement opposed the Leninists because they did not go far enough in ex-ploiting the Russian upheavals for strictly proletarian ends. They became prisoners of their environment and used the international radical movement to satisfy specifically Russian needs, which soon became synonymous with the needs of the Bolshevik Party-State. The "bourgeois" aspects of the Russian Revolution were now dis-covered in Bolshevism itself: Leninism was adjudged a part of international social-democracy, differing from the latter only on tactical issues.

This evaluation of Bolshevism found support in the Leninist conceptions of socialism and of the role of the party in social actions. State-capitalism, that is, the nationalization of the productive resources, was for Lenin the first and most necessary step in the social transformation process. Marx also spoke of the nationalization of the means of production, but for him this was only a revolutionary act undertaken as a prelude to the institution of socialism. For Marx, capitalism was private-property capitalism, and where it seemed to lose its strictly private-enterprise nature, as in state-industries and even in the joint stock companies, he saw this as a partial abolition of the capitalist mode of production within the capitalist mode of production, a sign of that system's decay. He did not contemplate systems of state-capitalism such as prevail in the so-called socialist part of the world.

For Lenin, however, "socialism is nothing but the next step forward from state-capitalist monopoly. Or, in other words, socialism is nothing but state-capitalist monopoly *which is made to serve the interests of the whole people* and has to that extent ceased to be capitalist monopoly."[1] Monopoly-capitalism itself tended to turn into state-capitalism; so that, in Lenin's view, the function of social revolutions consisted mainly in completing those developments already occurring. The reformists too thought that the development of capitalism would lead to some form of state-capitalism which could then be transformed into socialism via existing democratic institutions. The situation in Western Europe gave even more credence to this idea than the rather backward conditions in Russia, which was largely agricultural. Precisely for this reason, Lenin believed in the Bolshevik dictatorship more firmly, assuming that the centralistic determination of economic development might be instrumental in bringing Russia nearer the advanced economies of the West.

A liberal bourgeoisie, addicted to the traditional ways of capital accumulation, could not develop Russia's economy in this way. But the functions formerly assigned to private enterprise and competition were now the functions of the Bolshevik State. Appropriating part of the social product and allocating productive resources turned the party which had fought capitalist control over production and distribution into the controller of labor and capital. If the capitalists' "peace of mind" requires some form of general

---

1 Lenin, *Questions of the Socialist Organization of the Economy*, Moscow, p. 46.

agreement on the indispensability of capital and private initiative, the new Russian situation needed a socialist ideology that could make the interests of the controllers and the controlled appear identical. Marxian ideology satisfied this need until the distinction between controllers and controlled hardened again into that of exploiters and exploited. The successful centralization of production and distribution secured by the power of the state may eliminate some of the social antagonisms of the private enterprise system, but new antagonisms of even greater magnitude arise through the polarization of society into controllers and controlled; in fact, the old antagonisms are not eliminated but only modified.

The controlled majority can imagine, and in fact is told, that the control exercised over them serves their interests too. If this were actually the case it would show up in the relationships between the authorities and the population at large, in politics, in field and workshop, and in the sphere of distribution. But nothing that would indicate a trend toward socialism is observable in Russia. There are excuses, of course, such as the Marxian proposition that socialism presupposes a high level of social production. This was in part contradicted by early Bolshevik theory, which held that central planning would improve living standards almost immediately, simply by enforcing equalization of consumption at the existing level of production. It was such arguments that induced the spokesmen of the bourgeoisie to claim that all the Bolsheviks were able to create was an "equalization of misery." Since only the miserable are inclined to believe in an equal sharing of a miserable situation, the Bolshevik elite soon realized that income differentiations serve as incentives for greater individual effort and thus are a blessing for all. This argument, which justifies the inequalities of capitalism on behalf of capital formation on the ground that the latter satisfies a social need, became Bolshevism's main excuse. In order to improve the life of all in the long run, it was necessary to improve that of some immediately. Capital competition was merely replaced by competition for social positions, highly remunerative either openly in money terms or in the hidden form of privileges. Presumably, these positions were allotted according to the social importance of the functions exercised by their recipients.

To hasten productive development even more, both the "positive" incentives of power and income and the "negative" incentives of forced labor and terrorism were continually advanced. And the more the interests of the controllers and the controlled diverged, the more insistently did ideology proclaim their identity. While it at first expressed a general hope for the future, this socialist ideology became more and more an instrument of control in the present. Though still considered the organization of the "transformation period," the new social structure soon presented itself as the desired "status quo" in need of defense against further change. The controllers no longer advocate changes in the basic social relations; any promises which remain unfulfilled relate merely to the betterment of individual existence within the prevailing social structure. If the socialist state can be made secure against external foes and can develop its production, it is said, the day will come when all people will be able to consume more and work less. But differentiations in living standards will remain for a long time to come, until the final step from "socialism" to "communism" can be effected and the *socialist* principle, "to each according to his work," can be changed into the *communist* principle, "to each according to his needs."

Meanwhile, there exists "equality of opportunity," which makes the individual responsible for the improvement of his lot. Of course, this principle cannot be realized in a society of widespread labor division, unequal in all respects save that of "opportunity;" but as ideology it supports the inequalities in the "socialist" countries just as it does elsewhere. It is in fact the ideological expression of the reality of fierce competition for power and privilege.

To compete is itself the privilege of a minority. The actions of the masses are controlled by a variety of organizations arrayed against them. By excluding all uncontrollable activities and expressions of social importance, the state perpetuates itself unaltered. And by giving permanence to its social relations and their ideological and terroristic bases it retains every social contradiction that gave rise to it in the first place. In this way totalitarian society reveals itself as one attempt among others to maintain the conditions of exploitation by modifying them. The unorganized control exercised by private capital is abolished in favor of the organized control of the whole of social life by the omnipotent state.

At the same time a parallel trend developed in the form of a strong tendency to idealize the new status relations associated with state control. This tendency serves to unify the privileged layers and to disorganize the exploited even more, since it raises the prestige value of advancements and opportunities which are not inconsiderable in times of social transformation and economic expansion. The direction and volume of production becomes increasingly more determined by the specific needs of the new ruling class. Scarcity will have to be maintained, whether objectively necessary or not, in order to secure a division of labor which leaves privileges intact despite all the existing "equality of opportunity." Such a social system cannot reach that state of abundance which it supposedly desires. Indeed, it must make this abundance impossible in order to safeguard itself. However, this question has become purely academic because imperialist competition removes or mitigates the need for artificial scarcities. In this situation the preservation of the conditions of exploitation appears as national defense.

A society which could reduce its necessary labor to minimum would lose all objective reasons for social antagonisms. In all class societies, and this embraces all existing forms of capital-producing societies, the development of the social forces of production[2] will be stopped when it threatens to endanger the welfare and existence of the socially dominating class. Economic abundance would render the social class structure pointless. The expectation of socialism is based on the possibility of such an abundance; but it presupposes the elimination of social class relations. This condition cannot be achieved within either the mixed or the state-capitalist economy.

In distinction to the competitive Western economies, however, the centralized economies of Russia and her satellites do not seem

---

2 By social forces of production we mean, of course, nothing other than the activities of men in their various efforts to increase social production and productivity. In capitalism, this is done through the accumulation of capital. Being activities of men, the social forces of production can be arrested or furthered. Because socialism promises to be a more productive system than capitalism, Marx considered the existence and the emancipatory efforts of the working class as the greatest of all productive forces in capitalism.

to fear the consequences of automation. Their production and productivity are still below those of Western nations, and automation, to the degree possible under these conditions, could not lead to large-scale unemployment. Roughly half of Russia's population, for instance, is still engaged in agriculture and — in view of the size of the country and its population — there is a general lack of means of production, not to speak of consumers' durables or even plain consumers' goods. To be sure, highly automated industries also exist, but there are not as yet enough to raise the social average productivity to the level prevailing in the West.

In principle, of course, the centralized nature of state-capitalism allows for a wider application of automation to social production processes than is possible in the Western economies. And this, in turn, promises a quickening of automation concurrent with the general rise of productivity. Economic planning, for example, is one of the most important areas of application of cybernetics. While in the competitive economies "planning" implies "counter-planning," in the centralized economies planning may be unitary, nation-wide, and all-comprehensive. This is why many of the Western advocates of abundance through cybernation emphasize the need for national planning.

Although the exploitative character of state-capitalist social relations is fairly obvious, questions as to what particular social group constitutes its new ruling class are always raised anew. The answer may be found in the developmental process of capitalism itself; since state-capitalism has adopted the relationship between "capitalist" and manager, and between "ownership" and control, from the modern corporation. In Marx's theory, the capitalist is not a creator of value but a consumer of labor-power. He is a capitalist because he is freed from the actual laboring process. And "just as at first the capitalist is relieved from actual labor so soon as his capital has reached that minimum amount with which capitalist production as such begins, so now, he hands over the work of direct and constant supervision of the individual workmen, and groups of workers, to a special kind of wage-labor. An industrial army of workmen, under the command of a capitalist requires, like a real army, officers (managers), and sergeants (foremen), who, while the work is being done, command in the name of the capitalist."[3] The latter retains leadership, but "it is not because he is a leader of industry that a man is a capitalist; on the contrary, he is a leader of industry because he is a capitalist."[4]

However, capital accumulation and the structural and technological changes associated with it freed (or deprived) capitalists in increasing measure of their industrial leadership. The "de-privatization" of capital by way of the credit system, stock companies, pyramided stock ownership, interlocking directorates, holding companies, bureaucratized management and increasing governmental determination of production and capital expansion replaced the entrepreneurial capitalist with the managerial direction of industry. The manager's decisions are often not directly determined by capital owners, even though they continue to be determined by the principle of profitability. "The perfectly bureaucratized giant industrial unit," wrote Joseph Schumpeter, "not only ousts the small or medium sized firm and 'expropriates' its owners, but in the end it also ousts the entrepreneur and expropriates the bourgeosie as a class which in the process stands to lose not only its income but also what is infinitely more important, its function."[5]

According to Marx, capital expansion is in the main the reproduction of capitalists and wage-workers. He regarded the idea "of some socialists that we need capital but not the capitalists" quite wrong, for "the concept of capital implies that the objective conditions of labor — though the product of labor itself — face the latter as persons, or, what is the same, appear as the property of other persons than the workers. The concept of capital contains the capitalists."[6] Although Marx recognized that "the capitalist mode of production itself has brought matters to such a point that the labor of superintendence, entirely separated from the ownership of capital, walks the streets,"[7] he saw the development of the management function as an indication that the capitalists had become as superfluous in production as they felt the money-lenders and real-estate owners to be. "A director of an orchestra," Marx wrote,

3 *Capital*, Vol. I., p. 364.
4 *Ibid.*, p. 365.
5 J. Schumpeter, *Capitalism, Socialism, and Democracy*, New York, 1947, p. 134.
6 K. Marx, *Grundrisse*, p. 412.
7 *Capital*, Vol. III, p. 455.

"need not be the owner of the instruments of its members, nor is it part of his function as a director, that he should have anything to do with the *wages* of the other musicians."[8] However, today's typical capitalist is no longer that of whom Marx spoke, and Marx's manager has become something more than just a commanding officer acting on the owner's behalf. The modern manager is not Marx's property-less "orchestra-leader" who has no say over wages. Though he may not own the instruments of production, he is certainly a buyer of labor-power and an appropriator of surplus-value. In contrast to the workers he is capital personified, and under his auspices value-expansion is still the production of capitalists and wage-workers. It is only that the former class now comprises, in addition to the clearly distinguishable private capital owners, part-owners and quasi-capitalists as well. But all of these types, nonetheless, make up a definite class interesed in perpetuating the exploitative wage-system. The transfer of entrepreneurial functions to the manager and the superfluity of the capitalist alter nothing in the capitalist relations of production.

Management functions are productive functions. The early capitalist was also a "working capitalist;" exploitation requires labor. The "wages" (i.e. profits) which he claimed were equal to the amount of realizable surplus-value extracted from his workers and did not depend upon the degree of his own exertions. The manager's reward, seen not as profit but as salary, is often larger than that of many capitalists. Most managers are also owners of capital stock, and thus exercise both capital and managerial functions. The manager's income in the form of salary, bonuses and dividends, like the capitalist's profits, has no connection with any special value-creating ability he may possess. In fact, his position more often than not rises with his distance from productive work. The typical executive calls upon subordinates to perform managerial functions and restricts himself to broader policy-making decisions. His income reflects the prestige of the firm; it may not be out of line with its profits but it is unrelated to the functions he performs. It is rather arbitrarily determined — constitutes a "political wage" so to speak — since it results from the manipulation within and between corporations and indicates, in some mea-

8 *Ibid.*

sure, the degree of control management has over the corporate stockholders.

The great bulk of capital is owned by individuals in the form of securities, covering one or several corporate enterprises, and bought and sold as commodities on the stock market. To a large extent "capital ownership" refers thus not to definite persons and their claims upon particular businesses and their profits, but to claims of successive persons upon a variety of businesses and their dividends. Both the capital itself and its part-owners are impersonal; generally, the part-owners know no more about their property than its market prices and the profit expectations based thereon. The corporations themselves do not know the owners as persons, save abstractly in their numbers. There still exist, however, smaller businesses whose whole capital stays in the hands of definite persons and families as well as very large businesses — in the extraction industries and in real estate in particular — where the whole assets are privately controlled. But the great mass of capital is concentrated in the larger corporations and has the form of widespread stock ownership. This type of ownership is in one way widely dispersed and in another very much concentrated — although many people own some stock, a very few people own the great bulk of it. The spread of stock ownership has had no effect upon the distribution of the national income, which has remained proportionally the same in spite of the rapid rise in the number of shareowners. Although the wide dispersal of stock ownership has been offset by its increasing concentration, the fact of the great number of stockholders gave rise to the concept noted above of "peoples' capitalism," which projects eventual part-ownership of the social capital for everyone. Meanwhile, however, in America (for example) only 2 per cent of all shareowners control about 58 per cent of all common stock, and one per cent of preferred stockowners control 46 per cent of all preferred stock.

Ownership in the large corporations is not identical with control. It is clear that there is no way for the 2 million stockowners of the American Telephone and Telegraph Company to exercise any kind of control over the company's transactions. The wide diffusion of stock ownership not only allows but demands minority control, and the greater the dispersal, the less stock is needed to maintain

working control of a corporation. In theory, the stockholders ultimately control management through their legal right to dismiss
unwanted managers. In practice, however, concentrated minority
holdings, in combination with management, usurp all decision-
making powers and can rarely, if ever, be challenged. Managers
and directors of corporations are usually also shareholders. But
their decision-making power comes not so much from their share-
ownership as from their possession of the managerial positions.

This new type of capitalism allegedly concerns itself with the
public interest rather than with profitability. The divorce of ownership from management supposedly subordinates the profit motive to the public good. According to Keynes, "Joint Stock Institutions, when they have reached a certain age and size, approximate to the status of public corporations rather than that of individualistic private enterprise. One of the most interesting and un-
noticed developments of recent decades has been the tendency of
big enterprise to socialize itself. A point arrives in the growth
of a big institution . . . at which the owners of capital, i.e., the
shareholders, are almost entirely dissociated from the management,
with the result that the direct personal interest of the latter in the
making of great profit becomes quite secondary. When this stage
is reached, the general stability and reputation of the institution
are more considered by the management than the maximum of
profit for the shareholders."[9] Actually it is the other way around:
the whole of the national economy is utilized to support the profitability of the big corporations.

Although ownership and control do not coincide in the modern
corporation, there is normally no divergence of interest between the
passive shareholders and the active business leaders. Both are
equally devoted to maximizing the corporation's profit. As for
capital generally so also for corporate capital: its operations must
be directed toward profit making and the formation of capital. A
lack of profitability, or losses, implies the eventual extinction of
the organization. Nor can there be a difference of interests between
the owners and the managers of a business, for the latter's position
and income depends on the existence and thus on the profitability
of the corporation under their management. For the managers

9 J. M. Keynes, *Laissez-Faire and Communism*, pp. 61-62.

to neglect the profit motive would mean to neglect their own interests. Actually, however, the managerial class forms the largest single group within the stockholding population, so that their interest in the profitability of corporate enterprise derives at once both from the side of management and from that of ownership.

Although management and stockholders have the same interest in making profits, they may differ on the issue of their distribution. Management, which is usually composed of company directors and professional managers, may use its power position within the corporation to vote itself very large salaries, expense accounts, bonuses, stock options, and retirement pensions at the expense of the stockholders' dividends. Stockholders and managers may also differ on the question whether to retain or to distribute profits, and on long-term policies which affect the distribution of dividends. But none of these differences affect the profit-motive of the corporation. Notwithstanding assertions to the contrary, the partial or even complete divorce of ownership from control alters nothing in the needs and necessities of corporations.

The uncompensated expropriation of private capital through nationalization constitutes a radical break with the principle of private appropriation of surplus-value. With the wage-system unaltered, the state bureaucracy now constitutes a new ruling class and its members "personify" capital. In this system the former relations between capital and management become relations between government and management. The State bureaucracy is as superfluous in production as the capitalists were formerly, but industrial managers have now less power than before. There is still some overlapping of management and control because of the inter-transferability of government and management functions. But for management to retain the degree of power it has gained within the private enterprise system, national planning must be prevented; for management relates to specific enterprises and corporations and not to a national, much less international, planning of production and distribution.

State-capitalist regimes treat the manager more like Marx's "orchestra-leader," that is, as one "wage-worker" among others. An opposition of interest between worker and manager still exists, of course, because of the institutional hierarchy which determines inequalities in power, income and prestige. But to exploit this social division, managers would have to fight politically within the State apparatus or within the Party, from which the State apparatus emerges and on which it is based. Such struggles could hardly serve the specific interests of one or another enterprise and its management. They could only serve them indirectly by a change of policy that affected the nation as a whole. It may be thought that managers as a group can demand special privileges, but to do that they would have to be indispensable, unassailable and organized. They have none of these qualities. The decisive power in the state-capitalist system rests with the coercive force of government, in its control over the military and the police. Having this the government has absolute control over all social groups, including the managers. To affect the decisions of government means to infiltrate into and to assume control over the State apparatus or the Party. All open sectional struggles, if possible at all, thus become struggles for the control of government and, within the government, for the displacement of some persons by others.

Because the capitalization process under the wage-system demands an industrial as well as a political hierarchy, management is, in a sense, an extension of government control in production. The manager's functions are geared to maximum production and their salaries are tied in with this goal. Control over the national capital — theoretically on behalf of society, practically on behalf of a new ruling class — places both economic and political power in the hands of the State. This close coordination of economic and political power does not exist in the "free" or even the "mixed" forms of capitalism, where political force is largely reserved for emergencies, as economic control is generally sufficient to secure the exploitation of labor. While destroying traditional capitalism, the new combination of political and economic coercion strengthens the capitalist mode of production. Whatever the particular arrangements, wage-labor characterizes the state-capitalist system just as it characterizes that of private enterprise. And, as Marx points out, "no form of wage-labor, even though one may be less obnoxious than another, can do away with the misery of wage-labor itself,"[10] or, for that matter, with the class determination of production and distribution.

10 *Grundrisse*, p. 43.

CHAPTER XXII

VALUE AND SOCIALISM

Lenin's Marxism did not express the practical necessities of the modern international, anti-capitalist class struggle, but was determined by conditions specific to Russia. Russia required not so much the emancipation as the creation of an industrial proletariat, and not so much the end of capital accumulation as its acceleration. The Bolsheviks overthrew Czarism and the Russian bourgeoisie in the name of Marx and by revolutionary means, only to become themselves a dictatorial force over the workers and peasants. And this in order to lead them, eventually, by way of intensified suppression and exploitation, into socialism. Lenin's Marxian "orthodoxy" existed only in ideological form, as the false consciousness of a non-socialist practice.

When dealing with the questions of the socialist organization of the economy, Lenin's proposals were therefore almost exclusively of a pragmatic type, and no attempt was made to relate them to Marxian theory. Of all the socialists who have written about socialism, Lenin said rightly, none had dealt concretely with the issues involved. For him, however, "socialism was gazing at us from all the windows of modern capitalism; socialism is outlined directly, *practically,* by every important measure that constitutes a forward step on the basis of modern capitalism."[1] Socialism consisted in doing what capitalism was doing for itself, but doing it better and in the interest of the working class.

This required an increase in the productivity of labor and a better organization of production. Thus, Lenin wrote, although "the Taylor system, the last word of capitalism in this respect, like

---

1 Lenin, *Questions of the Socialist Organization of the Economy,* Moscow, p. 47.

all capitalist progress, is a combination of the refined brutality of
bourgeois exploitation and a number of the greatest scientific
achievements in the field of analysing mechanical motion during
work," nonetheless "the possibility of building socialism depends
exactly upon our success in combining the Soviet power and the
Soviet organization of administration with the up-to-date achievements of capitalism. We must organize in Russia the study and
teaching of the Taylor system and systematically try it out and
adapt it to our ends."[2] As regards administration, "the foundation
of socialism called for absolute and strict *unity of will,* which di-
rects the joint labor of hundreds, thousands and tens of thousands
of people. The technical, economic and historical necessity of this
is obvious, and all those who have thought about socialism have
always regarded it as one of the conditions of socialism. But how
can strict unity of will be ensured? By thousands subordinating
their wills to the will of one."[3] It is for this reason "that all direct
interference by the trade unions in the management of factories
must be regarded as positively harmful and impossible."[4] In brief,
things should be run as they always have been run in capitalism;
only now for "society as a whole," no longer for the accumulation
of private capital. For Lenin the social reconstruction is no longer
concerned with social but only with technical issues, such as the
revival of industry, the increase of agricultural production, sound
financial policies, electrification, and so forth.

Apart from a few general remarks, Marx did not concern himself
with the organization of a socialist society. His economic writings
were not intended to enrich the "science of economics," but to lay
bare the actual social relations that found their fetishistic expression in political economy. Although political economy "is for the
proletariat first and foremost an enemy country,"[5] it has to be
entered in order to show that "economic relations" are mere disguises for capitalist exploitation relations, and to reveal the class
contradictions in the economic contradictions that beset bourgeois
practice and capitalist development. For Marx, the "economic
laws" propounded by political economy are irrelevant to socialism

2   *Ibid.,* p. 117.
3   *Ibid.,* p. 127
4   *Ibid.,* p. 341.
5   K. Korsch, *Karl Marx,* p. 90.

which, in fact, will bring them to an end. Instead, there will be conscious regulation of production and distribution by the associated producers themselves, and the instrumentalities to this end will be of a technical-organizational nature.

When planning became a possibility for the Bolshevik state, it nevertheless found its theoretical starting-point in Marx, that is, in his idea of social production as a reproduction process. The planners thought Marx's schemata of simple and enlarged reproduction, which Marx had developed from the physiocrat Francois Quesnay's *Tableau Economique,* and which he presents in the second volume of *Capital,*[6] applicable to all social formations and particularly useful in solving the problems of a socialist economy. It was on the basis of these schemata that Soviet economists constructed macro-economic models depicting the feasibility of a balanced planned economy.[7]

Marx's reproduction schemes serve to show the relationships in the production and exchange process which are required to consummate the process of capital production with respect to both the value and use-value of commodity production. "So long as we looked upon production of value and the value of products from the point of view of individual capital," he wrote, "it was immaterial for the analysis which was the natural form of the product in commodities. So far as reproduction was concerned, it was sufficient to assume that that portion of the products in commodities, which represented capital in the sphere of circulation, found an opportunity to reconvert itself into its elements of production and thus into its form of productive capital. It likewise sufficed to assume that both the laborer and the capitalist found in the market those commodities for which they spend their wages and surplus-value. This merely formal manner of representation does not suffice in the study of the total social capital and of the value of its products. The reconversion of one portion of the value of the product into capital, the passing of another portion into the individual consumption of the capitalist and working classes, form a movement within the value of the product itself which is created

6 Chapters XX and XXI
7 English translations of some of these endeavors are to be found in N. Spulber, ed., *Foundations of Soviet Strategy for Economic Growth,* Bloomington, 1964.

by the total capital; and this movement is not only a reproduction of value, but also of material, and is, therefore, as much conditioned on the relative proportions of the elements of value of the total social product as on its use-value, its material substance."[8]

There is no need here to display Marx's diagrams; it suffices to recall that he divided total social production into two sections — one producing the means of production and the other the means of consumption. Each department is composed of constant and variable capital and produces surplus-value. The transactions between the two departments are such as to reproduce the total capital, leaving the surplus-value for capitalist consumption. "Simple reproduction," Marx wrote, "is essentially directed toward consumption as an end," and "insofar as simple reproduction is a part . . . of annual production on an enlarged scale, consumption remains as a motive accompanying the accumulation of wealth as an end and distinguished from it."[9] The difference between simple and enlarged reproduction consists in the fact that part of the total surplus-value is not consumed by the capitalists but is turned into additional capital. The shift from simple to enlarged reproduction involves "not the quantity, but the destination of the given elements of simple reproduction . . . and this change is the material basis of a subsequent reproduction on an enlarged scale."[10]

Whatever the methodological merits of Marx's reproduction schemes, they cannot be construed as a system of general equilibrium akin to bourgeois equilibrium theory. The process of reproduction depicted by them, Marx pointed out, "may take place when society controls the material requirements of its own production. But in capitalist society it is an element of anarchy."[11] The control of the material requirements of society's own reproduction presupposes the abolition of the value aspect of capitalist production; for it is the contradictory movement between value and use-value production which accounts for capitalism's anarchy, i.e., its inability to organize production and reproduction rationally. "The fact that the production of commodities is the general form of capitalist production," Marx wrote, "implies the role which money is playing

---

8 *Capital,* Vol. II pp. 455-56.
9 *Ibid.,* p. 476.
10 *Ibid.,* pp. 591-92.
11 *Ibid.,* p. 546.

not only as a medium of circulation but also as money capital, and creates conditions peculiar for the normal transactions of exchange under this mode of production, and therefore peculiar for the normal course of reproduction, whether it be on a simple, or on an enlarged scale. These conditions become so many causes of abnormal movements, implying the possibility of crisis, since a balance is an accident under the crude conditions of this production."[12]

The "equilibrium" of the reproduction scheme, in which both value and material production are in harmony, illustrates the essentials of a frictionless capitalist reproduction process. This "equilibrium" is possible in theory but not in practice; like the equality between supply and demand, or value and price, it will exist only by accident. Russian economists, in basing their models of a socialist economy on Marx's reproduction schemes, conceived these models in strictly material, not value, terms. The relationships of production and distribution, it was said, "must be studied in their material representation, that is, as the sum of concrete products in their concrete movement from producer to consumer. . . . Since the balance studies the relationships of production and circulation in material terms, it must consider the social economy as a kind of natural economy measuring production as the sum of materials and things produced in the course of the year and exploring the distribution of products in their material expression."[13] Even if money "must play the role of yardstick, a means of reducing the assorted fruits of social production to a common denominator . . . the balance studies the relationships in the production and consumption of products as a material process."[14]

The actual organization of the Russian economy was, indeed, a planning in material terms to realize economic goals set by the government. These goals emphasized economic growth and the development of industry, or, in bourgeois parlance, the accumulation of capital. With wages and prices administered, it can be approximately but directly determined what portion of the total social product shall fall to the producers as consumption goods, how these goods shall be distributed among the consumers, and

12 *Ibid.*, p. 578.
13 P. I. Popov, "Introduction to the Balance of the National Economy," in Spulber, *Foundations of Soviet Strategy for Economic Growth*, p. 18.
14 *Ibid.*

what portion of the total shall serve to enlarge the productive
apparatus. Wages and prices are here media for bringing forth
and distributing a social product in accordance with a central plan
conceived in physical terms, as material production. The authorities determine production and distribution in those proportions
which they deem necessary or desirable.

According to Marx, the "measure of work is time. Only because
products require labor can these products be measured by labor-
time."[15] In capitalism, however, "price is not the equivalent of
value and the value-determining element — labor-time — cannot be
the element which expresses prices."[16] Because in capitalism "labor-time as a measure of value exists only ideally, it cannot serve
as the element for the comparison of prices."[17] Yet it has often
been said that the indirect regulation of the whole of the capitalist system by the law of value, as assumed in Marx's value scheme
of capital development, can be the basis of the direct regulation of
production in the socialist system. Supposedly, this will be achieved
by a kind of "re-transformation" of prices into values; though these
values are no longer indirectly established through market competition but are instead set by socialist planning agencies. The possibility of such a "re-transformation" is, for instance, implicit in
Sweezy's claim that "Marx's value theory has the great merit, unlike some other value theories, of close correspondence to the actual
accounting categories of capitalistic business enterprises."[18] If this
is so, then it is of course possible to assume that it is only the
imperfect price-form of value, but not value itself, which will disappear in a socialist society. Joan Robinson, for instance, felt it
apt to say that while little, if anything, can be done with the law
of value in capitalism, Marx may be right in believing that "it
would come into its own"[19] in socialism.

Although Marx held no such belief, some Russian economists
did indeed express the opinion that the law of value applies to
both capitalism and socialism. Value is here equated with cost-of-
production; and, it is said, without a knowledge of production

15   *Grundrisse*, p. 507.
16   *Ibid.*, p. 58.
17   *Ibid.*, p. 59.
18   P. M. Sweezy, *The Theory of Capitalist Development*, p. 63.
19   J. Robinson, *An Essay on Marxian Economics*, p. 23.

costs social planning would be impossible. Other economists, most prominently N. I. Bukharin and E. A. Preobrazhensky, maintained that the law of value was operative only in a market-determined commodity-producing society and not under conditions of socialism, where all the bourgeois categories like money, prices, wages, interest, rent and profits disappear to make room for a direct accounting of economic processes in material terms. According to Preobrazhensky, those who hold that the law of value has general validity merely confuse the regulatory economic processes under commodity production with the regulatory role of labor-expenditure in any system of social production. To acknowledge the law of value as the unique regulator of the economic system of the U.S.S.R. was to deny her socialist character. "We need only try to imagine the law of value as regulator of socialist production," he wrote, "or the planning principle as regulator of commodity production, to see that we cannot separate the regulatory mechanism from the whole structure of the given society."[20]

The assertion of the validity of the law of value in socialism led to much discussion, which was authoritatively terminated by Stalin himself. Wherever commodities and commodity production exist, Stalin wrote, "there the law of value must also exist. In our country, the sphere of operation of the law of value extends, first of all, to commodity circulation, to the exchange of commodities through purchase and sale, the exchange, chiefly, of articles of personal consumption. Here in this sphere, the law of value preserves, within certain limits, of course, the function of the regulator. But the operation of the law of value is not confined to the sphere of circulation. It also extends to production. True, the law of value has no regulative function in our socialist production, but it nevertheless influences production. In this connection, such things as cost accounting and profitableness, production costs, prices, etc., are of actual importance in our enterprises. Consequently, our enterprises cannot, and must not, function without taking the law of value into account."[21]

What does it actually mean to take the law of value into account? According to Stalin it means, first of all, "to train business

20 E. A. Preobrazhensky, *The New Economics*, London, 1965, p. 29.
21 J. Stalin, *Economic Problems of Socialism in the U.S.S.R.*, p. 18.

executes to count production magnitudes . . . to improve methods of production, to lower production costs, to practice cost accounting, and to make enterprise pay."[22] Although in Marx's definition the labor theory of value refers exclusively to capitalist production, and the concept of surplus-value to labor exploitation, in Stalin's definition value theory need not be in contradiction with the requirements of socialism. All that is necessary is to discard "certain concepts taken from Marx's *Capital,* such as 'necessary labor' and 'surplus labor,' 'necessary' and 'surplus' product, 'necessary' and 'surplus' labor time."[23] Stalin found it rather strange "to use these concepts now, when the working class is not only not bereft of power and means of production, but, on the contrary, is in possession of power and controls the means of production. Talk of labor power being a commodity and of 'hiring' of workers sounds rather absurd now, as though the working class, which possesses means of production itself, sells its labor power to itself. It is just as strange to speak of 'necessary' and 'surplus' labor; as though, under our conditions, the labor contributed by the workers to society for the extension of production, the promotion of education and public health, the organization of defense, etc., is not just as necessary to the working class, now in power, as the labor expended to supply the general needs of the workers and their families."[24]

In its essentials, Stalin's position on the problem of value in socialism still prevails in post-Stalinist Russia. There have been discussions since 1956 as to whether or not the law of value has only partial or general validity, that is, whether it applies only to the consumer market, or to the totality of goods circulating in the whole of the economy. Voices have been heard which deny the commodity character of production in the U.S.S.R., and, in consequence, wish to apply the law of value in the sense of Marx's "economics of time" as the objective criterion for measuring, economizing, and allocating the social product. Contrariwise, it is held that just because the Russian economy is considered to be a "planned form of commodity production" it should be "based on the law of

---

22 *Ibid.,* p. 20.
23 *Ibid.,* p. 17.
24 *Ibid.,* p. 18.

value and commodity-monetary relations."[25] This general bewilderment is further confounded by economists who want to avail themselves of the marginalism of bourgeois theory and wish to deal with factors of production other than labor, as well as with the application of linear programming and computer techniques in economic planning. Bourgois economists, for their part, celebrate these events as the abandonment of Marx's labor theory of value by the "Marxists" themselves; as if the theory of value had actually been the theory of Russian economic practice, or could be the economic theory of socialism.

The confusion which surrounds the labor theory of value does not reflect the theoreticians' muddled thinking alone; it results from their attempt to describe a non-socialist system of production and distribution as a socialist society. They do so because, by their definition, socialism *is* state-control over the means of production and centrally-planned determination of the national economy. It seems to them then that planning which fits the social needs and economic necessities, is planning in accordance with the law of value. Under capitalism, it is said, "the law of value acts as an elemental law of the market, inevitably linked with the destruction of productive forces, with crisis, with anarchy of production. Under socialism it acts as a law of the planned administration of the national economy, under the conditions of the development of an economy free from crises."[26]

To say that the law of value underlies economic processes is to say that there is some definite regulation of social production despite the lack of concern for, and the practical impossibility of, such regulation under private property relations. The "regulation" is brought about by way of market competition and crises. But if there is no private ownership of capital. no competition, no private accumulation; if production is centrally planned; if prices and wages are regulated, and the expansion of production consciously determined — then there cannot arise those *results* of competition and crises which manifest the operation of the law of value. To apply the law of value "consciously" in socialism could only mean

25 Y. Liberman, "The Soviet Economic Reform," in *Foreign Affairs,* New York, October, 1967, p. 53.
26 *Teaching of Economics in the Soviet Union,* The American Economic Review, September, 1944, p. 525.

to incorporate the effects of competition and crisis into the planning mechanism — in other words, to re-institute the market and private property, which is obviously nonsense.

It is perhaps for this reason that Stalin spoke of a law of value "strictly limited and placed within definite bounds," i.e., one which fully operates only in the sphere of circulation confined to personal consumption, and which "influences" the sphere of production only because the latter cannot disregard the principle of profitability, even though this principle is modified by conscious decisions on the part of the planning authorities. But even though the "modified" law of value presumably affects production and regulates distribution, Stalin saw no social division between value and surplus-value, and none between necessary and surplus labor, because *by definition* the whole social product belongs now to all of society.

In the U.S.S.R. the planned total output is expressed either in physical terms or in terms of money-values. Although prices, wages, and profits are still economic categories, they no longer play an independently active part: they are merely expressions for aggregate physical magnitudes that are directly determined by the decision-makers. Resource allocation here has nothing to do with price relations; rather, prices, wages, and profits are used to assure the allocation of resources required by the plan. As this is, practically, a difficult task, the plan comprises only rough approximations, subject to continuous change. Thus far, all economic planning has been, so to speak, makeshift planning, and has been attempted under conditions not very susceptible to over-all control of the economy. Planning has been used in industrially underdeveloped countries whose foremost need is the rapid accumulation of capital. Forced industrialization by political means proceeded from government direction to direct government control and, in the process, created the conditions for a planned economic development. The plans reflected the general backwardness; they could not be any better than the conditions they tried to alter.

The total social income in the U.S.S.R. is supposed to equal the total value of the total material product, which equates with the sum total of the final selling prices of material goods — aside from the amortization of fixed capital. Social demand is controlled through the control of personal incomes, as well as through control of the allocation of productive resources. Prices are supposedly based on the average costs of production of all enterprises producing identical commodities. Retail prices for all goods and services are fixed to match the level of personal incomes. These prices move in relation to supply and demand for consumption goods that enter the market. Money-wages are manipulated by pricing policies. Profits fall to the government mainly through a turnover tax which is derived from the difference between retail prices and actual costs of production.

With wages and prices administered, it can be approximately but directly established what portion of total social production shall fall to the workers and in what particular commodity form. Consumption goods may be priced in such a way that the workers' choice of commodities is *practically* limited to what the government thinks their choice should be, and scarce commodities can be made even scarcer by a pricing policy which reserves them for the privileged layers of society. The necessity of keeping the laboring population alive and working prevails in all forms of continuous social production; in capitalism, it is expressed in the value of labor-power, which determines and limits the surplus-value or surplus-labor time extractable out of a given laboring population. But if necessary- and surplus-labor is *at once* the common property of the socialized producers, it is quite pointless to speak of a law of value as the regulator of social distribution and of the effect of this regulation upon the process of production. If the total social product is the common property of the whole of society, its compartmental division into consumption, reproduction, and expansion could just as well be expressed in direct labor-time quantities, which would refer no longer to value relations but to strictly technical arrangements enabling the social production and reproduction process to function properly.

There is only one compelling reason for retaining the law of value in its Russian definition, and that is to give the conditions of inequality, such as prevail in the state-capitalist economy, the semblance of an "economic law." Because "Marxism" is here the state-enforced ruling ideology, it is not only necessary to explain that production implies reproduction, and that progress means enlarged reproduction, for which purpose present consumption must be restricted to assure a better future consumption; it is also necessary to explain that the wage differentiations between the workers, and the income differentiations between the workers and the administrative layers of society are not arbitrarily instituted by the whims of a new ruling class, but are determined by an "economic law" which gives each his due in accordance with his particular contribution to society. As there are nominally none but productive people in Russia, their different living standards must be explained by differences in their productivity, and by the economic necessity to take these differences into account — at this historical stage of development, at any rate.

Rewarding labor in accordance with its productivity means that skilled labor receives more than unskilled labor. Because of training expenses, the reproduction costs for skilled labor are higher than those for unskilled labor. Income differentiations may thus be explained by the different productivity of different kinds of labor, and by the varying intensity in the performance of a particular type of labor. Because actual work is unequal, equal incomes would imply the "exploitation" of more-productive by less-productive labor. In the Bolshevik as well as in the bourgeois mind, this would destroy the incentive to prepare for and engage in more skilled and therefore more productive activities, to the detriment of the whole of society. There is then a social need for income differentiations as the inescapable requirement of social development.

We will here recall that in Marx's value theory all labor is reduced to abstract simple labor. The concept of value refers to *abstract social aggregates* of necessary labor time and surplus labor time. This allows for the consideration of skilled labor as multiplied simple labor, just as it allows for the identity of value and price. Both wages and prices deviate from labor-time values. To say that the capitalist law of value applies to the planned economy could only mean that here, too, it refers to the social aggregates of abstract necessary and surplus labor, which are now, however, no longer unknown quantities but data given through a social inventory in terms of labor-time units, or expressed in money-terms representing these units. This would not reveal the concrete contribution of individuals, or categories of individuals, to the total mass of products incorporating the total quantity of labor-time expended on their production. It would, however, reveal, through the changing relationship between the social aggregates of necessary labor-time and surplus-labor time, whether the exploitation of labor-power is increasing or decreasing. This increase or decrease of exploitation would be an observable phenomenon in the state-controlled economy, though it is not in the competitive private-enterprise economy. The latter discovers it only through market movements from prosperity to depression, but the former could — in theory — rearrange social aggregates as it sees fit by political decisions, to either speed up or slow down the exploitation process.

According to Marx, *social labor-time in general* determines value. The value of commodities refers not to the specific quantity of labor contained in them but to that relative portion of the general social labor-time which they represent. It follows from this that it is not possible to separate the economy into a value-determined sphere and another sphere not so determined. Either the whole of the economy is regulated by the law of value or it is not. It is not possible to say with Stalin, for instance, that the law of value regulates the sphere of consumption but not the sphere of production; either it regulates the whole of the economy or it regulates none of it.

The abstract value of labor-power does not explain actual wages and their differentiations. Marx showed no interest in the actual supply and demand determination of one or another wage. The wage differentials encountered in reality relate roughly to different reproduction costs of different types of labor. But these differences disappear in the equation of skilled as multiplied simple labor used to analyze the social aggregates of value and surplus-value and their changing relationship in the course of capital accumulation. The abstract value concept is quite useless in the determination of individual wages and to deal with the latter as actual entities is to accept them simply as historically-given facts.

In state-capitalism the law of value could have validity only with respect to the social aggregates of constant capital, variable capital, and the surplus-value brought forth in production, and their changing relationships in the course of capital formation. Under conditions of competitive private capital accumulation, the physical expansion of capital can only proceed as the accumulation of exchange-value. In state-capitalism, where all means of production are centralized, this need not be so. Such a society can choose between measuring its increasing wealth in the abstract form of added capital values, and organizing its social production and distribution in real, physical terms, without regard to value relations.

Marx did not foresee the emergence of state-capitalist systems such as are presently recognized as actualizations of "Marxian socialism." For him, socialism was, first of all, the end of value production and thus also the end of the capitalist relations of production. "Within a co-operative society based on common ownership of the means of production," Marx wrote, "the producers do not exchange their products. Neither does the labor employed on the products appear here as the value of these products, as one of their material qualities — since now individual labors are directly component parts of the total labor, and not indirectly, as in capitalist society."[27] In Marx's view, no real social change — as regards the conditions of the working class — was possible unless it involved a change in the social relations of production. "The distribution of the means of consumption at any period," he wrote, "is merely the consequence of the distribution of the conditions of production themselves . . . Capitalist methods of production for example depend on the condition that the material conditions of production are distributed among non-workers under the form of capital and land ownership, while the masses are only owners of the personal conditions of production, i.e., labor-power. If the elements of production are so distributed, then the contemporary [capitalistic] distribution of the means of consumption results automatically. But if the material conditions of production are the collective property of the workers themselves, then, naturally, a different distribution of the means of production from the present one will result."[28]

According to Marx, then, the mode of distribution depends on the mode of production. In a society in which the workers have no control over the means of production but sell their labor-power

27 K. Marx, *Critique of the Gotha Programme*, New York, 1933, p. 29.
28 *Ibid.*, p. 32.

to others who have this control, the system of distribution will be as antagonistic as are the relations in the production process between the producers and the appropriators of surplus-labor. The state-capitalist system neither is capitalistic in the traditional sense nor represents the socialism of Marx's vision. From the point of view of private capitalism, it may be described as *state-socialism* simply because it centralizes capital in the hands of the state; but from the point of view of working-class socialism, it must be described as *state-capitalism,* since it retains the capitalistic division of the conditions of production between workers and non-workers. Both terms can be used interchangeably since they denote indentical conditions.

For Marx, the law of value "regulates" market capitalism but no other form of social production. To speak of a law of value as the "regulator" of the economy in the absence of specifically capitalistic market relations can only mean that the *terms* "value" and "surplus-value" are retained though they express no more than the relation between labor and surplus-labor. In capitalism, labor-power is a commodity like any other, and because all commodities are socially interrelated only by means of the exchange process they must be realized as exchange-value before they can become articles of utility. In the centralized state-economy, however, capital and labor can be allocated apart from market relations and value considerations by a direct regard for social utility as understood by the controlling authorities. If this is partly done and partly not done, it is because the state-capitalist system refuses to acknowledge itself for what it is, namely, a system of exploitation based on the direct control of a ruling minority over the ruled majority.

What distinguishes capitalist exploitation from every previous form of exploitation is the extraction of surplus-labor in the absence of direct coercion. Deprived of the means of production, the workers have no choice but to sell their labor-power to the capitalists at the prevailnig market prices. Social production is carried on by way of buying and selling. Thus the social life process appears dependent on market relations. Short of changing the whole of society, this is, of course, true. Within the frame of this society, the workers will accept the conditions of inequality as determined by market relations, and they will not necessarily recognize the fact of their exploitation. They will attempt to utilize the market relations for their own ends, in the competition for lucrative jobs and in the struggle for higher wages. It is the market, and — within definite limits — the competitive utilization of the market, which assures a more subtle extraction of surplus-labor than direct physical coercion. The more subtle way is of course also the more advanced, even for the workers; since wage-labor is generally preferable to forced labor. Neither willing nor able to end the system of labor exploitation, the state-capitalist system too prefers wage-labor to forced labor and for that reason adopts the mechanism of the market economy wherever possible.

It is the *semblance* of capitalistic market relations within the state-controlled economy which suggests the continued validity of the law of value under the now modified conditions of capital production. Actually, however, the law of value cannot be "operative" because the market relations are artificial, not real. The planning authorities merely *orient their plans on the model of the capitalist market economy,* for they cannot organize production and distribution in accordance with socialist principles, and they no longer dare to deal with the realities of exploitation and capital accumulation in open forms such as characterized the first period of the Russian state-socialist regime. During that period — later to be denigrated as the externally-enforced period of war-communism — the whole of commodity production with its categories of value, price, profit and wages was to be replaced by a centralized natural economy administered in terms of physical necessities and possibilities with respect to both production and distribution.

Under the conditions prevailing in underdeveloped capitalist nations, centralized administration must make the expansion of production, and therewith the formation of capital, its first concern. If this is to be accompanied by the destruction of market relations, both production and consumption must be determined by governmental decisions with or without the consent of the population thereby affected. The productive resources are allocated by decree and dictatorially enforced. Wage-labor becomes forced labor and, for better or worse, the conditions of production and distribution are determined by the deliberations of individuals in social power positions. And thus, while the change from the market to the planned-economy is undoubtedly an advance, the methods by which this advance is attained are regressive. But as Leon Trotsky wrote, "we can have no way to socialism except by the authoritative regulation of the economic forces and resources of the country, and by the centralized distribution of labor-power in harmony with the general State plan. The Labor State considers itself empowered to send every worker to the place where his work is necessary. And not one serious socialist will begin to deny to the Labor State the right to lay its hands upon the worker who refuses to execute his labor duty."[29]

Moreover, according to Trotsky, "the principle of compulsory labor has just so radically and permanently replaced the principle of free hiring as the socialization of the means of production has replaced capitalist property."[30] We will "retain, and for a long time retain, the system of wages. In the present difficult period the system for wages is for us, first and foremost, not a method for guaranteeing the personal existence of any separate worker, but a method of estimating what that individual worker brings with his labor to the Labor Republic. Consequently, wages, in the form of money and goods, must be brought into the closest possible touch with the productivity of individual labor. Those workers who do more for the general interest than others receive the right to a greater quantity of the social product than the lazy, the careless, and the disorganizers . . . All these measures must assist the development of rivalry in the sphere of production."[31]

But what is an objective measure of the productivity of individual labor? Trotsky neither raised nor anwered the question. In practice, differences in reward for different types of labor were analogous to the wage differentials in capitalism, even though wage-rates were set by government and not by the labor market. However, complete regimentation of labor proved to be an impossibility and was soon replaced by a combination of market relations and government planning, indirect and direct methods of control, and money and physical measurements, all of which freed the

---

29 L. Trotsky, *Dictatorship vs. Democracy,* New York, 1920, p. 142.
30 *Ibid.,* p. 137.
31 *Ibid.,* p. 149.

social production and distribution process from *regulation* by the law of value without, however, leading to a value-free socialist economy.

With wages administered and strikes excluded, with prices set to stimulate the consumption of some commodities and discourage that of others, with the rate and trend of accumulation consciously determined, it is merely a question of convenience whether to command labor into certain occupations or to induce workers to choose these jobs of their own free will by differential valuation of various types of work. In the latter case there is a limited freedom of choice of occupation. To be sure, as in the capitalism of old, the choice of occupation is more the exception than the rule. Obviously, it does not include such large-scale transfers from agricultural to industrial pursuits as were brought about by the enforced collectivization and modernization of agriculture. Various administrative hurdles placed in the way of individually-desired changes from one job to another discourage such changes — not to speak of wage-rates so low as directly to forbid both mobility and individual initiative. However, since the industrializing society is an expanding economy, it does offer opportunities to acquire skills, prepare for new professions, reach for high positions, and to compete for better jobs. The social climate of competition deliberately fostered by a hierarchial income-structure is indistiguishable from that in capitalism.

To sum up: The state-socialist society neither is "regulated" by the law of value nor orders its economic relationships on the basis of the law of value. But even if it "leaned on the law of value," as Stalin asserted, in order to assure rational cost and profit calculations and a method of social book-keeping for the proper allocation of resources, this still would not justify its designation as socialism. In any case, the law of value cannot be *made* operative in either the capitalist or the socialist society. In capitalism it asserts itself like a "natural law" because *private* exchange relations exclude the conscious *social* organization of production; and in socialism, where this proportioning of the social labor is done consciously and directly, the law of value no longer determines social conditions.

A value analysis of capital production considers the general need for rationality in the social production process in the specific form in which this general need expresses itself in capitalism. Even so, the value analysis does not deal with the concrete capitalist exchange relations, but with the disregarded and actually unknowable realities underlying these exchange relations. Because "in the analysis of economic forms," Marx wrote, "neither microscopes nor chemical reagents are of use, the force of abstraction must replace both."[32] Labor-time value is the "scientific expression" of the economic relations of capitalism. It is not an empirical description of these relations, but it is an abstraction from them; and it is only by way of abstract thought that the concrete situation becomes comprehensible.

This does not mean, however, that labor-time value could actually become the organizational principle of a non-capitalist, or socialist, system of production and distribution. In criticizing the Ricardian socialists[33] and, notably, Proudhon for advocating an exchange system of private producers based on labor-time value, Marx pointed out that products which are produced as commodities can only be exchanged as such, that is, in terms of prices; they cannot be exchanged according to labor-time values. Of John Gray's proposed theory of labor-time as the direct measure of money, Marx wrote that it is based on the illusion "that commodities could be related directly to each other as products of social labor. But they can relate to each other only in their capacity as commodities. Commodities are the direct products of isolated independent private labors, which have to be realized as universal labor through their alienation in the process of private exchange. That is to say, labor based on the production of commodities becomes social labor only through universal alienation of individual labor. But by assuming that the labor-time contained in commodities is *directly social* labor-time, Gray assumes it to be the *common labor-time* or labor-time of *directly associated* individuals. Under such conditions a specific commodity like gold or silver

32 *Capital,* Vol. I., p. 12.
33 T. Hodgskin, *Labour Defended Against the Claims of Capital,* 1825; W. Thompson, *An Inquiry into the Principles of the Distribution of Wealth most conducive to Human Happiness,* 1824; J. F. Bray, *Labour's Wrongs and Labour's Remedy,* 1839; J. Gray, *The Social System: A Treatise on the Principles of Exchange,* 1831.

could not confront other commodities as the incarnation of universal labor, and exchange value would not be turned into price; but, on the other hand, use-value would not become exchange-value, products would not become commodities and thus the very foundation of the capitalistic system of production would be removed."[34]

To put this in a slightly different way: If the labor-time contained in the social product is the *common labor-time of directly associated* producers, these products do not take on the character of commodities. They do not need, then, to be transformed into products of universal social labor (which they are already), nor do they require a definite money-commodity to express their social nature in the form of prices. If labor-time, Marx asked, "is the intrinsic measure of value, why should there be another external measure side by side with it?"[35] The fact that there is the measure of price indicates that social products (as commodities) are not *directly* part of the *common social labor* but can only become part of it via the exchange and money relations in a market economy of *disassociated* producers. The theory of value, as the theory of bourgeois society, Marx told Proudhon, cannot become "the revolutionary theory of the future."[36]

In a communist society, Marx wrote, "the money-capital would be entirely eliminated, and with it the disguises which it carries into the (economic) transactions. The question is then simply reduced to the problem that society must calculate beforehand how much labor, means of production, and means of subsistence it can utilize without injury for such lines as, for instance, the building of railways, which do not furnish any means of production or subsistence, or any useful thing, for a long time, a year or more, while they require labor, and means of production and subsistence out of annual production."[37] Although the "economics of time" and the planned distribution of labor-time over the different spheres and branches of production are still an economic necessity, this has nothing to do with *labor-time value,* that is, with the exchange-value of labor-power or its products.

34   K. Marx, *A Contribution to the Critique of Political Economy,* pp. 104-105.
35   *Ibid.,* p. 104.
36   K. Marx, *The Poverty of Philosophy,* p. 45.
37   *Capital,* Vol. II, p. 362.

As regards individual labor, it is impossible to measure specific contributions to the total social product and divide the latter accordingly in both socialism and capitalism. The labor of different individuals in identical occupations, and the work between diverse occupations, differs quantitatively as well as qualitativly. Because there exists no actual common denominator for different types of labor, Marx saw their only possible common denominator in labor-time. With respect to specific kinds of labor, quantitatively different accomplishments during a given time (as in piecerate systems) do, of course, reveal productivity variations of individuals. But such differences are rather small and present no real problem either with regard to wage differences, or with respect to entrepreneurial calculations, which concern themselves with the average productivity of the working force in terms of the total wage bill.

Since it takes time to acquire a skill, the production costs of skilled and simple labor differ. But as costs of learning are ascertainable, it is not difficult to account for them in actual wage-rates. In fact, differences between wages for simple and skilled labor are not wide enough to throw doubt upon labor-time as the common denominator of the value of labor-power. Great income differences exist only within and between occupations in which it is practically impossible to measure differences of productivity or special contributions to the general social wealth. Objections raised to labor-time as the common value-denominator for all types of labor are, then, rarely related to wage differences within the labor force, but to types of work and services performed by non-working-class people, most often to payments received for activities that have nothing at all to do with the social production process.

The productivity of different types of labor is inseparably connected with the productivity of total *social labor* and changes in the social production process. In capitalism, of course, this problem is approached not from a social but from an individual point of view because of the commodity character of labor-power and the capitalistic division of labor, which includes the division between mental and manual labor or, rather (since mental and manual labor cannot really be divorced), between office and factory, science and industry. Specialization in one-sided activities has been found profitable; but whether it is socially more productive than interchangeability of occupations remains to be tested. Meanwhile, the differing evaluations of mental and manual labor, skilled and simple work, in terms of prices established by supply and demand relations on the labor market, are taken quite seriously; they divide the laboring population into different income groups, blurring the dominance of social relations by capital-labor relations.

According to Marx, the individual's labor is a necessary component of the total social labor because labor has become socialized labor, indirectly in capitalism, and directly in socialism. In socialism, kinds of labor will be differentiated only with respect to their utility, and this utility will not find expression in an attached exchange-value. Although bourgeois society propounds the principle of equality in exchange, Marx views this as an unrealizable principle in capitalism as well as in socialism. Because the classical value concept had given rise to the idea of an exchange of equal labor-time quantities, which assured all producers the whole proceeds of their labor, Marx pointed out that the existence of a non-working population (children, aged, sick, etc.), the necessity of unproductive activities, and the requirements of social development in general prohibited the appropriation by individuals of the whole proceeds of their labor. The proceeds of labor, Marx wrote, could only be part of its product, "even if what is taken away from the producer as a private individual is given back to him directly or indirectly in his capacity as member of the co-operative commonwealth."[38]

After these necessary deductions, however, the individual could get back "what he has given society in his individual amount of labor. For example, the social working-day consists of the sum of the individuals' hours of work. The individual working-time of the individual producer is that part of the social working-day contributed by him, his part thereof. He receives from society a voucher that he has contributed such and such a quantity of work (after deductions from his work for the common fund) and draws through his voucher on the social storehouse as much of the means of consumption as the same quantity of work costs. The same amount of work which he has given to society in one form, he

38 K. Marx, *Critique of the Gotha Programme*, p. 28.

receives back in another."[39] In this way equal quantities of labor-time would "exchange" for equal quantities of labor-time, and "the right of the producers would be proportional to the amount of labor they contribute; the equality consists in the fact that everything is measured by an *equal measure,* labor."[40] But this "equal right" to the proceeds of labor would actually be an unequal right for unequal work, due to unequal personal situations. "It is therefore a right of inequality in its content, as in general is every right."[41]

If labor-time is adopted as a measure to determine the distribution of the returnable part of the social product destined for consumption, there would arise an equality of remuneration, for, in fact "it is in the nature of large-scale industry that working hours should be equal for all."[42] Yet personal situations, such as the marital status of a worker or the number of his dependents, would turn this equal share of consumption goods measured by his labor-time contribution to the social product into an inequality of living standards. To achieve real equality in this respect the right to the proceeds of labor would have to be unequal.

Moreover, Marx pointed out, some excel physically or intellectually and contribute in the same time more labor than others. Yet, "labor, to serve as a measure, must be defined by its duration or intensity, otherwise it ceases to be a standard of measure."[43] If labor is measured by its *intensity* it is no longer measured by labor-time but by the diverse productivity of different persons in different occupations. In that case, however, the arising inequalities would not be the result of an *equal measure,* but the result of measuring unequal individual contributions to the total social labor product. Not labor-time, but the specific product of labor, would be measured. This is probably what Marx meant in saying that the right to one's particular labor "is still based on the same principle of bourgeois right, although principle and practice are no longer at daggers drawn, while the exchange of equivalents in commodity exchange only exists for the *average* and not for the

39 *Ibid.,* p. 29.
40 *Ibid.,* p. 30.
41 *Ibid.*
42 K. Marx, *The Poverty of Philosophy,* p. 77.
43 K. Marx, *Critique of the Gotha Programme,* p. 30.

individual case."[44] If the individual's labor is still seen as embodied in his individual product and not as a component of the whole of social labor, it is still seen from a bourgeois, not a socialist, point of view. It is, then, this distinction between *duration* and *intensity* of labor which serves as an apologia for inequalities in the nominally socialist nations.

Because of the vagueness of his formulation, Marx's position on this issue has been subjected to different interpretations. It can be accepted as meaning that, whether labor serves as a standard of measurement in its duration or in its intensity, in either case there will be inequality in living conditions for unequally-endowed or unequally-situated individuals. To avoid these inequalities, the right to the proceeds of labor would have to be unequal instead of equal, which could either mean that the individual's contribution to general social labor should be ignored in order to assure an equitable distribution of consumption goods, or that the inequitable distribution of consumption goods is unavoidable because labor is still measured with regard to its duration or its intensity. It does not mean that Marx opposed equality. But it does mean that he realized that the principle of equality based on labor contributions *was not a socialist principle,* even though it might be the ruling principle in the transitory stages of a socialist society.

Marx thought that the idea of the individual's right to his labor-product may still dominate the society emerging from capitalism and "in every respect still tainted economically, morally, and intellectually with the hereditary diseases of the old society."[45] Yet, in his mind, equalitarianism was a question not of remuneration as bound to an abstract principle of equality, but of rational social relations that exclude exploitation and promote the free sharing of goods and services. In his view, the development of society in the post-capitalist world would find expression not in a rigid and

44 *Ibid.*
45 *Ibid.*, p. 29.

narrow realization of an always greater equality in "exchange" in accordance with the individual's contribution to the social labor process, but in a tendency toward the realization of the principle "from each according to his ability, to each according to his needs."[46] Sociality is itself a developmental process in which the "narrow bourgeois horizon of private rights" would wither away because of an increasing abundance of consumption goods that would render economic accounting based on individual contributions to production both superfluous and ridiculous.

46 *Ibid.*, p. 31.

EPILOGUE

Marx did not envision an intermediary stage between private-enterprise capitalism and socialism. His rather clean-cut differentiation between feudalism, capitalism, and socialism made for a certain "orderliness" and "simplicity" in his revolutionary expectations. He recognized, however, that his history of the rise of capitalism pertained solely to Western Europe, and he opposed any attempt to turn it into "a general historical-philosophical theory of development valid for all nations, no matter what their historical conditions might be."[1] Marx, as well as Engels, allowed for courses of development different from those in Western Europe, and for a shortening of the road to socialism for pre-capitalist nations, in the wake of successful proletarian revolutions in the West. They recognized the state-capitalist tendencies in developed capitalist nations as indications of the coming socialist revolution without foreseeing their role in transforming pre-capitalist into state-capitalist systems of production.

We know now that social revolutions in capitalistically-under-developed countries do not, and cannot, repeat the pattern of development of Western capitalism, but tend to introduce state-capitalist structures. They are not socialist revolutions in the Marxian sense even if they do avail themselves of Marxian ideology. The idea that state-capitalist revolution means the victory of socialism even in industrially-advanced nations gains some credibility because such revolutions appear to bring to its logical conclusion the increasing government-determination of production and of social life in general, and because they follow the pattern set by the established state-capitalist systems, which are quite generally perceived as socialist. In these systems, however, the institution of state-capital-

1 K. Marx, "Letter to the Editors of Otetschestwennyj Sapiski," *Marx-Engels Werke*, Vol. 19, Berlin, 1962, p. 111.

ism had the function not of abolishing the proletarian class but of aiding in its quick formation and thereby in the formation of capital. In industrially-advanced countries, state-capitalism would be as irrational a system as that which preceded it, for the difficulties of capital production can here be resolved not through an increase of exploitation but only through its abolition.

However, industrially-advanced countries could maintain a system of class differences under state-capitalist regimes just as capital-poor nations do. They would not have the "excuse" of the under-developed states, but they could create a political apparatus of repression which would eliminate the need for one. There would thus have been a revolution, but not a socialist revolution. For a socialist revolution must mean precisely the creation of a social structure in which the producers *themselves* control their product and its distribution. It is conceivable only as one made by the working-class which ends social class relations. "What Marx — and before him, in 1843, Flora Tristan — formulated in one single proposition, namely, that 'the emancipation of the working class must be conquered by the working class itself', remains the implicit postulate of all genuine socialist thought."[2]

It was Marx's conviction that the contradiction between the growing social forces of production and the narrow capitalist relations of production would be overcome through a revolution which, by ending the class structure of society — its basic antagonism — would open the way towards a socialist world. Such a social revolution has not taken place; neither has the contradiction of social- as capital-production been resolved. Production is still everywhere the production of capital, and the capitalist world remains a world of crises.

Within this context, Keynesianism merely reflects the transition of capitalism from its free-market to a state-aided phase and provides an ideology for those who momentarily profit by this transition. It does not touch upon the problems Marx was concerned with. As long as the capitalist mode of production prevails, Marxism will retain its relevance, since it concerns itself neither with one or another technique of capital production, nor with social

2 M. Rubel, "Reflections on Utopia and Revolution," in *Socialist Humanism*, ed. by E. Fromm, New York, 1966, p. 216.

changes within the frame of capital production, but only with its final abolition.

It may well be that socialism is an illusion and that society is condemned to remain class-society. But this conclusion cannot be derived merely from the fact that recent revolutions have not destroyed exploitative class relations. The revolutions of the twentieth century have been directed against a capitalism unable to extend the conditions of its own existence, powerless to enlarge the industrial proletariat and, therewith, its own domain. Yet capitalism disturbed and destroyed earlier forms of social organization and modes of production by subordinating world production to a world market determined by the special interests of the great centers of capital production. The old ruling classes of the ravaged nations lacked both the interest and the power to withstand the inroads of foreign capital. It was left to the impoverished themselves to rebel against the double yoke of foreign and native exploitation, as well as the still greater misery of unemployment resulting from the lack of such exploitation. Because their wretchedness was due to both class and national subjugation, the character of their revolution was, and still is, both revolutionary and nationalist.

There is as yet no way to transcend the limited nationalist character of these revolutions, because of the total absence of an international revolutionary working-class movement capable of providing these national struggles with a wider frame of operations and with goals more extensive than mere capitalization by revolutionary means. Whatever else these revolutions may accomplish, they cannot lead to socialism as an alternative to modern capitalism. They are but one of many expressions of the disintegration of the capitalist market economy as a world system, and it is only as such that they support the general need for a more rational social system of production. The problems of the backward nations cannot be solved apart from those that beset the developed ones. The solution for both still lies in a revolutionary change in the latter, which would prepare the way for a socialist integration of world economy. For just as the underdeveloped countries cannot develop socialistically in a world dominated by capital production, so they could not develop capitalistically in a world dominated by socialist systems of production. The key to a socialist development of the underdeveloped nations is the socialist transformation of the advanced capitalist part of the world.

Yet this key does not seem to fit the real situation. It is quite obvious that the industrially-advanced parts of the world have the means to industrialize the underdeveloped regions in a rather short time and to eliminate hunger and poverty almost immediately merely by diverting the expenses of waste-production into productive channels. But there are as yet no social forces in sight willing to realize this opportunity and thus bring peace and tranquility to the world. Instead, the destructive aspects of capital production take on an increasingly more violent character — internally, by more and more waste production; and externally, by laying waste to territories occupied by people unwilling to submit to the profit requirements of foreign powers, which could only spell their own doom.

It cannot be expected that those who profit by the *status quo* and whose existence and future depends on its perpetuation will alter their ways by abdicating their dominating class positions. It is by means of the "mixed economy" that they have thus far succeeded in preventing the rise of social conditions which could lead to anti-capitalist social movements. In this sense, Keynesianism has been the "savior" of capitalism, even though by its own nature, and by the nature of capitalism, it can be only of temporary avail. With or without full employment, the mixed economy is a social fact in all capitalist nations, and in some of them has proved itself capable not only of avoiding large-scale depressions but of bringing about conditions of "prosperity" such as have never been experienced before, thus making it possible for the well-off to describe capitalism as a society of affluence.

Practically and ideologically, World War II and its aftermath led to an almost total eclipse of working-class socialism. But a continuing absence of any effective opposition to capitalism presupposes the system's ability to maintain the given living conditions of the laboring population. If this should turn out to be impossible, the present social cohesion of the capitalist system may well be lost again — as it has been in previous crises of long duration. It is only on the assumption that all arising social problems can be resolved within existing institutions that it is possible to deny the

working class — the vast majority of the population in the industrially-advanced countries — their role in history, which must of
necessity be an oppositional role and thus find expression in a revived or newly-emerging revolutionary consciousness.

The temporary success of Keynesian policies has given rise to
the conviction that a way has finally been found to deal effectively with capitalism's difficulties and thus dissolve the system's
revolutionary potentialities. But this conviction is an illusion based
on the money veil that covers all capitalistic activities. If the veil
is lifted, it becomes apparent that the continuous application of
Keynesianism implies the self-destruction of capital production.
The optimism of the "new economics" merely mistakes the postponement of a problem for its disappearance.

If revolutionary consciousness depends on misery, there can be
little doubt that the suffering awaiting the world's population will
go beyond anything thus far experienced, and that it will eventually engulf even the privileged minority of workers in the industrially-advanced countries who still think of themselves as immune
to the consequences of their own activities. As the general level
of oppression increases, the special situation of "affluence" will
dissolve, for the blessings of increased productivity will be dissi-
pated in slaughterous competition for the diminishing profits of
world production. Even previously, war and its aftermath brought
with them an extent of social misery unknown during the darkest
days of the Industrial Revolution and exceeding anything Marx
himself was able to relate about the miserable condition of the
laboring population. Only by excluding the human costs of war
and depression has it been possible to assert that capitalist development did not imply the growth of "the mass of misery, oppression, slavery, degradation, and exploitation;" and only by restricting the argument to the narrow field of wage statistics in a few
countries could it be said that Marx was wrong in predicting an
increasing misery during the course of capital accumulation. But
surely, this prediction is derived from his *General Law of Capitalist
Accumulation* and its *Historical Tendency* and not merely from
the commodity-character of labor-power and its changing fortunes
on the labor market. It encompasses all aspects of capitalist development by way of competition, crises, and wars. It is not reasonable

to maintain that the conditions of prosperity in a few countries in the wake of World War II, and the consequent further improvement of the living standards of their populations, is sufficient compensation for the rather permanent crisis conditions in the larger part of the world and for the almost incomprehensible suffering, exploitation, and degradation of hundreds of millions of people during and after the war.

The high standards of living attained by large layers of the working-class in industrially-advanced countries may themselves become detrimental to capital expansion. For the maintenance of such standards under conditions of decreasing profitability requires a continuous extension of non-profitable production. This in turn implies an increasingly greater need to raise the productivity of labor, which, under present conditions, means the steady growth of unemployment. Provision for the unemployed itself becomes an increasing expense which, together with all the other expenses of "affluence," will sooner or later tax to the utmost even the greatest economic and technical capacities. This is not to say that "affluence" breeds revolution, but only that no absolute impoverishment is required to produce oppositional sentiments. People need not be reduced to starvation levels before they begin to rebel; they may do so with the first deep inroads into their customary living standards, or even when access to what they consider their living standards should be is denied them. The better off people are, the harder it is to bear any deprivation, and the more tenaciously they cling to their accustomed style of life. It is in this sense that the partial loss of the prevailing "affluence" may be enough to destroy the existing consensus.

Marx once said that "the proletariat is revolutionary or it is nothing." At present it is nothing and it may well be that it will continue to be nothing. But this is not certain. Obviously, subversive ideas flourish only under conditions of dissatisfaction such as do not as yet exist in the prosperity — false though it is — of present-day society. Though the poverty-stricken in the mixed economies are a large minority they are still a minority, and their opposition remains inarticulate. They cannot become a social force strong enough to oppose the material interests represented by the ruling ideology. The sporadic rebellions of despair are easily handled by the authorities representing the smug majority, which still includes the mass of the proletariat. The substratum of the impoverished can be decimated by the very conditions of existence provided for them. But as their number grows — and it is growing — the frequency of their rebellious acts will also increase, as will the awareness on the part of many of the smug that perhaps they, too, will soon find themselves on the refuse heap of capitalism. To judge by the past, the growth of social misery gives power to this misery and power leads to conscious actions aimed at ending the misery. Of course, the patterns of the past may not hold for the future; the age of revolutions may well be over. But if we cannot judge by past experiences, we cannot judge at all. In that case, everything is possible — even a working-class revolution.

This possible revolution presupposes the continued existence of the proletariat, which, however, is allegedly already coming to an end with respect not only to its non-existing class consciousness but to its social functions as well. A distinction is often made between the "classical working-class," i.e., the industrial proletariat in the Marxian sense, and the modern working population, of which only the smaller part is occupied in production. But this distinction is artificial, for what differentiates the proletariat from the bourgeoisie is not a particular set of occupations, but the former's lack of control over their existence resulting from the lack of control over the means of production. Even if more workers are now engaged in non-productive, so-called service industries, their social position vis-a-vis the capitalists remains unaltered. Because of the concentration of capital and the elimination of the proprietory middle-class there are more proletarians now than ever before. It is of course true that a good portion of these people receive incomes which provide them with bourgeois or petty-bourgeois living standards. But the vast majority, as far as living standards are concerned, fall into the category of wage-workers, no matter how unproductive their work may be.

When Marx declared that the "historical mission" of the working class was to end the capitalist system, he was speaking, as may be gathered from his theory of accumulation, of the expropriation of the few by the many. He rightly saw that the expansion of capital is also the polarization of society into a small minority of capitalists and a vast majority of propertyless workers forced to sell their labor power in order to exist. The industrial proletariat of a hundred years ago has today swollen into an amorphous mass of wage-receiving occupations and professionals, all of whom are dependent on the vicissitudes of market events and the changing fortunes of the accumulation process. However they think of themselves, they belong not to the ruling class but to the ruled.

Capitalism is basically a two-class society, notwithstanding the various status differentiations within each separate class. The ruling class is the decision-making class; the other class, regardless of its inner differentiations, is at the mercy of these decisions, which are made with a view to the special needs of capital and determine the general conditions of society. The ruling class cannot act otherwise than it does: stupidly or intelligently, it will do everything to perpetuate itself as a ruling class. Those outside the decision-making process may disagree with the decisions made, since they may not correspond with their own interests, or because of convictions that things should be done differently. But to change these decisions they must have power of their own.

Whatever the decision-makers decide upon has to be actualized in the sphere of production because the manner of distribution depends on that of production. Without control over the production process, no decisions can be made, no class can rule. Control of production is exercised by control of the means of production, by ideology and by force. But property, ideology, and force alone can produce nothing. It is upon productive labor that the whole social edifice rests. The productive laborers thus have more latent power at their disposal than any other social group, or all other social groups combined. To turn this latent into actual power demands no more than the producers' recognition of social realities and the application of this knowledge to their own ends.

To deny this fact is the main job of bourgeois ideology, as is evidenced by its economic theories and by the general disparagement of productive labor. However, despite the prevailing notion of the decreasing importance of the industrial proletariat, more attention is devoted to it than ever before, because its potential power to control society has actually never been so great as it is now. The technical-organizational "socialization" of production,

i.e., the interdependence of the whole of the population in an uninterrupted flow of production, provides the working class with
almost absolute power over the life and death of society simply by
ceasing to work. While this could not be their intention, as they
are members of the same society, they could nevertheless shake
society to its foundations if they were determined to alter its structure. It is for this reason that labor unions have been adapted to
the capitalist establishment — in order to control industrial dis-
putes — that governments, including labor governments, pass anti-
strike legislation, and that those most aware of the latent power
of industrial action, the totalitarian regimes, outlaw strikes altogether.

Because the industrial proletariat has the power to change society if so inclined, it is now, as before, the class on whose action the
actual transformation of society depends. If this power did not
exist, if its application were not a real possibility, there would be
no hope of overcoming the existing material forces of repression.
To be sure, all social struggles are also ideological struggles; yet
success in the fight for a new society requires a material lever with
which the defenses of the *status quo* may be overturned. It is not
entirely inconceivable that the growing irrationality of capitalism
will lead to a wide-spread revulsion among the population at large,
regardless of class affiliations, and to a growing conviction that
there is no longer any need for, nor any sense in, exploitative class
relations, since society could be reorganized so as to benefit all
people. Still, such a society will have to be fought for with all
available weapons both in the ideological sphere and in the field
of real power relations.

With the record of working-class behavior before us, the workers'
indispensability for the actualization of socialism makes socialism
seem farther off than ever. But it is more than doubtful that the
working class will indefinitely endure all that the capitalist system
has in store for it. One has only to think of what in all probability

is bound to happen without a socialist revolution in order to accept the possibility of a different kind of behavior on the part of the laboring population. What is bound to happen is in some measure already happening, and the quantitative projection of the present into the future points to the utopianism of solving capitalism's social problems by capitalistic means. The present American war in Southeast Asia, for instance, may well engulf the Far East and finally the whole world. In view of this perspective, not to speak of unavoidable new economic crises of world capitalism, the phrase "socialism or barbarism" states the only real alternatives.

BIBLIOGRAPHY

Baran, P. A., *The Political Economy of Growth*, New York, 1960.

Berle, A. A., *Economic Power and the Free Society*, New York, 1957.

Berliner, J. S., *Soviet Economic Aid*, New York, 1958.

Bernstein, E., *Evolutionary Socialism*, New York, 1961.

Beveridge, W. H., *Full Employment in a Free Society*, New York, 1945.

Böhm-Bawerk, *Karl Marx and the Close of his System*, New York, 1949.

Bucharin, N., *Oekonomik der Transformations Periode*, Hamburg, 1922.

Burns, A. F., *The Frontiers of Economic Knowledge*, Princeton, 1954.

Clark, J. M., *Alternative to Serfdom*, New York, 1960.

Crosser, P. K., *State Capitalism in the Economy of the United States*, New York, 1960.

Denian, J. F., *The Common Market*, New York, 1960.

Deans, V. M., *New Patterns of Democracy in India*, Cambridge, 1959.

Dillard, D., *The Economics of John Maynard Keynes*, New York, 1948.

Doane, R. R., *The Measurement of American Wealth*, New York, 1933.

Drucker, P. F., *Landmarks of Tomorrow*, New York, 1959.

Eaton, J., *Marx Against Keynes*, London, 1951.

Einzig, P., *The Economic Consequences of Automation*, New York, 1957.

Engels, F., *Anti-Dühring*, Chicago, 1935.

Flanders, R. F., *The American Century*, Cambridge, 1950.

Gesell, S., *Die Natürliche Wirtschaftsordnung durch Freiland und Freigeld*, Berlin, 1916.

Gillman, J. M., *The Fall of the Rate of Profit*, New York, 1958.

Gillman, J. M., *Prosperity in Crisis*, New York, 1965.

Grossmann, H., *Das Akkumulations und Zusammenbruchsgesetz des Kapitalistischen Systems*, Leipzig, 1929.

Hansen, A. H., *America's Role in the World Economy*, New York, 1945.

Harris, S. E., *Saving American Capitalism*, New York, 1950.

Hawtrey, R. G., *The Gold Standard in Theory and Practice*, London, 1931.

Harrod, R. F., *The Life of John Maynard Keynes*, London, 1951.

Heilbroner, R. L., *The Worldly Philosophers*, New York, 1953.

Heilbroner, R. L., *The Making of Economic Society*, Englewood Cliffs, 1962.

Hickman, B. G., *Investment Demand and U.S. Economic Growth*, Washington, 1965.

Hilferding, R., *Das Finanzkapital*, Wien, 1910.

Keynes, J. M., *Laissez-Faire and Communism*, New York, 1926.

Keynes, J. M., *The Economic Consequences of the Peace*, New York, 1920.

Keynes, J. M. *A Treatise on Money*, New York, 1930.

Keynes, J. M., *The General Theory of Employment, Interest and Money*, New York, 1936.

Klein, L. R., *The Keynesian Revolution*, New York, 1947.

Kautsky, K., *Aus der Frühzeit des Marxismus*, Prague, 1935.

Kolko, G., *Wealth and Power in America*, New York, 1962.

Korsch, K., *Karl Marx*, London, 1938.

Kuznets, S., *Capital in the American Economy*, New York, 1961.

Kritsman, *Die Heroische Periode der Grossen Russischen Revolution*, Wien, 1929.

Kurihara, K. K., *The Keynesian Theory of Development*, New York, 1959.

Lange, O., *Political Economy*, New York, 1963.

Lange, O., *On the Economic Theory of Socialism*, Minneapolis, 1938.

Lerner, A. P., *The Economics of Control*, New York, 1944.

Lerner, A. P., *Everybody's Business*, New York, 1964.

Lenin, V. I., *Questions of the Socialist Organization of the Economy*, Moscow, no date.

Lichtheim, G., *Marxism*, London, 1961.

Lister, L., *Europe's Coal and Steel Community*, New York, 1960.

Lundberg, E., *The Business Cycle in the Post-War World*, London, 1955.

Luxemburg, R., *The Akkumulation des Kapitals*, Leipzig, 1921.

Luxemburg, R., *The Russian Revolution*, Ann Arbor, 1961.

Maddison, A., *Economic Growth in the West*, New York, 1964.

Marcuse, H., *Soviet Marxism*, New York, 1961.

Marx, K., *A Contribution to the Critique of Political Economy*, Chicago, 1904.

Marx, K., *Capital*, Vol. I to Vol. III, Chicago, 1906, 1909.

Marx, K., *Theorien über den Mehrwert*. Vol. I to Vol. III, Stuttgart, 1905.

Marx, K., *Letters to Dr. Kugelmann*, Moscow, 1934.

Marx, K., *The Poverty of Philosophy*, Moscow, no date.

Marx, K., *Critique of the Gotha Programme*, New York, 1933.

Marx, K., *Grundrisse der Kritik der Politischen Oekonomie*, Berlin, 1953.

Marx, K. and Engels, F., *Briefe über das Kapital*, Berlin, 1954.

Marx, K. and Engels, F., *Selected Correspondence*, Moscow, no date.

Marx K. and Engels, F., *Selected Works*, 2 Volumes, Moscow, 1958.

Means, G. C., *The Corporate Revolution in America*, New York, 1964.

Mende, T., *China and Her Shadow*, New York, 1962.

Michael, D. N., *Cybernation: The Silent Conquest*, Santa Barbara, 1962.

Moulton, H. G., *The Formation of Capital*, Washington, D. C., 1935.

Myrdal, G., *Beyond the Welfare State*, New Haven, 1960.

Nove, A., *The Soviet Economy*, New York, 1962.

Norman, E. H., *Japan's Emergence as a Modern State*, New York, 1946.

Nurske, R., *Problems of Capital Formation in the Underdeveloped Countries*, London, 1953.

Pigou, A. V., *The Political Economy of War*, London, 1940.

Pollock, F., *Automation*, Frankfurt am Main, 1964.

Preobrazhensky, E., *The New Economics*, London, 1965.

Robinson, J., *An Essay on Marxian Economics*, London, 1942.

Rowse, A. L., *Mr. Keynes and the Labour Movement*, London, 1936.

Stalin, J., *Economic Problems of Socialism in the U.S.S.R.*, New York, 1952.

Schlesinger, R., *Marx: His Time and Ours*, New York, 1950.

Spulber, N., *Foundation of Soviet Strategy for Economic Growth*, Bloomington, 1964.

Strachey, J., *Contemporary Capitalism*, New York, 1956.

Strachey, J., *The End of Empire*, New York, 1960.

Schumpeter, J. A., *Capitalism, Socialism and Democracy*, New York, 1947.

Sweezy, P. M., *The Theory of Capitalist Development*, New York, 1942.

Tinbergen, J., *Shaping the World Economy*, New York, 1962.

Tinbergen, J., *Central Planning*, New Haven, 1964.

Thorp, W. L., *Trade, Aid, or What?*, Amherst, 1954.

Trotsky, L., *Dictatorship vs. Democracy*, New York, 1920.

Vernon, R., *Trade Policy in Crisis*, Princeton, 1958.

Wilkinson, J. D., *Politics and Trade Policy*, Washington, D. C., 1960.

Williams, F., *Socialist Britain*, New York, 1949.

Williams, J. H., *Economic Stability in a Changing World*, New York, 1953.

Worsley, P., *The Third World*, London, 1964.

INDEX

EHB NEW TITLES 1969

THE NEW LEFT: A COLLECTION OF ESSAYS
Priscilla Long, Ed. Introduced by Staughton Lynd
$6.00 cloth   500 pages $3.00 paper

Written entirely by New Left activists, these essays sum up,
define and explain the New Left point of view. Theory,
issues, the Movement, and the New Society are discussed in
28 essays on women in society, racism, organizing, Marxism,
capitalism, anarchism, communal living, and many more
topics.

MARX & KEYNES: THE LIMITS OF THE MIXED ECONOMY
by Paul Mattick. 350 pp. $6.95 cloth

Keynesian economic theory aimed to refute Marx's predictions about
the end of capitalism. Mr. Mattick undertakes a critical interpretation of Keynes alongside an analysis of the actual conditions of
contemporary capitalism. He sees Keynes' mixed economy as a
temporary system which does not solve capitalism's inherent difficulties. A major theoretical work.

THE NATURE OF CIVILIZATIONS by Matthew Melko.
250 pp. $4.95 cloth

The first comparative history to support the term "civilizations" and
construct a model of them—based on the arguments of Dr. Melko's
six predecessors, and a world-wide range of examples. In the light
of comparative history he weighs up hopes and fears for the future
of Western civilization. His clear style and dispassionate approach
recommend the book for young students.

VALUES IN HUMAN SOCIETIES by F. R. Cowell.
350 pp. $7.50 cloth

What was Sorokin's achievement? Cowell shows that Sorokin (Har-
vard sociologist) formed a revolutionary sociology by making its
essence the theory of values. Sorokin's sociology has content as a
source of answers to our social problems.

PORTER SARGENT PUBLISHER
11 Beacon Street, Boston, Mass. 02108

EXTENDING HORIZONS BOOKS—A Library of Writings to aid those working for Man's more hopeful future:

SARGENT HANDBOOK SERIES — Scope and Emphasis of Thousands of Schools and Facilities:

THE HANDBOOK OF PRIVATE SCHOOLS — An Annual Descriptive Survey of Independent Education

PRIVATE SCHOOLS ILLUSTRATED — Profusely illustrated presentation of hundreds of Independent Schools, Summer Schools and Summer Camps

SCHOOLS ABROAD — A World Wide Guide to Private International Education in all areas of the world

THE UNDERACHIEVER — A Guide to Tutorial, Remedial, Diagnostic and Academic Resources

GUIDE TO SUMMER CAMPS AND SUMMER SCHOOLS— A Comprehensive Reference to hundreds of Summer Programs of Academic Study, Summer Camps, Travel, etc.

SPECIAL EDUCATION SERIES — A Basic Library of References for Education of the Exceptional:

DIRECTORY FOR EXCEPTIONAL CHILDREN — Basic Data on thousands of Educational and Training Facilities and Guidance Clinics for all Exceptional Children

IF YOUR CHILD IS HANDICAPPED — Collection of personal accounts written by parents of handicapped children — edited by William C. Kvaraceus and E. Nelson Hayes

FORGOTTEN CHILDREN — An answer to the plight of the Multi-Handicapped Child — by Merle E. Frampton, Ellen Kerney, Regina Schattner

NEW HOPE FOR THE RETARDED — Enriching the Lives of Exceptional Children by Morris P. and Miriam Pollock

SPECIAL EDUCATION FOR THE EXCEPTIONAL — Three Volumes — Resources and Reference Books for all dealing with the exceptional — edited by Merle E. Frampton and Elena Gall

A NEW LOOK AT READING — A Comprehensive Manual on Reading and the Language Arts — by Willard Abraham

Circulars of any of the above and announcements of forthcoming publications will be sent on request

PORTER SARGENT PUBLISHER
11 Beacon Street, Boston, Massachusetts 02108